Fatal Consumption

The Sustainability and the Environment series provides a comprehensive, independent, and critical evaluation of environmental and sustainability issues affecting Canada and the world today.

SUSTAINABILITY
AND THE
ENVIRONMENT

*Edited by Robert F. Woollard
and Aleck S. Ostry*

Fatal Consumption:
Rethinking Sustainable
Development

UBCPress · Vancouver · Toronto

Printed in Canada on acid-free paper ∞

ISBN 0-7748-0786-5
ISSN 1196-8575 (Sustainability and the Environment)

Canadian Cataloguing in Publication Data

Main entry under title:

Fatal consumption

    (Sustainability and the environment, ISSN 1196-8575)
    Includes bibliographical references and index.
    ISBN 0-7748-0786-5

1. Sustainable development. 2. Sustainable development – Case studies. 3. Sustainable development – British Columbia – Lower Mainland – Case studies. I. Woollard, Robert F. II. Ostry, Aleck Samuel, 1952- III. Series.
HC117.B8F37 2000   333.7   C00-910443-7

This book has been published with the help of a grant from the Humanities and Social Sciences Federation of Canada, using funds provided by the Social Sciences and Humanities Research Council of Canada.

UBC Press acknowledges the financial support of the Government of Canada through the Book Publishing Industry Development Program (BPIDP) for our publishing activities.
Canadä

We also gratefully acknowledge the support of the Canada Council for the Arts for our publishing program, as well as the support of the British Columbia Arts Council.

Printed and bound in Canada by Friesens
Copy editor: Judy Phillips
Proofreader: Fran Aitkens
Indexer: Elizabeth Bell

UBC Press
University of British Columbia
2029 West Mall
Vancouver, BC V6T 1Z2
(604) 822-5959
Fax: (604) 822-6083
E-mail: info@ubcpress.ubc.ca
www.ubcpress.ubc.ca

Consumption:

1. The action or fact of consuming or destroying, destruction.
4. Wasting of the body by disease; a wasting disease; now applied specifically to pulmonary consumption or phthisis (Tuberculosis).
7. Pol. econ. The destructive employment or utilization of the products of industry.

– *Oxford English Dictionary*, 1971

"No, 'tis not so deep as a well, nor so wide as a church door; but 'tis enough, 'twill serve. Ask for me tomorrow, and you shall find me a grave man."

– Mercutio in *Romeo and Juliet* III.I.100

Contents

Part 3: Case Examples and the Reason for Hope

Acknowledgments

The editors and authors wish to acknowledge the assistance of the Science Council of British Columbia, the Canadian Tri-Council Eco-Research Fund, the Government of British Columbia, and the City of Richmond, who provided funding and ancillary support for the research contained in this book.

We would also like to thank the many students whose work we hope is fairly represented within the chapters of this volume – four of them have contributed chapters or major portions of chapters to this volume. A particular appreciation goes to Janette McIntosh and Dr. Matis Wackernagel, whose contributions have had a sustaining influence on the group and its ideas. The dedicated work of Shirley Tam in preparing much of the initial manuscript is gratefully acknowledged.

Finally, we would like to express our appreciation to our various families and friends who were alternately tolerant and supportive during the years of research and subsequent writing.

This book was published with the assistance of the Aid to Scholarly Publications Programme.

Fatal Consumption

Introduction: Fatal Consumption (When Too Much Is Not Enough)
Robert F. Woollard

Somewhere along the road to our present crisis we lost the idea of "enough." Somehow the twentieth century's version of progress lost its compass and began to see "more" as the only desirable direction. Like the idea of the west that continually followed the sun and shaped the North American consciousness, we never sought to reflect on where we were but became obsessed with where we might be. The predictable consequences of a century of excess surround us (from the collapse of the Atlantic and Pacific fisheries, through ozone depletion, precarious world food production, to global warming, and so on). The degradation of the global commons on which we all depend is increasingly impossible to deny. It is equally obvious that a significant portion of this degradation is unnecessary and is related to excessive consumption of energy and resources by the wealthiest countries and peoples in the world. While containing significant and unacceptable clusters of poverty, the urban centres of Canada and the United States are among the most egregious centres of consumption in the world. Much of the adverse consequences of this overconsumption can be traced to a disproportionately high consumption of fossil fuels in remarkably inefficient transportation systems based on the private automobile. By and large, these same cities have formal statements expressing their intent to reduce automobile dependency and air pollution associated with hydrocarbon consumption. In spite of this, the situation worsens and, in 1999 for the first time in history, the majority of new automobiles sold in North America are sports utility vehicles and trucks – vehicles that are significantly less fuel-efficient than the average car. This is but one specific example of a paradox this volume seeks to explore. Why, in the face of its obvious unsustainability, do we persist in levels of consumption far beyond what is necessary or even healthy?

As we approach the end of this century, concern about these issues is well established in the public consciousness. This consciousness is so well developed that there is little serious debate at the level either of policy development or public consultation that the city of the future must contain far fewer automobiles burning far fewer hydrocarbons than the city of today. Indeed, there is a growing understanding that transportation must consume less energy of any sort if cities are to survive and thrive. While the postwar boom years of the midcentury and the virtual explosion of automobile-dependent suburbs had been looked at with some nostalgia up until the beginning of the current decade, there is a growing concern even in the popular media (for instance, the 1995 *Newsweek* cover issue on *The Ugly Suburb)* that something is terribly wrong with this vision.

Despite this evolving consciousness, current development patterns in the Lower Fraser Basin of British Columbia show limited recognition of these concerns and the ecological realities that are behind them (Wackernagel 1996). While general public discussions about the preferred future are full of well-articulated hopes for a liveable region with fewer automobiles, better integrated planning requiring less transportation of people, and communities sensitive to the necessities of social support, when particular issues such as the replacing of Vancouver's Lions Gate Bridge appear in the public and policy making domain, the debate is almost entirely given over to discussions of how best to facilitate traffic flow of automobiles with a mild genuflexion toward public transportation. This occurs in spite of almost a half century of evidence (Jacobs 1992) that the facilitation of automobile traffic is precisely the wrong policy direction and that cities should be looking to the attrition of automobiles instead.

This seemingly perverse paradox is not unique to the Lower Fraser Basin, and in fact, is a standard feature of urban development in contemporary North America. With few notable exceptions stimulated mostly by necessity and occasionally by unusual perspicacity (Roseland 1992), there is in North America a continued increase in the number of automobiles, automobiles per capita, and average commuting distance. Since the example of Los Angeles and the even more egregious example of Mexico City are there for everyone to see, does it not seem self-destructive that the people of this region we call home seem incapable of effective, collective action to avoid a future we seem to have agreed is undesirable?

This is the central question that has motivated the researchers who have worked together over the past four years and whose reflections you now hold in your hand. These reflections, like the problems they consider, are both general and specific, relate to both process and status, and attempt to give an integrated view of both why we can and why we must correct our self-destructive path – our fatal consumption.

Each of the chapters in this volume represents a piece of the puzzle with which we are grappling. When taken together, they create a picture of a significant North American bioregion whose human population is just beginning to realize the enormity of the problems it is creating and the urgency with which those problems must be addressed. The picture includes some understanding of how our behaviours make the search for solutions more difficult. But it also shows some ways in which barriers can be overcome and charts the beginning of some paths that may lead to alternative and more sustainable futures.

Chapter 1 describes the ecological significance of our current consumption patterns. It demonstrates in graphic terms why it is physically impossible for us to continue our current rates of consumption and waste production.

Chapter 2 demonstrates that populations in other areas of the world enjoy a health status that is at least as good as ours while consuming only a fraction of what we consume. It also illustrates that the correlation between health and wealth exists only up to a certain point, beyond which increases in consumption become superfluous and even dangerous. It therefore raises the possibility that dramatic reductions in our own consumption need not in principle compromise our current very high health standard.

Chapter 3 provides insight into the way in which societies are constructing themselves in order to provide a quality of life that is even higher than that which we enjoy, while at the same time consuming far fewer ecological resources. The development of social capital or the nurturing of social caring capacity is presented as a practical and feasible alternative to what otherwise seems our inevitable, fatal drive toward increasing consumption and increasing social distance.

Chapter 4 provides a detailed analysis of the failure of the City of Vancouver to implement an integrated policy to reduce the impact of the city on the global atmospheric commons. It promotes an understanding of how the barriers to implementation might be classified, analyzed, and overcome. As such, it provides an antidote to the nihilism and cynicism that often attends the failure of such complex initiatives.

Chapter 5 contains the developmental history of a number of trends and tools that have had an impact on policy, as society has struggled with the problem of making decisions in a socially and ecologically complex world. It gives further impetus to our search for ways of overcoming some of the barriers to change outlined in the previous chapter.

Chapter 6 outlines the way in which sound policy decisions in the area of health and sustainability might be translated into action. It offers insights into the translation of policy into action at the community level in a way that allows and promotes the ability of the individual to behave in a healthy and sustainable fashion.

Chapter 7 describes a four-year-long case study of Richmond, a growing urban centre attempting to come to grips with the concept of sustainability. It describes a partnership between a multidisciplinary academic task force and a group of responsible policy makers in a real life, real time attempt to understand and apply theories surrounding health and sustainability. This experience has informed the content of the entire volume.

Chapter 8 describes a careful longitudinal study of the way in which technological and social trends have affected the health of a large cohort of sawmill workers and the communities in which they have resided. It provides a thoughtful and practical analysis of the relationship between technology, economic trends, social health, and intergenerational equity. These key factors in long-term social, physical, and ecological sustainability are brought into practical relief when we look at the hinterland on which any city depends.

The Conclusion reflects on the four-year experience of the task force in an interdisciplinary study and brings together some of the elements of solutions to the dilemma of sustainability.

The Dilemma

The point of departure for all that follows is that if we are to achieve health and sustainability, we must dramatically reduce our consumption and do so in a way that enhances our social capacity for caring about one another.

Even should we wish to, we cannot continue to consume at our current and predicted rates. We cannot demand more from the ecosystems on which we all depend nor can we ask those systems to absorb any more waste. We will demonstrate why this is so but, more importantly, we will discuss why we have arrived at our current crisis, and in which directions we might search for effective responses. In the same way that solutions to automobile congestion cannot be found by adding lanes to existing bridges and freeways, solutions to our central problem of overconsumption will not be found by looking for more technologically efficient ways of consuming. This is particularly true in a society that has long revered increased consumption as the road to progress and the automobile as the most revered form of consumption. This has been the unfortunate and even tragic direction taken by North America in the twentieth century. Mere evidence of its failure is unlikely to effect a significant change in direction in the short term, especially when the majority of us are insulated by economic and trade arrangements from the harsh ecological realities of our lifestyles. What is required is a broader context in which to place the evidence and some ideas about how it can be translated into action.

The University of British Columbia Task Force on Healthy and Sustainable Communities[1] brings to this exercise a sufficient number of disciplines and perspectives to address both the evidence and its context. The evidence shows that North Americans in general and British Columbians in particular must significantly decrease the rate at which we consume our natural resources and pollute our local and global environments. The context in which we do this will determine both our success and the social consequences. Our studies show that it is possible and even likely that if properly managed, the change toward lower consumption can lead to a better rather than a worse society. In such a society, enhanced social cohesion, interdependence, mutual aid, and trust act as substitutes for the frantic consumption of natural resources that marks the path of our current search for happiness and progress. Examples abound where small steps have been taken in this direction already. In this volume we seek to explore how to build upon those successes and avoid the pitfalls that have marked what Eric Hobsbawm terms "The Short Twentieth Century" (Hobsbawm 1994). This requires a redefinition of progress as our century draws to a close. Future historians must judge us as they must judge the success and failure of the twentieth century. An effective transition away from excessive consumption and toward an idea of progress, measured by increasing interpersonal commitment to a sustainable Fraser Valley, may lead such historians to describe our current period as "the time when too much was not enough."

If this is an accurate assessment of where our society currently stands, there are two descriptors that must be addressed: "too much" consumption, and the belief that even that is "not enough." Previous publications by the task force and others (Boothroyd et al. 1994; Vitousek 1997; Healey et al. 1999; Pierce and Dale 1999), as well as chapters within this volume, make a strong case that finite global resources make it impossible for us to continue consuming at our current rate, and unthinkable that these rates of consumption could be extended to an expanding global population. Since we are consuming *orders of magnitude* more energy and resources than all the poorest communities in our world, any reasonable concept of fairness would affirm that we are consuming too much. Evidence within this volume demonstrates we could undergo massive reduction in our rate of consumption without major adverse effects on the health of our population, as long as issues of distributive justice are attended to.

If we are consuming, owning, and using "too much," we are at the same time claiming that it is "not enough." We need look no further than the tax revolt among the affluent middle class to see affirmation of a belief that even our current and recent wealth is insufficient for sharing (see Chapter 2). This same thread weaves itself from the provision of schools at the local level through resistance of wealthy provinces to transfer payments to the less fortunate provinces, and even to a small and diminishing commitment to international aid development on the part of Canadians as a whole. At the international level, the stated economic policy of Organization for Economic Co-operation and Development (OECD) countries is that the only way out of our current economic, social, unemployment, and deficit problems is through the growth and expansion of our consumer economy. While vague and hopeful references are made to increasing efficiency, as recently as March of 1996, the OECD is poised to write off sustainable development as a failure and to commit itself to what it terms "sustained economic growth." This does not leave us much hope that history will be kind to our short-sighted era.

On the other hand, a look at our own history and the current actions of many communities around the globe gives us some hope that we might dramatically restructure our society and move toward sustainability. Much of the data contained in this volume indicate that the quality of life within the Lower Fraser Basin could be significantly improved through the development of social capital and the enhancement of our social caring capacity (see Chapter 3). Indeed, our data show that should we decide to move in that direction, our overall rates of consumption could, and very likely would, diminish significantly. It is quite possible that our current rates of consumption and relative monetary wealth actually compromise the quality of life experienced by all but the poorest citizens in the Lower Fraser Valley. The social transformation implied by a move in this direction is not trivial. However, given that a social transformation is already upon us because we have reached the limits of consumption, specifically the collapsing West Coast fishery and forestry base, we should at least start to shape our future rather than be condemned by our past.

We are therefore presented with a fundamental dilemma: How do we drastically reduce the consumption of a society that is based on consumption, while moving toward a sustainable social system?

Elements of the Dilemma

While the overarching dilemma is framed by the collision of overconsumption and ecological limits, it is important to recognize that there are many elements to this dilemma and that each of them must be addressed simultaneously if we are to move beyond our present crisis. What follows is a brief description of these elements and some reflection on their origins and tractability. The individual chapters expand on the nature and possible solutions each of them represent.

Separation of Action and Consequence

One of the fundamental reasons societies have difficulty coming to grips with the problems of sustainability is that with few exceptions, human actions are separated from their ecological and social consequences. When this state exists, the self-correcting action we might expect from intelligent systems does not take place because the necessary feedback loops are never closed. This separation of action and consequence can take place in a number of dimensions and manners:

Temporally

The effects of ecological degradation and environmental contamination can be delayed in a number of ways. The contaminants may take some time to reach the organism in which its biological effect is expressed. There may be a delay in its incorporation into the biological system it will ultimately affect. The consequence of its biological influence may not be demonstrated for years; for example, exposure to radioactive carcinogens and the development of cancer. The effect on populations may be cumulative, meaning that it may be many years before the realization of irreversible biological effect is seen as related to a particular event; for example, the link between lung cancer and asbestos. All this can leave uncertainty as to the consequences of any single human-made event or series of events.

Geographically

Since we are firmly situated in an era of global trade with massive movement not only of goods but also of components of goods, there is an effective separation of both consumption and waste products from their points of origin and final disposal. Thus, the expression of choice through market mechanisms is not a meaningful exercise except in the most immediate local exchange.

Socially

Goods and services required to avoid overconsumption are frequently not distributed where they would be most used. Thus, employment, housing, daycare, and retired family members are often widely separated, when they could support one another if they were in close proximity.

Intellectually

As will be demonstrated in later chapters of this volume, both individually and collectively, we practise denial by preventing conscious understanding of the obvious connections between current actions and their adverse consequences.

Ethically

Intellectual development, whether in terms of technology or social manipulation such as advertising, tends to be separated from any consideration of its ethical desirability or even acceptability.

We must move beyond our present blind groping and occasional high-profile connections, such as the linkage between "mad cow disease" and Creutzfeld-Jakob disease in the British beef industry. If we are to do this, we must make efforts to overcome the many sources of separation between our actions and their ecological and social consequences. This volume contains a number of tools that may prove useful in bridging this separation.

Globalization

The globalization of trade has served as a powerful insulator between the collective actions of the affluent societies of the world and the ecological and social consequences of their affluence. As is amply demonstrated in this volume and elsewhere, the affluence of the Lower Fraser Basin is dependent on ecologically productive land, water, and air far removed from our valley. Thus many of our daily amenities, from our morning orange juice to our evening coffee, are drawn from land, water, and air scattered over the globe. Our sense of stewardship for this scattered environment is limited. Our influence is frequently far from benign. The pattern of monoculture and cash crop substitution for long-standing subsistence agriculture in the Third World is well documented and almost universally results in the loss of established civil societies. As individuals, we are generally spared this knowledge and, as a consequence, our dilemma persists.

Globalization in another form allows the Fraser Valley to produce disproportionately large amounts of greenhouse gases and fluorocarbons. While we will, in concert with our Third World partners, suffer the consequences of global warming and stratospheric ozone depletion, the somewhat distant and uncertain effects leave us collectively unmoved. While ground-level air-pollution effects move up the valley and have some immediate consequences on agriculture and human health (Bates 1994), our contributions to stratospheric decline are wafted away in a global movement that does not motivate us to solve the dilemma.

Who Is to Blame?

We are in an unusual predicament as a global civilization. The maximum that is politically feasible, even the maximum that is politically imaginable right now, still falls short of the minimum that is scientifically and ecologically necessary.
– US Vice-President Al Gore (McKibbin 1995)

There are a number of levels at which political ineffectiveness is demonstrated. While there is some interest and perhaps some hope at the global, international, and national levels of government, the World Summit on Environment and Development and its aftermath are not a potent source for optimism. Nor, for that matter, should they be expected to be. Very early in our studies, it became apparent that many of the political levers capable of having an impact on the consumption causing global environmental degradation exist at the municipal level. A detailed discussion of this can be found in Chapters 4 and 7, on Vancouver and Richmond, respectively.

If in this book you seek the principal villains, or even the most culpable fools, to explain our current collective lurching toward ecological disaster, you might better turn your search toward other sources. The authors of this book, in their four-year search for understanding of how humankind simultaneously acknowledges the stupidity of our current path while continuing to tread it, did not find any simple answers. Certainly we found scores of examples of short-sightedness, self-serving justification, misguided collective endeavours, venal individuals, and malformed systems that could not deliver on the perfection they promised. Yet all this still failed to yield a set of answers that could safely transfer both the blame and the solutions to someone other than ourselves and the way in which we collectively live. In the words of what passed for a sage early in our self-destructive half-century – "We have seen the enemy and they is us" (Kelly, W.). Unfortunately, the decades that followed this insight from our popular culture have not been marked by an assiduous search for self-understanding nor by an acknowledgement of our collective propensity for self-destruction. Instead they have been marked by an increasingly loud, sometimes quite literate, cacophony of claims that the "us" of which the 1960s comic-strip character Pogo spoke is not as inclusive as all that, and only rarely includes the personal "us." Thus, we have had a prolonged and unseemly search for the enemy within, beginning with the tragic buffoonery of the McCarthy witch hunts but practised in increasingly subtle and self-deceptive ways for the past half-century. The enemy within can be characterized by a breathtaking kaleidoscope of colours and shapes depending on whether our lenses are ideological, religious, class, or gender based, economic, professional, or simply muddied by deliberate ignorance of the subtleties and the richness of the world we are fortunate enough to inhabit.

Much of the anguished concern that has arisen in response to the increasingly self-evident knowledge that humankind is rapidly overwhelming the limits of what our sustaining ecosphere can support has been focused through the various lenses noted above and has provided both powerful insights and articulate cries for action in various spheres. Unfortunately, these have often been drowned out by more strident and urgent cries from elsewhere, cries that often have a more immediate appeal to self-interest, especially economic, or externalization of blame. Despite this, there would appear to be a prolonged and fairly consistent feeling among the North American population, its youth in particular, that all is far from well in our relationship with our natural environment. The consistency with which this is seen as a major concern in public opinion polls over the past three decades would argue for a sense of disquiet about the general direction of modern consumer societies. When coupled with signal events like the collapse of the fish stocks, massive deforestation, and the final, seemingly grudging admission by the meteorological community that global warming is indeed occurring, it becomes increasingly difficult to excuse the public from knowing the precarious state of current ecological affairs and our collective part in pushing us toward an irreversible edge.

How then do we explain our continued inability to take action to mitigate even the worst examples of our continued path toward ecosystem destruction? We are unable even to stop those actions such as the malignant growth of automobile-dependent, urban concentrations that are most obviously and urgently connected with both local and global environmental degradation (Bates 1994; Task Force on Atmospheric Change 1990). It is necessary but far from sufficient to acknowledge the superficiality and inability of the popular media to act as a serious conduit for simple information about the nature of the ecological crisis, let alone the wisdom required to address it. Applied discourse on the problem occurs in few other fora. The political enterprise is marked by the same superficial and short-term considerations as its supporting media. The economic enterprise has, on the whole, exacerbated the problems surrounding the "tragedy of the commons" (Hardin 1968) by knowingly creating and abetting a culture of self-maximizing consumption.

These observations are not made with the intention of externalizing the blame for the current untenable collective position. Far from it. They are made with the intention of acknowledging the failure of individual and sectoral attempts to come to grips with what is an exceedingly complex set of problems. That attempts are being made should be a source of hope. That they have been unsuccessful should be a source of redoubled effort. The various sectors are not the enemy within that is carrying us to our destruction; they are simply parts of an exceedingly complex human presence that must be understood if we are to move from our present eco- and self-destructive course onto one that we might claim to contain hope for sustainability.

The Question of Scale
An understanding of global limits and global effects might naturally lead us to assume that we must seek answers at the global level. While this would transfer our search for solutions into a seductively distant realm, many of the practical levers necessary to effect change in human behaviour exist at another level altogether.

It was the municipal and regional levels of government that made the decisions that led to the dramatic suburbanization and automobile dependency characterizing human development in the Lower Fraser Basin and most of North America for the past 50 years. The cumulative impact is there for all to see and has been alluded to above. Our studies would demonstrate that not only is it the scale at which effective action might be taken, but it is also the scale at which the greatest disjunction takes place between stated national and international policy and the ongoing daily activities that belie stated policy. This is explored more completely in the chapters on Vancouver and Richmond.

Paralysis by Analysis

A dilemma that compounds our primary dilemma is the fact that science and knowledge can be simultaneously a tool and a weapon. As shall be discussed later in the volume, the absence of provable causal relationships between particular human activities and adverse ecological events can be a powerful disincentive for regulatory action. This is especially true if those human activities are seen to have significant and immediate economic benefits.

One of the most potent excuses for the massive denial that we practise in relation to our primary dilemma is our appeal to the complexity of the issues presented. We become inured to apocalyptic claims of consequence when we are continuously shielded from an understanding of how the choice we make today in relative innocence may move us incrementally but definitely in an unsustainable direction. There is no denying that these problems are complex. Nor is there any denying that the problems are real. At issue is whether we can understand and adapt to changing circumstances in order to move collectively toward, rather than away from, long-term survival.

Attempts to focus on the particular are often fraught with debilitating confusion. However, when we turn our attention to the system in which that particular occurs, the confusion can sometimes be lessened. Nature is full of self-organizing systems and the task force has come to view the theories and data surrounding *complexity theory* or *the theory of complex adaptive systems* as a fruitful area for enhancing our understanding of sustainability (Waldrop 1992; Gell-Mann 1994; Kauffman 1995). This theory and its relevance have been explained in previous publications but a simple example may allow some optimism.

The human disease diabetes mellitus is a complicated, confusing, multisystem disease that is frequently fatal in its untreated form. Despite this complexity, a patient innocent of any knowledge of biochemistry or endocrinology can come to understand three inputs – food, exercise, and insulin, and a single measurement, blood sugar – in order to gain effective control of what otherwise might be a disintegrating body. Similarly, our current dilemma may be susceptible to simpler solutions than we imagine. Another example might be the famous case of Dr. John Snow, one of the founding fathers of public health. In observing a cholera epidemic raging through early industrial London, Dr. Snow came to the conclusion that drinking water sources might be the means of spread of this debilitating and fatal epidemic. This was before the development of bacteriology or even an understanding of the causes of the disease itself. He struck upon the expedient of removing the handle of the Broad Street pump, which was the source of drinking water for the most seriously affected area of the city. In spite of a hostile public and an uncomprehending political class, he persisted and the epidemic resolved. We do not know what the equivalent of the Broad Street pump is in the area of our epidemic of consumption but, in principle, there does not appear to be any reason why we might not expect to find one.

Our search is compromised by the culture surrounding technology, its development, and its deployment. A metaphor for the difficulty we have in addressing complex issues can be found in the observations of Diane Vaughan in her book *Challenger Launch Decision: Risky Technology, Culture and Deviance at NASA* (Vaughan 1996). The explosion of the space shuttle, a flagship of complex human technology and control, together with the social and political response, presents a useful metaphor for complex systems and the issue of individual, sectoral, and systemic culpability. Because of the spectacular and public nature of this failure, there arose an intense need to at least understand if not find blame for this direct challenge to the *hubris* that has characterized the culture of our relationships with technology. Two major investigations were launched. Vaughan, with the benefit of a decade on which to reflect and the increased objectivity thus gained, provides a powerful insight into how our television age culture wrestles with complex issues.

The received versions of both the US Congressional Committee on Science and Technology and the Blue Ribbon Presidential Commission tended to make, in Vaughan's terminology, "amoral calculators" of the NASA middle managers. Vaughan, on the other hand, takes care to explore the decision support system and points out that no one violated the rules, understandings, or cultural assumptions of the design and control systems. While there was disquiet among some, especially the Morton Thiokol engineers, and a hunch that things might go wrong, the experience to that point was that they had not. Even the close calls of previous flights did not prove that a failure of the famous O-rings would be as catastrophic as it subsequently proved to be. Failures of these seals with ejection of hot gases against the fuel tanks were the final pathway that led to the explosion. The investigative committees and their supporting media sought, and found, a simplified explanation. This consisted of saying that NASA was under pressure to perform, and under that pressure chose to ignore the problem of the O-ring and overrode the prelaunch advice of the Morton Thiokol engineers. While delightfully simple for mass media consumption, this did not reflect the true series of events that resulted in the disaster – not that systems failed, but that they worked. The launch was not delayed because the burden of proof was on the dissenters to provide evidence sufficient to stop the launch. In the absence of such evidence and in the cultural belief that sufficient provision had been made for dissent, there was no choice but to proceed with the launch. This is a useful metaphor for the general cultural pattern of North American society when confronted with the promise of new technology.

If, as is currently the case, the burden of proof to delay the launching of a technology rests on the shoulders of those who may have some disquiet, it is likely that continued Challenger disasters and worse lie before us. The current series of disastrous ecological collapses (e.g., fish stocks, rain forest) may be the consequences of such a cultural approach to complexity and technology.

Another salient feature of the metaphor of the Challenger disaster is how the issue of the near miss of O-ring failures in previous launches appeared to be dealt with. Instead of being interpreted as a warning, they in fact provided a degree of reassurance in that they held. Thus, instead of being evidence in support of the concerns of the Morton Thiokol engineers, they become an argument against what could be conceived as excessive concern. Once these near failures had been deemed acceptable and within the safety margin of previous launches, it became extremely difficult to argue against future launches. As Vaughan points out, "for the workgroup to reverse itself to any point prior to the 1986 Challenger launch teleconference would have required a rejection of the scientific paradigm advanced ... for all previous launches" (Vaughan 1996, 249). A more graphic and colloquial expression of this slippery-slope dilemma can be found in the testimony of Larry Wear, the Solid Rocket Motor manager at the Marshall Space Center: "If we had stood up one day and said, 'We are not going to fly anymore because we are seeing erosion on our seal,' they would have all looked back in the book and said, 'Wait a minute. You've seen that before and you told us that it was okay. And you saw it before that, and you said that was okay. Now, what are you? Are you a wimp? Are you a liar? What are you?'" (Vaughan 1996).

It does not take a rocket scientist to recognize an analogy with expressed concerns about the environment in North American culture. Concerned citizens and scientists bear the burden of proof in stopping the launches of expanded technology. This, like the Challenger launch decision, represents a significant cultural shift from the previous rationale that the proponents of technological innovation must prove their claim of safety and efficacy. When the unseen hand of the neoclassical marketplace then becomes the arbiter of any residual controversy, we see that we have come a significant cultural distance from that time when a disinterested science could form the basis of any conclusion. In a perverse way, the Chernobyl nuclear disaster is an example of this cultural shift. The massive and undeniable adverse environmental and health effects have been diluted by distance and time to the point where the industry claims some reassurance for its continued existence, in spite of the fact that a similar episode in a more densely populated and open society will make the Challenger tragedy a triviality. It is for this reason that the task force believes that the scientific evidence cannot be divorced from the value judgments society must make regarding its choices for the future.

The final metaphorical lesson that we might gain from the deaths of the Challenger astronauts is a cautionary tale about vilification and the fixing of blame. Our search for an understanding of complex systems must be subject to ongoing scientific and ethical scrutiny. Our investigations have shown that sustainability will be found when a detailed and multidimensional scientific assessment is combined with an ethical consensus of what the long-term future of any given community should be.

Sustainability and Persistence

Let us close this introductory chapter by reflecting on the deeper meaning of sustainability as it applies to the human community and its sustaining ecosystems. Sustainability is not an end state to be found in either an Arcadian past or a utopian future. Its essence is the ability to adapt and persist in the face of changing circumstances. Survival is an essential element of sustainability, but since each individual must at some point die, and even cultures must come and go, we must look beyond the lives of ourselves or even our species if we are to arrive at a deeper meaning for the term sustainability. Even if, as is most unwise, we restrict ourselves to the human dimension of persistence, we can see the words of a poet such as Joseph Brodsky and achieve some perspective on our own lives:

> I who write these lines will cease to be, so will you who read them, but the language in which they are written and in which you read them will remain, not merely because language is a more lasting thing than man, but because it is more capable of mutation ... One who writes a poem writes it because the language prompts, or simply dictates the next line. (Nobel lecture, Brodsky 1996, 57)

> The revulsion, irony or indifference often expressed by literature toward the state is essentially the reaction of the permanent – better yet, the infinite – against the temporary. (Ibid., 47)

Brodsky gives us a useful example of the difficulties we encounter when we use only scientific tools to approach the idea of sustainability. Such a broad vision cries out for the cohesive application of an equally broad range of intellectual disciplines as our society seeks to grapple with the idea of its persistence or demise. Even this anthropocentric view may not be large enough to encompass the solutions we must find in response to our current dilemma. As later chapters in this volume will demonstrate, it is likely that persistence of human culture will be achieved precisely to the extent that we are able to identify with and nurture the persistence of non-human, natural systems (Chapter 3). Chapter 1 demonstrates that in aggregate, humankind is appropriating an increasing share of the fixed quantity of resources necessary for all life. The implications of this for our own health are explored in Chapter 2. But woven throughout the book to its conclusion is a belief that our own health is inextricably tied to the health of all life on the planet. We do not see this as a romantic harking back to some simpler time and place represented by a visionary such as Chief Seattle (Gifford and Cook 1992); instead, we see this understanding as absolutely fundamental to any solutions to the problems surrounding sustainability.

This book seeks to look beyond the romantic and to start to give shape to a practical reality. It represents the first attempt of which we are aware to address simultaneously the key factors that are required for a society to move toward sustainability, and the reasons that it might not do so. If successful, it will demonstrate a variety of examples of the ideas, intellectual approaches, observations, successful applications, and outstanding challenges to a sustainable future for the Lower Fraser Basin and, by extension, much of the "developed" world. In aggregate, it presents a coherent if somewhat crude vision of what a hopeful future for humankind might resemble.

In the Conclusion, we will reflect upon the effectiveness of our four-year relationship as an interdisciplinary research team and the next steps that will be required to move forward on a path toward sustainability rather than on the path we seem to have chosen.

Note
1 Members of University of British Columbia Task Force on Healthy and Sustainable Communities: R. Woollard (cochair), W. Rees (cochair), P. Boothroyd, M. Carr, L. Green, C. Hertzman, J. Lynam, S. Manson-Singer, J. McIntosh, J. Moore, A. Ostry, and J. Shoveller.

References
Bates, D. 1994. *Environmental Risks and Public Policy.* Vancouver: UBC Press.
Boothroyd, P., L. Green, C. Hertzman, J. Lynam, S. Manson-Singer, J. McIntosh, W.E. Rees, M. Wackernagel, and R. Woollard. 1994. "Tools for Sustainability: Iteration and Implementation." In C.M. Chu and R. Simpson, eds., *Ecological Public Health from Vision to Practice*, Chapter 10. Nathan, Queensland: Institute of Applied Environmental Research, Griffith University (Australian edition); Toronto: Centre for Health Promotion, University of Toronto (Canadian edition).

Brodsky, J. 1996. *On Grief and Reason.* New York: Farrar Strauss Giroux.

Gell-Mann, M. 1994. *The Quark and the Jaguar: Adventures in the Simple and the Complex.* New York: W.H. Freeman.

Gifford, E., and R.M. Cook, eds. 1992. *How Can One Sell the Air? Chief Seattle's Vision.* Summertown, TN: The Book Publishing Company.

Hardin, G. 1968. "The Tragedy of the Commons." *Science* 162: 1243-8.

Healey, M., J. Robinson, R. Shearer, B. Wernick, and R. Woollard. 1999. "Sustainability Issues and Choices in the Lower Fraser Basin." In M. Healey, ed., *Seeking Sustainability in the Lower Fraser Basin: Issues and Choices.* Vancouver: Institute for Resources and the Environment / Westwater Research.

Hobsbawm, E. 1994. *Age of Extremes: The Short Twentieth Century, 1914-91.* London: Michael Joseph; Toronto: Penguin Books Canada.

Jacobs, J. 1992. *The Death and Life of Great American Cities* [Vintage Books 1961]. New York: Random House.

Kauffman, S. 1995. *At Home in the Universe.* New York: Oxford University Press.

Kelly, W. 1960s. *Pogo.* Syndicated newspaper comic strip.

McKibbin, W. 1995. *Hope, Human and Wild.* Boston: Little, Brown and Co.

Pierce, J.T., and A. Dale, eds. 1999. *Communities, Development, and Sustainability across Canada.* Vancouver: UBC Press.

Roseland, M. 1992. *Towards Sustainable Communities: A Resource Book for Municipal and Local Governments.* Ottawa: National Round Table on the Environment and the Economy.

Task Force on Atmospheric Change. 1990. *Clouds of Change.* Vancouver: City of Vancouver, June.

Vaughan, D. 1996. *Challenger Launch Decision: Risky Technology, Culture and Deviance at NASA.* Chicago: University of Chicago Press.

Vitousek, P.M., H.A. Mooney, J. Lubchenco, and J.M. Melillo. 1997. "Human Domination of the Earth's Ecosystem." *Science* 277: 494-9.

Wackernagel, M., and W.E. Rees. 1996. *Our Ecological Footprint: Reducing Human Impact on the Earth.* Philadelphia and Gabriola Island, BC: New Society Publishers.

Waldrop, M.M. 1992. *Complexity: The Emerging Science at the Edge of Order and Chaos.* Toronto: Simon and Schuster.

Part 1:
The Global Reality of Sustainability

Part 1 provides the scientific and intellectual basis for the relationship between consumption and sustainability. The first chapter provides ample evidence that the rates of material and energy consumption enjoyed by currently rich societies are clearly unsustainable. The role of modern cities and some examples of alternatives are outlined in such a way as to provide both alarm and hope. The hope resides primarily in our ability to reduce consumption while not adversely affecting the health of our societies. Chapter 2 demonstrates that reduced consumption need not be purchased at the expense of diminished health or indeed happiness. It does, however, necessitate a social transformation from our present consumer society to one which is potentially more socially effective and happier. The elements of this transformation are outlined in Chapter 3.

Part 1 thus provides both the necessity of and the basis for effective adaptation – the necessary but not sufficient conditions for sustainability.

1
Ecological Footprints and the Pathology of Consumption
William E. Rees

This chapter examines key aspects of the human ecology of the City of Vancouver and its region in the Lower Fraser River Basin of British Columbia, Canada. Ecology is about relationships and the particular relationships to be examined here are the resource flows that connect the citizens of the Vancouver region to the rest of the biophysical world. My basic objective is to establish a framework from which to assess the long-term ecological sustainability of the human society living in the Lower Fraser Basin.

The work of our task force is directed toward building "healthy and sustainable communities." Thus, a primary question to be asked is whether the people of the Lower Fraser exist in healthy relationship with the natural environment. We believe, that for all our technological wizardry, human beings are still very much dependent on nature for survival. In fact, much of our work is premised on the belief that individual health and well-being depends on community health and that both of these, in turn, are dependent on the health of local ecosystems and the ecosphere.

Prevailing Perceptions

In this context, it may surprise some readers to know that for all the concern in recent years about the so-called "environmental crisis," human ecology is an ill-developed field. By this I mean that there are relatively few studies that examine human beings as ecological entities in their own right, as if they were *integral components* of particular ecosystems. True, more environmental studies and assessments have been conducted in the past thirty years than in all previous human history. However, these studies almost invariably focus on the impact of human beings *in here* on the quality of the environment *out there*. In short, "environmental science" as practised today reflects a deep-seated bias that permeates scientific industrial society: the tendency to perceive human beings as somehow separate and apart from nature.

Following the popular media for a week would convince anyone that our culture sees "the environment" as an optional backdrop to human affairs. The latter is the real play. We acknowledge nature for its aesthetic and recreational value, and everyone agrees that a clean environment is preferable to a dirty one. However, there is little appreciation that the integrity of ecosystems may actually be essential to human survival. We may worry about polluted beaches or fret about the collapse of a fishery, but most of the concern is over the potential effect on human health or the economy. Rarely do we interpret such trends or events as signalling a fundamental dysfunction in the relationship between industrial "man" and the ecosphere. More rarely still do we seriously consider changing our ways to enable nature to recover – when push comes to shove, it's economic growth and human wants that take precedence over the environment. "You can't stop progress" captures the popular sentiment pretty well.

One major consequence of this human-centred cultural bias is already implicit in the above. If industry pollutes our favourite stream, poor logging practices destroy vital salmon habitat, or CFCs deplete the ozone layer, we say we have *environmental* problems. We "externalize" the issue (to use the economists' unconsciously revealing term). There is little real appreciation that the problem – and ultimately the solution – resides within us. Indeed, when we do act to improve matters, the frequent response is a technical fix aimed at enabling society to carry on pretty much as before. Stream contaminated? Build a swimming pool and chlorinate the drinking water (or import it in bottles from France). Fishery in trouble? "Fix" nature by building a hatchery.

An Alternative Perspective
The ecological approach advanced in this chapter presents a very different perspective from that of mainstream environmental science. To begin, it recognizes that, whatever we may think, the fact is that humankind is still very much a part of nature. We can therefore analyze humanity's ecological niche in much the same way as we would that of any other species. What are the important connections and dependencies between humans and other species? What biophysical processes in nature are essential for maintenance of the human enterprise?

As we begin to answer such questions, we find that far from being independent of nature, people today make greater demands on the natural world than at any previous time in history. What mammal is the dominant predator in the sea? Why humans, of course! We don't usually think of ourselves as marine mammals, but no other species comes close to matching humanity's take from the world's oceans. The global fish catch represents 8 percent of total net marine primary production (net photosynthesis) and 25 to 35 percent of the productivity of estuaries and coastal shelves. (These rich habitats represent only 10 percent of the area, but 96 percent of the humanity's ocean "harvest") (Pauly and Christensen 1995). So it is on land. Humans are the greatest macroconsumer in most of the world's grasslands and forests, directly consuming or otherwise diverting for their own use about 40 percent of the net product of terrestrial photosynthesis (Vitousek et al. 1986). Indeed, human beings may well be the dominant consumer organism in all the major ecosystems on Earth. Peculiar situation for a species that considers itself unconstrained by nature!

Other examples of humanity's expanding role in nature abound. More artificial nitrate is now applied to the world's croplands than is fixed from the atmosphere by microbial activity and other natural processes combined (Vitousek 1994); the rate of human-induced species extinctions is approaching the extinction rates driven by "the great natural catastrophes at the end of the Paleozoic and Mesozoic era – in other words, [they are] the most extreme in the past 65 million years" (Wilson 1988); "residuals" discharged by industrial economies are depleting stratospheric ozone and altering the preindustrial composition of the atmosphere, and both these trends contribute to the threat of climate change, itself the most potent popular symbol of human-induced global change.

These data bring us back to the question posed at the outset. Just how healthy or sustainable is the ecological niche that industrial society has carved for itself? The empirical evidence cited above suggests that the aggregate scale of economic activity is already capable of altering global biophysical systems and processes in ways that jeopardize both global ecological stability and geopolitical security. Yet the problems so far are mainly the result of production and consumption by just the richest quarter of the world's human population. What then can we say about a global development path (as set by the United Nations, the World Bank, and other mainstream institutions) that suggests that a five- to ten-fold increase in industrial output can be anticipated over the next half-century as the population increases to nine or ten billion and the rest of the world catches up to European and North American levels of material well-being (WCED 1987)?

Coming to Grips with Reality

Driven by an uncritical worship of economic growth, it seems that consumption by humans threatens to overwhelm the ecosphere from within. This is clearly a pathological relationship. The continuous growth of any species in nature is an unnatural condition that can be purchased only at the expense of other species and the integrity of the ecosystem as a whole.

Indeed, any relationship in which the vitality of one organism is sustained by sapping the vitality of another is, by definition, a parasitic one. The distinguishing feature of parasitism is "the subversion, co-option, or undermining of the self-regenerative or autopoietic capacity of the host" (Peacock 1995). "Looked at from the point of view of other organisms, humankind therefore resembles an acute epidemic disease, whose occasional lapses into less virulent forms of behaviour have never yet sufficed to permit any really stable chronic relationship to establish itself" (McNeill 1976, cited in Peacock 1995).[1] While it may seem extreme to interpret humans and their economy in such unsavoury terms, it may also be wholly realistic. If we don't understand the problem, we have little chance of finding workable solutions.

Simply acknowledging the truth is a necessary first step in stimulating new thinking about human development options. Noting that many of our so-called environmental problems are now global in scope or common to every continent, World Bank ecologist Robert Goodland (1991) emphasizes that humanity is confronting a whole new class of limits to growth. Similar data bring economist Herman Daly to argue that the world has reached an historic turning-point, a point at which the world must shift from the assumptions of "empty-world" to those of "full-world" economics (Daly 1991).

I agree unambiguously with Goodland and Daly. My starting premise in this chapter is that humanity is facing an unprecedented crisis that is slowly (for now) but inexorably undermining the integrity of the ecosphere and with it the full potential of humankind. This creeping malaise is driven by the dominant values and behaviours of an increasingly global consumer society. However, temporarily shielded by seeming material abundance from the ecological and social consequences of their own lifestyles, the business and political leaders, and many of the citizens of those high-income countries in a position to address the problem, remain in a state of deep denial. Worse, the ecologically naïve models of their technical and economic advisors have convinced them that the "surest way to improve [the] environment is [for everyone] to become rich" (Beckerman 1992, cited in Ekins 1993).

A major objective of this chapter, therefore, is to explain and illustrate an analytic tool that graphically depicts human ecological reality. This tool, ecological footprint analysis, gains its strength by focusing on the continuous stream of energy and material resources that connect humans and their economy to the ecosphere at both ends (inputs and outputs) of the production and consumption stream.[2] Converting estimates of the material flows associated with any defined population to the area of land and water required to produce or assimilate these flows produces an estimate of the true ecological footprint of that population on the Earth. In short, ecological footprint analysis produces a simple and readily understandable area-based index of sustainability. This method enables direct comparisons of the ecosystem area needed to support the specified population with available supplies of productive land. Emphasizing physical reality in this way clarifies and quantifies the ecological dimensions of the global crisis, points to related problem areas, and suggests policy directions that might contribute to resolving the dilemma.

The primary ecological question in today's world is: Are humans living within nature's means? Conventional analyses of the economy are not even capable of asking this question, but the methods outlined in this chapter provide one way of answering it. Some of the science and terminology may be intimidating. However, the concepts themselves are not difficult to understand and the analysis is facilitated by a case example from Vancouver and the Lower Fraser Basin. The final sections further ground the analysis by outlining some concrete policy implications for both local and higher political levels.

Framing the Analysis

Many biophysically oriented scientists agree that the "full-world economics" proposed by Herman Daly will be an economics based on principles of ecology and the second law of thermodynamics. While the second law is arguably the ultimate governor of all economic activity, it is totally ignored in conventional economic models. This is partially because neoclassical economics seems fixated by the first law (which says that energy may be transformed from one form to another but is never created nor destroyed) and by the law of conservation of mass (which says that the mass of the inputs to any chemical reaction are precisely equal to the mass of the outputs). These physical laws seem to suggest that we can never run out of anything. Unfortunately, this simplistically optimistic interpretation ignores the *qualitative* changes that occur in every energy and material transformation. Simply put, the use of any rich source of energy or matter changes it in ways that reduce its potential for any future use – ashes and smoke are not the equivalent of the original lump of coal. This peculiar reality is a property of the second law. The following section links the second law firmly to human ecology through the much-maligned concept of carrying capacity.

Introducing the Second Law

In a sufficiently long time-frame, it becomes evident that the most important [potential] scarcity is of thermodynamic potential.
– R.S. Berry (Berry 1972)

The second law of thermodynamics states that the entropy of any isolated system always increases. This means that if a system is cut off from supplies of high-grade energy and matter, it will gradually run down – internal energy spontaneously dissipates, gradients disappear, and the system becomes increasingly unstructured and disordered in an inexorable slide toward thermodynamic equilibrium. The latter is a state in which "nothing happens or can happen" (Ayres 1994).

What is often forgotten is that *all* systems, whether isolated or not, are subject to the same forces of entropic decay. In other words, any complex differentiated system has a natural tendency to erode, dissipate, and unravel. The reason self-producing, self-organizing systems such as the human body or modern cities do not "run down" in this way is that they are able to import available energy and material (essergy)[3] from their host environments which they use to maintain their internal integrity. Such systems also export the resultant entropy (waste and disorder) back into their hosts. Modern formulations of the second law therefore suggest that all highly ordered systems develop and grow (increase their internal order) "at the expense of increasing disorder at higher levels in the systems hierarchy" (Schneider and Kay 1994).[4] Because such *systems* continuously degrade and dissipate available energy and matter, they are called "dissipative structures."

Of what relevance is this to sustainability? The human economy (or any subset such as a modern city) is a prime example of a highly ordered, dynamic, far-from-equilibrium dissipative structure. At the same time, it is an open, growing, subsystem of the materially closed, nongrowing ecosphere (Daly 1992). It follows that the economy can grow and develop (i.e., remain in a dynamic nonequilibrium state) only because it is able to extract useful energy and material (essergy) from the ecosphere and discharge its wastes back into it. Unfortunately, the hierarchical nature of this relationship implies that beyond a certain point, *the cost of continuous economic growth is the increasing entropy or disordering of the ecosphere.* (Note that the ecosphere develops and maintains itself by dissipating solar energy, i.e., by increasing the entropy of the solar system.) Thermodynamic law thus suggests a new physical criterion for sustainable development: an economy or a community exists in a sustainable state *if there is no significant increase in the net entropy of its host ecosystem(s).* In other words, essergy production by the ecosphere must be adequate to balance entropy output by the economy.

Revisiting Carrying Capacity
The notion that humanity may be up against a new kind of physical limit has rekindled the Malthusian debate about human carrying capacity (see, for example, *Ecological Economics* 15: 2 [November 1995]). Carrying capacity is usually defined as the maximum population of a given species that can be supported indefinitely in a defined habitat without permanently impairing the productivity of that habitat. However, because we humans seem to be capable of continuously increasing the human carrying capacity of Earth by eliminating competing species, by importing locally scarce resources, and through technology, conventional economists and planners generally reject the concept as irrelevant to people. As Herman Daly (1986) critically

observes, the prevailing vision assumes a world in which the economy floats free of any environmental constraints. This is a world "in which carrying capacity is infinitely expandable" – and therefore irrelevant.

By contrast, we have already noted that the economy is an inextricably embedded subsystem of the ecosphere. Despite our technological and economic achievements, humankind remains in a state of "obligate dependence" on the productivity and life-support services of the ecosphere (Rees 1990). The trappings of technology and culture aside, human beings remain biophysical entities. From a trophodynamic perspective, the relationship of humankind to the rest of the ecosphere is similar to those of thousands of other consumer species with which we share the planet. We depend for both basic needs and the production of cultural artifacts on energy and material resources extracted from nature, and *all* this energy/matter is eventually returned in degraded form to the ecosphere as waste.

The major material difference between humans and other species is that, in addition to our biological metabolism, the human enterprise is characterized by an industrial metabolism. In second law terms, all our toys and tools (the human-made "capital" of economists) are "the exosomatic equivalent of organs" and, like bodily organs, require continuous flows of energy and material to and from "the environment" for their production and operation (Sterrer 1993).

The second law forces thus an uncomfortable reinterpretation of the nature of economic activity. In effect, it shows that what we usually think of as economic production is actually consumption – nature is the real producer. As Georgescu-Roegen (1971) observes, "valuable natural resources [from nature] enter the economic process, and valueless waste is thrown out." Moreover, because of the thermodynamic inefficiency of energy/ material transformations, any economic activity necessarily consumes more essergy than is contained in the useful product. At best, therefore, the economic process can be said to extract economic goods and services – rather inefficiently – from energy and material produced elsewhere in the ecosphere.

The Constant Capital Stocks Criterion for Sustainability

Because of humanity's continuing functional dependence on ecological processes, some analysts have stopped thinking of natural resources as mere "free goods of nature." Ecological economists now regard the species, ecosystems, and other biophysical entities that produce required resource flows as forms of "natural capital" and the flows themselves as types of essential "natural income" (Pearce, Markandya, and Barbier 1989; Victor 1991; Costanza and Daly 1992). This capital theory approach provides a valuable insight into the meaning of sustainability: no development path is sustainable if it depends on the continuous depletion of productive capital.

From this perspective, society can be said to be economically sustainable only if it passes on an undiminished per capita stock of essential capital from one generation to the next (Solow 1986; Pearce et al. 1989; Victor 1991; Pearce 1994).[5] This "constant capital stocks" criterion is obviously closely related to the "no increase in net entropy" criterion described above.

In the present context, the most relevant interpretation of the constant stocks criterion is as follows: "Each generation should inherit an adequate per capita stock of natural capital assets no less than the stock of such assets inherited by the previous generation."[6]

Because of its emphasis on maintaining natural (biophysical) capital intact, the foregoing is a "strong sustainability" criterion (Daly 1990). The prevailing alternative interpretation would maintain a constant *aggregate* stock of human-made and natural assets. This latter version reflects the neoclassical premise that manufactured capital can substitute for natural capital and is referred to as "weak sustainability" (Daly 1990; Pearce and Atkinson 1993; Victor, Hanna, and Kubursi 1995).

Ecologists advocate strong sustainability because it best reflects known biophysical principles and the *multifunctionality* of biological resources "including their role as life support systems" (Pearce et al. 1989). Most importantly, strong sustainability recognizes that manufactured and natural capital "are really not substitutes but complements in most production functions"(Daly 1990). In other words, many forms of biophysical capital perform critical functions that cannot be replaced by technology.[7] For sustainability, therefore, a critical minimal amount of natural capital must be conserved intact and in place. This will ensure that the ecosystems upon which humans depend remain capable of continuous self-organization and production.[8]

In this light, the fundamental ecological question for sustainability is whether remaining *natural* capital stocks (including other species populations and ecosystems) are adequate to provide the resources consumed, and assimilate the wastes produced by the anticipated human population into the next century, while simultaneously maintaining the general life-support functions of the ecosphere. In short, is there adequate human carrying capacity? At present, of course, both the human population and average consumption are increasing while the total area of productive land and stocks of natural capital are fixed or in decline. Shrinking carrying capacity may therefore soon become the single most important issue confronting humanity.

Carrying Capacity as Maximum Human Load

> An environment's carrying capacity is its maximum persistently supportable load.
> – William Catton (Catton 1986)

The issue becomes clearer if we define human carrying capacity not as a maximum population but rather as the maximum (entropic) "load" that can safely be imposed on the environment by people (Catton 1986). Human load is clearly a function not only of population but also of average per capita consumption. Significantly, the latter is increasing even more rapidly than the former because of (ironically) expanding trade, advancing technology, and rising incomes. As Catton (1986) observes, "the world is being required to accommodate not just more people, but effectively 'larger' people." For example, in 1790, the estimated average daily energy consumption by Americans was 11,000 kilocalories per capita. By 1980, this had increased almost twenty-fold to 210,000 kilocalories per day (Catton 1986). As a result of such trends, load pressure relative to carrying capacity is rising much faster than is implied by mere population increases.[9]

Ecological Footprints: Measuring Human Load

By inverting the standard carrying capacity ratio and extending the concept of load, my students and I have developed a powerful tool for assessing human carrying capacity. Rather than asking what population a particular region can support sustainably, the critical question becomes, How large an area of productive land and water is needed to sustain a defined population indefinitely, *wherever on Earth that land is located* (Rees 1992; Rees and Wackernagel 1994)? In the language of the previous section, we ask how much of the Earth's surface is appropriated to support the load imposed by a referent population, whatever its trading relationships or technological status. Most importantly, this approach overcomes the economists' argument that trade and technology can eliminate local resource constraints, making carrying capacity irrelevant to human beings. Ecological footprinting recognizes (1) that trade does not actually increase global productive capacity but merely shuffles it around, and (2) that all material transformations have a material basis whatever the level of technological sophistication.

Since most forms of natural income (resource and service flows) are produced by terrestrial and aquatic ecosystems,[10] it should be possible to estimate the area of land/water required to produce indefinitely the quantity of any resource or ecological service used by a defined population at a given level of technology. The sum of such calculations for all significant categories of consumption would provide a conservative area-based estimate of the "in-place" natural capital requirements of that population. We call this area the population's true "ecological footprint."

A simple two-step thought experiment serves to illustrate the ecological principles behind this approach. First, imagine what would happen to Vancouver, as defined by its political boundaries, if it were enclosed in a glass or plastic bell-jar completely closed to material flows. This means that the human system so contained would be able to rely only on whatever remnant ecosystems were trapped within the hemisphere.

It is obvious to most people that the city would cease to function and its inhabitants would perish within a few days. The population (and economy) contained by the bell-jar would have been cut off from both vital resources and essential waste sinks, leaving it to starve and suffocate at the same time. In other words, the ecosystems contained within our imaginary human terrarium would have insufficient carrying capacity to service the ecological load imposed by the contained population.

The second step pushes us to contemplate urban ecological reality in more concrete terms. Let's assume that our experimental city is surrounded by a diverse landscape in which cropland and pasture, forests and watersheds – all the different ecologically productive land types – are represented in proportion to their actual abundance on the Earth, and that adequate fossil energy is available to support current levels of consumption using prevailing technology. Let's also assume our imaginary glass enclosure is elastically expandable. The question now becomes, How large would the bell-jar have to grow before the city at its centre could sustain itself indefinitely and exclusively on the land and water ecosystems and the energy resources contained within the capsule?[11] In other words, what is the total area of different ecosystem types needed continuously to support all the consumption activities carried out by the people of our city as they go about their daily activities? Answering this question would provide an estimate of the de facto ecological footprint of the city. Formally defined, the ecological footprint (EF) is the total area of productive land and water required on a continuous basis to produce the resources consumed and to assimilate the wastes produced by a specified population, wherever on Earth that land is located.

The ecological footprint is an area-based measure of the population's demand for goods and services provided by self-producing natural capital. Thus, ecological footprinting recognizes that photosynthesis and dependent ecological processes are the major means by which the ecosphere neutralizes the disorder produced by economic production/consumption processes. (For sustainability, the net essergy produced by the ecosphere must at least offset the entropy pumped out by the economy.) This, in turn, requires that an adequate area of productive ecosystem remain in place for every significant increment of consumption.

The Method in Brief
The basic calculations for ecological footprint estimates are conceptually simple. Typically, we estimate average annual consumption (c_i, usually in kilograms) of each major consumption item (i) used by the study popula-

tion, usually from published data. Much of the data needed for preliminary assessments is readily available from national statistical tables on, for example, energy, food commodities, or forest products production and consumption. For many categories, national statistics provide both production and trade figures from which consumption can be trade-corrected as follows:

trade-corrected consumption = production + imports - exports

The next step is to estimate the land/water area (a_i) "appropriated" by the study population for the production of each consumption item. We do this by dividing annual consumption of each item (c_i) by land productivity or yield for that item (y_i, usually in kilograms per hectare).[12] Thus:

$$a_i = c_i / y_i = (kg_i / kg_i \times ha^{-1})$$

Similar calculations can be made for the land/water required to assimilate certain waste products such as carbon dioxide.

We then compute the total ecological footprint of the population (F_p) by summing the ecosystem areas appropriated by all the individual consumption goods or services. Thus:

$$F_p = \sum_{i=1}^{n} a_i$$

Finally we obtain the per capita ecological footprint (f_c) of individuals in the study population by dividing the population eco-footprint by population size (N): Thus:

$$f_c = F_p / N$$

Figure 1.1 provides a sample calculation showing the land requirement for paper consumption by the average Canadian (in this example, consumption and yield are in cubic metres per year).

Our eco-footprint calculation is structurally similar to the more familiar representation of human environmental impact, $I = PAT$, where P is population size, A is a measure of affluence, and T represents technology (Ehrlich and Holdren 1971; Holdren and Ehrlich 1974). The ecological footprint is, in fact, a measure of population impact expressed in terms of appropriated land area. The size of the footprint will of course, reflect the affluence (material consumption) and technological sophistication of the subject population.

So far, our EF calculations are based on items in five major categories of consumption – food, housing, transportation, consumer goods, and ser-

Figure 1.1

Productive forest area required for paper production by an average Canadian

Question: How much productive forest is dedicated to providing pulp-wood for the paper used by the average Canadian? ("Paper" includes food wrappings, other packaging, reading material, and construction paper.)

Answer: Each Canadian consumes about 244 kilograms of paper products each year. In addition to the recycled paper that enters the process, the production of each metric ton of paper in Canada currently requires 1.8 m³ of wood. For ecological footprint analyses, an average wood productivity of 2.3 m³/ha/yr is assumed. Therefore, the average Canadian requires:

$$\frac{244 \text{ kg/cap/yr} \times 1.8 \text{ m}^3/\text{t}}{1{,}000 \text{ kg/t} \times 2.3 \text{ m}^3/\text{ha/yr}} = 0.19 \text{ ha/capita of forest in continuous production for paper.}$$

---

vices – and on eight major land-use categories. However, we have examined only one class of waste flow in detail. We account for carbon dioxide emissions from fossil energy consumption by estimating the area of average carbon-sink forest that would be required to sequester them ([carbon emissions/capita]/[assimilation rate/hectare]), on the assumption that atmospheric stability is a prerequisite of sustainability. (Ours is a relatively conservative approach. An alternative is to estimate the area of land required to produce the biomass energy equivalent [ethanol] of fossil energy consumption. This produces a larger energy footprint than the carbon assimilation method.) Full details of EF calculation procedures and more examples can be found in Rees and Wackernagel (1994); Wackernagel and Rees (1996); Rees (1996a); and Wackernagel et al. (1999).

The Ecological Footprints of Modern Cities and High-Income Regions
Canada is one of the world's wealthiest countries. Its citizens enjoy very high material standards by any measure. Indeed, ecological footprint analysis shows that the total land required to support present consumption levels by the average Canadian is at least 4.3 hectares (2.3 hectares for carbon dioxide assimilation alone). Thus, the per capita ecological footprint of Canadians (their average "personal planetoid") is almost three times their "fair Earthshare" of 1.5 hectares[13] (Rees 1996a; Wackernagel and Rees 1996).

Footprinting Vancouver and Its Region
Let's apply this result to our study area – the Lower Fraser Basin of British Columbia. In many respects, it is typical of high-income regions anywhere. Within this area, the City of Vancouver had a 1991 population of 472,000

and an area of 11,400 hectares (114 square kilometres). Assuming a per capita land consumption rate of 4.3 hectares,[14] the 472,000 people living in Vancouver require, conservatively, 2 million hectares of land for their exclusive use in order to maintain their current consumption patterns (assuming such land is being managed sustainably). However, the area of the city is, again, only about 11,400 hectares. This means that the city population appropriates the productive output of a land area *nearly 180 times larger than its political area* to support its present consumer lifestyles.

We can also estimate of the marine footprint of the city's population based on fish consumption. Available data suggest a maximum sustainable yield from the oceans of about 100 million tonnes of fish per year. First we divide the global fish catch by total productive ocean area. About 96 percent of the world's fish catch is produced in shallow coastal and continental shelf areas that constitute only 8.2 percent of the world's oceans (about 29.7 million square kilometres). Average annual production is therefore about 32.3 kilograms of fish per productive hectare (.03 hectares per kilogram of fish). Since Canadians consume an average of approximately 23 kilograms of marine fish annually, their marine footprint is about 0.7 hectares each. If we add this per capita marine footprint to the terrestrial footprint, the total area of Earth needed to support Vancouver's population is 2.36 million hectares, or more than 200 times the geographic area of the city.

While these findings might seem extraordinary, other researchers using our methods have obtained similar results for other modern cities. British researchers have estimated London's ecological footprint for food, forest products, and carbon assimilation to be 120 times the surface area of the city proper (IIED 1995). Folke, Larsson, and Sweitzer (1994) report that the aggregate consumption of wood, paper, fibre, and food (including seafood) by the inhabitants of twenty-nine cities in the Baltic Sea drainage basin appropriates an ecosystem area 200 times larger than the area of the cities themselves. (While this study includes a marine component for seafood production, it has no energy land component.)[15]

Extending our Vancouver example to the entire Lower Fraser Basin (population of 1.78 million) reveals that even though only 18 percent of the region is dominated by urban land use (i.e., most of the area is rural agricultural or forested land), consumption by its human population "appropriates" through trade and biogeochemical flows the ecological output and services of a land area about 14 times larger than the region's 5,500 square kilometres. In other words, the people of the Lower Fraser Basin, in enjoying their consumer lifestyles, have overshot the terrestrial carrying capacity of their home territory by a factor of 14. Put yet another way, analysis of the ecological load imposed by the regional population shows that at prevailing material standards, *at least* 90 percent of the ecosystem area needed to support the Lower Fraser Basin actually lies outside the region itself.

Table 1.1

Estimated ecological footprints of Vancouver and the Lower Fraser Basin (terrestrial component only)

Geographic unit	Population	Land area (ha)	Ecological footprint (ha)	Overshoot factor
Vancouver City	472,000	11,400	2,029,600	178.0
Lower Fraser Basin	1,780,000	555,000	7,654,000	13.8

These results are summarized in Table 1.1.

In summary, the sustainability of the Lower Fraser Basin of British Columbia is dependent on imports of natural goods and services from an area elsewhere on Earth vastly larger than the study area itself. Lower Fraser Basin residents consume 14 times the natural income produced by their own natural capital. In effect, however healthy the region's economy appears to be in monetary terms, the Lower Fraser Basin is running a massive ecological deficit with the rest of Canada and the world.

The Hidden Foot of the Global Economy
This situation is typical of high-income regions and even of some entire countries. Most highly urbanized industrial countries run an ecological deficit about an order of magnitude larger than the sustainable natural income generated by the ecologically productive land within their political territories (Table 1.2). The last two columns of Table 1.2 represent low estimates of these per capita deficits. (N.B. More recent data produce greater eco-footprints and deficits [Wackernagel et al. 1999].)

These data throw new light on current world development models. For example, Japan and the Netherlands both boast positive trade and current account balances measured in monetary terms, and their populations are among the most prosperous on earth. Densely populated yet relatively resource- (natural capital) poor, these countries are regarded as stellar economic successes and held up as models for emulation by the developing world. At the same time, we estimate that Japan has a 2.5 hectare per capita and the Netherlands a 3.3 hectare per capita ecological footprint, which gives these countries national ecological footprints about eight and fifteen times larger than their domestic territories respectively. (Note that the larger figures in Table 1.2 are based on domestic areas of ecologically productive land only.) The marked contrast between the physical and monetary accounts of such economic success stories raises difficult developmental questions in a world whose principal strategy for sustainability is economic growth. Global sustainability cannot be deficit-financed; simple physics dictates that *not all countries or regions can be net importers of biophysical capacity*.

Table 1.2

Ecological deficits of the urban-industrial countries[1]

Country	Ecologically productive land (ha) a	Population (1995) b	Ecologically productive land per capita (ha) c = a/b	National ecological deficit per capita (ha) d = footprint - c	(in percent available) e = d/c
Countries with 2-3 ha footprints				**Assuming a 2.5 ha footprint**	
Japan	30,417,000	125,000,000	0.24	2.26	940
Countries with 3-4 ha footprints				**Assuming a 3 ha footprint**	
Belgium	1,987,000	10,000,000	0.20	2.80	1,400
Britain	20,360,000	58,000,000	0.35	2.65	760
France	45,385,000	57,800,000	0.78	2.22	280
Germany	27,734,000	81,300,000	0.34	2.66	780
Netherlands	2,300,000	15,500,000	0.15	2.85	1,900
Switzerland	3,073,000	7,000,000	0.44	2.56	580
Countries with 4-5 ha footprints				**Assuming Cdn 4.3 and US 5.1 ha footprints**	
Canada	434,477,000	28,500,000	15.24	(10.94)	(250)
United States	725,643,000	258,000,000	2.81	2.29	80

1 Footprints estimated from studies by Ingo Neumann of Trier University, Germany; Dieter Zürcher, Infras Consulting, Switzerland; and our own analysis using World Resources Institute (1992) data.

Source: Abstracted and revised from Wackernagel and Rees (1996). Ecologically productive land means cropland, permanent pasture, forests, and woodlands as compiled by the World Resources Institute (1992). Semiarid grasslands, deserts, and icefields are not included.

It is worth noting in this context that Canada is one of the few high-income countries that consumes less than its natural income domestically (Table 1.2). Low in population and rich in natural resources, this country has yet to exceed domestic carrying capacity. However, Canada's natural capital stocks are being depleted by exports of energy, forest, fish, and agricultural products to the rest of the world. In short, the apparent surpluses in Canada are being incorporated by trade into the ecological footprints of other countries, particularly those of deficit economies, such as Japan and the United States (although the entire Canadian surplus would be insufficient to satisfy just the US deficit!). How should such biophysical realities be reflected in local and global strategies for ecologically sustainable socioeconomic development?

Cities and Sustainability

Ecological footprint analysis underscores that as a result of the enormous increase in per capita energy and material consumption made possible by (and required by) technology, and universally increasing dependencies on trade, *the ecological locations of high-density regions no longer coincide with their geographic locations.* Twentieth-century cities and industrial regions are dependent for survival and growth on a vast and increasingly global hinterland of ecologically productive landscapes. Cities necessarily appropriate the ecological output and life-support functions of distant regions all over the world by means of both commercial trade and natural flows of energy and material through the ecosphere. This observation highlights a potentially critical reality that should be obvious but is often ignored or forgotten in conventional development planning: *no city or urban region can achieve sustainability on its own.* Regardless of the sensitivity of urban land use and environmental policies to ecological concerns, a prerequisite for sustainable cities is sustainability of the countryside.

The other side of this dependency coin is the impact urban populations and cities have on the ecosphere. Combined with rising material standards and the spread of consumerism, the mass migration of humans to the cities in this century has turned urban industrial regions into nodes of intense consumption. The wealthier the city and the more connected it is to the rest of the world, the greater the entropic load it is able to impose on the ecosphere through trade and other forms of economic leverage. However, most biophysical resources and life-support services are produced outside the cities. Seen in this light and contrary to popular wisdom, the seeming depopulation of many rural areas does not mean the latter are being abandoned in any functional sense. While most of the people may have moved elsewhere, rural lands and ecosystem functions are being exploited more intensely than ever in the service of newly urbanized populations. Indeed, while the countryside could be viable without the city, there could be no city without the countryside.[16]

Cities and the Entropy Law

The populations of so-called "advanced" high-income countries are 75 percent or more urban, and estimates suggest that over 50 percent of the entire human population will be living in urban areas by the end of the century. If we accept the Brundtland Commission's estimate that the wealthy quarter of the world's population consumes over three-quarters of the world's resources (and therefore produces at least 75 percent of the wastes), then the populations of wealthy cities are responsible for about 60 percent of current levels of resource depletion and pollution. The global total contribution from cities is probably 70 percent or more.

In effect, cities have become entropic black holes drawing in energy and matter from all over the ecosphere and returning all of it in degraded form back to the ecosphere. This relationship is an inevitable expression of the second law of thermodynamics (cities are prime examples of highly ordered dissipative structures). This means that in the aggregate, cities (and the human economy) can operate sustainably only within the thermodynamic load-bearing capacity of the ecosphere. Beyond a certain point, the cost of material economic growth will be measured by increasing entropy or disorder in the environment. Recall that this process is the essence of parasitism. The enormous drain imposed on the ecosphere by high-income societies has changed consumption by humans into a planetary disease.

We would expect this point – the point at which consumption by humans chronically exceeds available natural income – to be revealed through the continuous depletion of natural capital: reduced biodiversity; fisheries collapse; air, water, and land pollution; deforestation; ozone depletion; desertification; and so on. Such trends are the stuff of daily headlines. We seem to be witnessing the destructuring and dissipation of the ecosphere, a continuous increase in global net entropy. By this criterion, society should acknowledge that the present global economy is unsustainably bankrupt. With prevailing technology, it can grow and maintain itself only by simultaneously consuming and polluting its host environment. As argued by World Bank ecologist Robert Goodland, "current throughput growth in the global economy cannot be sustained" (Goodland 1991). We have already reached the entropic limits to growth.

This brings us back to Daly's (1991) warning that with the onset of global ecological change, the world has reached an historic turning point that requires a conceptual shift from empty-world to full-world economics (and ecology). Ecological footprint analysis underscores the urgency of making this shift. As noted, the productive land "available" to each person on Earth has decreased rapidly with the explosion of human population in this century. Today, there are only 1.5 hectares of such land for each person, including wilderness areas that probably shouldn't be used for any other purpose. At the same time, the land area "appropriated" by residents of richer countries has steadily increased. The present per capita ecological footprints of North Americans (4 to 5 hectares) represent at least three times their fair share of the Earth's bounty. By extrapolation, if everyone on Earth lived like the average North American, the total land requirement would exceed 26 billion hectares. However there are fewer than 9 billion hectares of such land on Earth. This means that we would need three such planets to support just the *present* human family. In fact, we estimate that resource consumption and waste disposal by the wealthy quarter of the world's population alone exceeds global carrying capacity by up to 30 percent (Wackernagel and Rees 1996). (Again, these are underestimates based on the assumption that our present land endowment is being used sustainably, which it is not.)

Cities and Global Trade

Acknowledging the energy and material dependence of cities also forces recognition of the city's role as an engine of economic growth and global trade. According to the conventional view, trade increases both incomes and carrying capacity. Individual trading regions can export local surpluses and thereby earn the foreign exchange needed to pay for imports of locally scarce resources. Hence, both the economy and the population are free to grow beyond limits that would otherwise be imposed by regional carrying capacity. The fact that 40 percent of global economic growth today is sustained by trade supports this argument.

There are, however, serious flaws in the conventional interpretation. First, trade reduces the most effective incentive for resource conservation in any import region, the regional population's otherwise dependence on local natural capital. For example, the Vancouver region's seasonal access to cheap agricultural imports from California and Mexico reduces the potential income from local agricultural land.[17] Fraser Valley farmers themselves therefore join developers in pressing for conversion of agricultural land to urban uses, which produce a higher short-term return. Because of trade, the consequent loss of foodlands in the Fraser basin proceeds without immediate penalty to the local population. Indeed, the latter are actually rewarded in the short term by the boost to the local economy. Ironically, then, while appearing to do the opposite, trade actually *reduces* both regional and global carrying capacity by facilitating the depletion of the total stock of natural capital. By the time market prices reflect incipient ecological scarcity, it will be too late to take corrective action.

By throwing new light on commercial trade and natural flows, ecological footprint analysis also suggests a disturbing interpretation of contemporary North-South relationships. Much of the wealth of urban industrial countries comes from the exploitation (and sometimes liquidation) of natural capital, not only within their own territories but also within their former colonies. The energy and material flows in trade thus represent a form of thermodynamic imperialism. The low entropy represented by commodity imports are required to sustain growth and maintain the internal order of the so-called "advanced economies" of the urban North. However, expansion of the human enterprise proceeds at the expense of "a net increase in [global] entropy as natural resource [systems] and traditional social structures are dismembered" (Hornborg 1992a, 1992b). Colonialism involved the forceful appropriation of extraterritorial carrying capacity, but today, economic purchasing power secures the same resource flows. What used to require territorial occupation is now achieved through commerce! (Rees and Wackernagel 1994).

In summary, the structure of trade, as we know it at present, is a curse from the perspective of sustainable development (Haavelmo and Hansen 1991). To the extent that competitive open global markets and liberated trade accelerate the depletion of essential natural capital, it is counterproductive to long-term sustainability. Trade only appears to increase carrying capacity. In fact, by encouraging all regions to exceed local limits, by reducing the perceived risk attached to local natural capital depletion, and by simultaneously exposing local surpluses to global demand, uncontrolled trade accelerates natural capital depletion, reducing global carrying capacity, and increasing the ultimate risk to everyone (Rees and Wackernagel 1994).

Toward Urban Sustainability
Ecological footprint analysis not only measures our ecological deficit or "sustainability gap" (Rees 1996a), it also provides insight into strategies for sustainable urban development. To begin, it is important to recognize that cities are themselves vulnerable to the negative consequences of overconsumption and global ecological mismanagement. How economically stable and socially secure can a city of ten million be if distant sources of food, water, energy, or other vital resource flows are threatened by accelerating ecospheric change, increasing competition, dwindling supplies, or civil or international strife? Does the present pattern of global development, one that increases interregional dependence on vital natural income flows that may be in jeopardy, make ecological or geopolitical sense? If the answer is "no" or even a cautious "possibly not," present circumstances may already warrant a restoration of balance away from the present emphasis on global economic integration and interregional dependency toward enhanced ecological independence and greater intra-regional self-reliance. (If all regions were in ecological steady-state, the aggregate effect would be global stability.)

To reduce their dependence on external flows, urban regions and whole countries may chose to develop explicit policies to invest in rehabilitating their own natural capital stocks and to promote the use of resources such as local fisheries, forests, and agricultural land. This would increase regional independence, creating a hedge against rising international demand, global ecological change, and potentially reduced productivity elsewhere.

Certainly in terms of food and fibre production, the Vancouver region is exceptionally well positioned to enhance its self-reliance. The metropolitan area (including the suburb cities of Richmond and Delta) is sprawling short-sightedly out over the richest farmland in Canada. As previously noted, prevailing short-term thinking (abetted by agricultural subsidies in the United State) results in the undervaluing of local croplands in agricultural use relative to urban residential or commercial use, despite the existence of the provincial Agricultural Land Reserve (ALR) system.

This could change. Rather than seeing the ALR as a barrier to development, Richmond, for example, could use its agricultural endowment to help move itself forward – that is, "develop" – as a prototype sustainable city. With appropriate policy support from the provincial and federal governments, maximizing food self-reliance could be part of this plan.[18] Increasing consumer interest in quality organic foods (low ecological impact), producer-consumer food co-ops, community truck gardens, and urban agriculture, along with growing consumer distrust of international agribusiness, suggest that the public may be ahead of the politicians on this issue.

Were the local and regional population to reinhabit its own landscape in this way, it would not only enhance the viability of the Lower Mainland agricultural community and help ensure the preservation of vital natural capital assets, it would also help reestablish regional urbanites' lost sense of connectedness to, and dependence on, the land. This could only stimulate greater interest in the broader issue of regional sustainability.

Although enhanced regional self-reliance is a desirable goal on several grounds, we are not arguing for regional closure. In any event, total self-sufficiency is not in the cards for most modern urban regions. The more important issue before us is to define an appropriate role of cities in achieving global sustainability. The key question is, How can we assure "that the aggregate performance of cities and urban systems within nations and worldwide is compatible with sustainable development goals" (Mitlin and Satterthwaite 1994)? And, we would add, compatible with shrinking global carrying capacity?

Ecological Strengths and Weaknesses of Cities
A major conclusion of ecological footprint analysis and similar studies is that urban policy should strive to minimize the disruption of ecosystems processes, and massively reduce the energy and material consumption, associated with cities. Various authorities share the view of the Business

Council on Sustainable Development that "industrial world reductions in material throughput, energy use, and environmental degradation of over 90 percent will be required by 2040 to meet the needs of a growing world population fairly within the planet's ecological means" (BCSD 1993). This "decoupling" of the economy from the ecosphere will require a continuous gain in energy and material efficiency for the next several decades. The most effective way of achieving this might be a sweeping overhaul of tax policy (ecological fiscal reform) to create the necessary economic incentives for conservation (see Rees 1995a).

Accelerating global change is increasingly accepted as evidence that remaining natural capital stocks are inadequate to support the material demands of even the *present* human population. This means that natural capital stocks must actually be *enhanced* to satisfy the basic needs of the presently poor and to restore global entropic balance. Moreover, since the richest quarter of the human population alone (mostly living in high-income cities) has appropriated virtually the entire productive capacity of the planet (Wackernagel and Rees 1996), it also challenges the presently rich to reduce their ecological footprints to free up needed ecological space for others. A sustainable world will be a more equitable world. (The need to arrest population growth is self-evident.)

Addressing these issues shows that cities present both unique problems and opportunities. First, the fact that cities concentrate both human populations and resource consumption results in a variety of ecological impacts that would not occur, or would be less severe, with a more dispersed settlement pattern. For example, cities produce locally dangerous levels of various pollutants that might otherwise safely be dissipated, diluted, and assimilated over a much larger area.

More importantly, from the perspective of ecosystems integrity, cities also significantly alter natural biogeochemical cycles of vital nutrients and other chemical resources. Removing people and livestock far from the land that supports them prevents the economic recycling of phosphorus, nitrogen, other nutrients, and organic matter back onto farm and forest land. As a consequence of urbanization, local, cyclically integrated ecological production systems have become global, horizontally disintegrated, entropic throughput systems. For example, instead of being returned to the land, Vancouver's daily appropriation of Saskatchewan mineral nutrients goes straight out to sea. As a result, agricultural soils are degraded (half the natural nutrients and organic matter from much of Canada's once-rich prairie soils have been lost in a century of mechanized export agriculture), and we are forced to substitute nonrenewable artificial fertilizer for the once renewable real thing. All this calls for much-improved accounting for the hidden costs of cities, of transportation, and of mechanized agriculture, and a redefinition of economic efficiency to include ecological factors.

While urban regions certainly disrupt the ecosystems of which they are a part, the sheer concentration of population and consumption also gives cities enormous leverage in the quest for global sustainability. Advantages of urban settlements include (based on Mitlin and Satterthwaite 1994):

- lower costs per capita of providing piped treated water, sewer systems, waste collection, and most other forms of infrastructure and public amenities
- greater possibilities for, and a greater range of options for, material recycling, reuse, remanufacturing, and the specialized skills and enterprises needed to make these things happen
- high population density, which reduces the per capita demand for occupied land
- great potential through economies of scale, cogeneration, and the use of waste-process heat from industry or power plants, to reduce the per capita use of fossil fuel for space heating
- great potential for reducing (mostly fossil) energy consumption by motor vehicles through walking, cycling, and public transit.

For a fuller appreciation of urban leverage, let's examine this last option in more detail. It is commonplace to argue that the private automobile must give way to public transportation in our cities and just as commonplace to reject the idea as politically unfeasible. However, political feasibility depends greatly on public support. The popularity of the private car for urban transportation is in large part due to underpriced fossil fuel, numerous other hidden subsidies (up to $2,500 per year per vehicle), and the absence of viable alternatives. Suppose we gradually move toward full-cost pricing of urban auto use and reallocate a significant proportion of the auto subsidy to public transit. This would make public transportation faster, more convenient, more comfortable than at present, and vastly cheaper than private cars. Whither political feasibility? People would demand improved public transit with the same passion they presently reserve for increased road capacity for their cars.

Most importantly, the shift in incentives and modal split would not only be ecologically more sustainable but also both economically more efficient and socially more equitable. (It *should* therefore appeal to both the political right and left.) Over time, it would also contribute to better air quality, improved public health, greater access to the city, more affordable housing, more efficient land use, the hardening of the urban fringe, the conservation of food lands, and levels of urban density at which at least direct subsidies to transit become unnecessary. In short, because of complex systems linkages, seriously addressing even a single issue in the city can stimulate change in many related factors contributing to sustainability. Rees (1995b) has previously called this the "urban sustainability multiplier." Again, if people come to understand that support for sustainability-oriented policies will actually increase their personal well-being while enhancing their communities, then nothing can hold us back.

Note, in this context, that ecological footprint analysis provides a useful tool to compare the relative effectiveness of alternative urban development patterns, transportation technologies, and so on, in reducing urban ecological impacts. For example, Walker (1995) has shown that the increased density associated with high-rise apartments compared to single-family houses reduces those components of the per capita ecological footprint associated with housing type and urban transportation by 40 percent. Urban structure and form clearly have a significant impact on individual resource consumption patterns.

At the same time, we should recognize that many human impacts that can be traced *to* cities have little to do with the structure, form, or other properties *of* cities per se. Rather, they are a reflection of societal values and behaviour and of individual activities and habits. For example, the composition of one's diet may not be much related to place of residence. Similarly, that component of a dedicated audiophile's ecological footprint related to his or her consumption of stereo equipment will be virtually the same whether he or she resides in a village or a metropolis. In short, if the fixed elements of an individual's footprint require the continuous output of two hectares of land scattered about the globe, it doesn't much matter where that individual resides. This impact would occur regardless of settlement pattern.

There are, of course, other complications. People often move to cities because of greater economic opportunities. To the extent that the higher incomes associated with urban life result in increased average personal consumption (*net* of any savings resulting from urban agglomeration economies), the urban ecological footprint may well expand beyond the base case. Ironically, many categories of elevated urban consumption may not even contribute to improved material welfare. Higher clothing bills, cleaning costs, and increased expenditures on security measures are all part of urban life that contribute little to relative welfare while adding to the city's total eco-footprint.

To reiterate, the real issue is whether the material concentrations and high population densities of cities make them inherently more or less sustainable than other settlement patterns. What is the materially optimal size and distribution of human settlements? Should we strive for single centres or multi-nucleated patterns of regional development? The evidence is mixed, and until we know the answer to these questions, it is pointless to speculate on ecological grounds whether policy should encourage or discourage further urbanization. In the meantime, we in the wealthiest cities must do what we can to create cities that are more ecologically benign (including, perhaps, learning to live more simply, that others may live at all). More on this below.

Investing in Social Capital

As noted, conventional approaches to sustainability require unbridled optimism in the power of technological innovation to reduce the material throughput of the economy. This is a predictable response from the industrial scientific or expansionist paradigm that prevails in international development circles today.

The problem is that technological fixes address neither the fundamental cultural values nor the growth ethic that have produced the ecological crisis and that lie at the heart of the mainstream paradigm. Arguably, therefore, by focusing exclusively on potential efficiency gains, policy makers may overlook other effective alternatives. One such option is to consider the efficacy of investing in social capital. If building up our stocks of social capital can substitute for the perceived need to accumulate manufactured capital, then *large reductions in society's ecological footprint may be possible even without technological efficiency gains* (see also Carr, this volume).

Welfare and Income

At least two lines of evidence encourage exploration of the social dimensions of sustainability. The first is revealed in the interesting relationship between income (consumption) and well-being. Available data show that life expectancy initially rises rapidly with per capita income but then levels off and is virtually flat between $10,000 and $25,000. It appears that 90 percent or more of the gain in life expectancy is "purchased" by the time income reaches $7,000 to $8,000 per annum[19] (World Bank 1993: Fig. 1.9; see also Hertzman and Kelly, this volume). Similar relationships hold for such other health and social indicators as reduced fecundity, infant survival, and literacy (Rees, unpublished data).

Seven to eight thousand dollars is only a quarter to a half of the per capita income of the world's wealthier countries. It seems clear, therefore, that quite substantial reductions in consumption by people in these countries might well be possible before there would be any significant deterioration in human welfare as measured by standard "objective" indicators. We should also note that various studies show that subjective happiness or well-being is not correlated with income in the middle and upper income range. Indeed, people's perception of their own social and health status seems more a factor of relative social position than of absolute material wealth.

These data pose a serious challenge to conventional assumptions about the social need for continuous economic growth. They suggest that a healthy and sustainable society may, in fact, be possible at relatively modest income levels, even without any dramatic restructuring of society or social relationships.

The Case of Kerala

The second argument for investing in social capital can be found in the state of Kerala, India. With an annual income per capita of only $US 350, Kerala has achieved a life expectancy of 72 years (the norm for states earning $US 5,000 or more per capita), a fertility rate of less than two, and a high-school enrollment rate for females of 93 percent. According to Alexander (1994), "extraordinary efficiencies in the use of the earth's resources characterize the high life quality behavior of the 29 million citizens of Kerala." Similarly, Ratcliffe (1978, 140) claims that Kerala refutes "the common thesis that high levels of social development cannot be achieved in the absence of high rates of economic growth ... Indeed, the Kerala experience demonstrates that high levels of social development – evaluated in terms of such quality of life measures as mortality rates and levels of life expectancy, education and literacy, and political participation – are consequences of public policies and strategies based not on economic growth considerations but, instead, on equity considerations." The state of Kerala invests much of its meagre public wealth in public health and education, with particular attention to the education of girls and women.

The point here is not to suggest that Kerala, with its unique political and cultural history, is a direct model for others to follow. Rather, it is simply to emphasize that every society and culture is in part a social construction, not entirely the product of natural laws. In short, *there is nothing sanctified about our high-throughput industrial culture.* Kerala shows that a high quality of life with minimal impact on the Earth is possible through the accumulation of social rather than manufactured capital. As such, it is a hopeful example that other people in other cultures – Vancouver, Richmond, possibly even in the global village as a whole – may also be able to organize in ways that distribute nature's limited bounty more equitably. There is no intrinsic reason why we cannot learn to live sustainably in a low throughput economic steady-state.

Policy Implications

Empirical evidence suggests that the economy has already exceeded carrying capacity, yet we seem more determined than ever to address the problems of sustainability and persistent poverty through a new round of vigorous growth.[20] This is a potentially dangerous path. It depends on the assumption that technological efficiency gains alone will succeed in reducing the human ecological footprint on the Earth, even as the consumption of goods and services rises by as much as ten-fold.

At the same time, there is clear evidence that meaningful social relationships and supportive community-based social infrastructure may be more effective than technology in reducing the demand for energy and material. Policy makers would therefore be well advised to consider the "soft" alternative toward sustainability. Relevant questions include:

- How can the state facilitate the community-level shift in personal and social values implicit in a more caring society?
- What circumstances facilitate the development of sharing and mutual aid as a mode of life even in the face of material scarcity?
- What kinds of formal and informal social relationships enhance peoples' sense of self-worth and personal security?
- Which of these personal relationships and community qualities reduce the compulsion to consume and accumulate private capital? In other words, what forms of social capital can substitute for manufactured capital?
- What sorts of policies would facilitate the development of these forms of social capital?

So far, material industrial society has avoided such questions in the production-consumption debate. However, addressing these issues would contribute not only to ecological sustainability but also to filling the spiritual void and general social malaise that increasingly seems to plague high-income, high-consumption societies.

Epilogue: Can We Get There from Here?

Ours is an urban industrial culture, and there can be no doubt that cities are among the brightest stars in the constellation of human achievement. At the same time, ecological footprint analysis shows that they act as entropic black holes, sweeping up the output of whole regions of the ecosphere much larger than themselves (Rees 1997a). There is a clear causal linkage between global ecological change and such concentrated local consumption. In this light, national and provincial and state governments should assess what powers might be devolved to, or shared with, the municipal level to enable cities better to cope with the inherently urban dimensions of sustainability.

Meanwhile, international agencies and national powers must recognize that policies for local, provincial or state, or national sustainability have little meaning without firm international commitment to the protection and enhancement of remaining common-pool natural capital and global life-support services. There can be no ecological sustainability without international agreement on the nature of the sustainability crisis and the difficult solutions that may be necessary at all geographic scales.

It seems that government intervention on behalf of the common good at all levels is an essential element of sustainability. The prevailing pattern of deregulation and freer markets fuels material growth, and we cannot depend on money prices to tell us much about ecological scarcity or the "invisible foot" of the marketplace. Indeed, if we stay our present course in the blind hope that things will all work out, humans may well become the first species to document in exquisite detail the factors leading to its own demise (without acting to prevent it).

This points to the wild card in the sustainability dilemma: will humanity be able to muster the political will to act decisively and coherently to address its most communal of problems? Are there any circumstances short of imminent global collapse in which the presently rich would be willing to consider any significant reduction in their own material prospects that the poor might live at all?[21] Are we even able to contemplate the international protocol needed to coordinate and facilitate the ecological fiscal reform required to stimulate the needed efficiency revolution? Kerala illustrates the plasticity of human social organization and provides reason to hope for cultural adaptation, at least on the local or regional level. On the other hand, as Lynton Caldwell (1990) observes, "the prospect of worldwide cooperation to forestall a disaster ... seems far less likely where deeply entrenched economic and political interests are involved. Many contemporary values, attitudes, and institutions militate against international altruism. As widely interpreted today, human rights, economic interests, and national sovereignty would be factors in opposition. The cooperative task would require behavior that humans find most difficult: collective self-discipline in a common effort."

In this light, empirical evidence on the relationship between ecological decline and sociopolitical stability provides cold comfort. Recent studies suggest that "in many parts of the world, environmental degradation seems to have passed a threshold of irreversibility" and "that renewable resource scarcities of the next 50 years will probably occur with a speed, complexity, and magnitude unprecedented in history" (Homer-Dixon, Boutwell, and Rathjens 1993). Meanwhile, work on environmentally related social strife suggests that "so long as [ecological] decline is seen as temporary, advantaged groups are likely to accept policies of relief and redistribution as the price of order and the resumption of growth. Once it is accepted as a persisting condition, however, they will increasingly exert economic and political power to regain their absolute and relative advantages" (Gurr 1985, 38-9). In short, in the absence of a concerted shift in values and material behaviour, the increasing disordering of regional ecosystems and the ecosphere may well be accompanied by increasing social entropy – the breakdown of civil order within countries and increasing turbulence in international relations. Global change and social inertia make poor bedfellows.

Acknowledgments
The author's and his students' work on ecological footprinting was supported by a
Canadian Tri-Council Eco-Research Grant to the University of British Columbia, in which
the author is a co-investigator. Special thanks to Mathis Wackernagel and Yoshi Wada for
their dedication and hard work. Portions of this chapter have been abstracted and revised
for publication in Rees 1996b, 1997a,b; and Rees and Wackernagel 1996.

Notes
1 Kent Peacock's (1995) paper is an excellent discussion of this concept.
2 This contrasts with economic analyses, which focus on monetary flows. Money, however,
   is an abstraction that tells us little about the state of the ecosphere (and the quantity of
   money knows no theoretical limits).
3 Energy and matter is "available" if it has potential to do real work. For example, some of
   the chemical energy in a stick of wood is available – it can be used to heat my coffee.
   However, I can do nothing with the much larger quantity of heat energy contained by a
   swimming pool at air temperature. The shorthand for available energy/matter is "essergy."
4 It is obviously the second law that makes the economy a potential parasite on the ecosphere.
5 Admittedly, the heterogeneity and interdependence of various forms of natural capital
   make this criterion difficult to operationalize. For example, ecosystems are constantly
   developing and evolving, and there are many combinations of natural capital stocks that
   could be sustainable. However, this does not detract from the general principle that for
   each potentially viable combination, sustainability requires some minimal individual and
   aggregate quantity of these component stocks.
6 "Natural assets" encompasses not only material resources (e.g., petroleum, the ozone layer,
   forests, soils) but also process resources (e.g., waste assimilation, photosynthesis, soils formation). It includes renewable as well as exhaustible forms of natural capital. Our primary
   interest here is in essential renewable and replenishable forms. Note that the depletion of
   nonrenewables could be compensated for through investment in renewable natural capital.
7 Moreover, manufactured capital is made from natural capital.
8 The only ecologically meaningful interpretation of constant stocks is in terms of constant
   physical stocks as is implied here. However, some economists interpret "constant capital
   stock" to mean constant monetary value of stocks or constant resource income over time
   (for a variation on this theme, see Pearce and Atkinson 1993). These interpretations allow
   declining physical stocks as value and market prices rise over time.
9 This increase in the entropic "size" of humans strengthens the argument of twentieth-century neo-Malthusian ecologists over that of the original nineteenth-century Malthusians.
   People were effectively smaller then!
10 Exceptions include the ozone layer and the hydrologic cycle, both of which are purely
   physical forms of natural capital.
11 For simplicity's sake, the question as posed does not include the ecologically productive land
   area needed to support other species independent of any service they may provide to humans.
12 We generally use world average productivities for this step in ecological footprint calculations. This is a reasonable first approximation, particularly for trade-dependent urban
   regions importing ecological goods and services from all over the world. Local productivities are necessary, however, to calculate actual local and regional carrying capacity.
13 There are only about 8.8 billion hectares of ecologically productive land on Earth (including those areas that should be left untouched to preserve biodiversity). If this were allocated
   evenly among the 1995 human population of 5.9 billion, each person would receive 1.5
   hectares.
14 Subsequent, more refined analyses have increased the per capita eco-footprint of
   Canadians to 7.7 hectares, including the marine component (Wackernagel et al. 1999).
15 The final (published) analysis showed these cities to have an ecological footprint 565 to
   1,130 times larger than the area of the cities themselves (Folke et al. 1997).
16 This is not to say that rural residents do not benefit from the products and services of cities.
   There is certainly a two-way exchange. However, rural "dependence" on cities generally involves nonessential factors. In contrast, cities are "obligate dependents" on their hinterlands.

17 The competitive advantage to imports comes from superior climate and longer growing season, abundant cheap labour, and direct and indirect subsidies (e.g., California producers pay a fraction of the real cost of providing their irrigation water).
18 The prevailing doctrine of efficiency through specialization and trade as reflected in present federal trade policy (e.g., NAFTA) militates against local self-reliance. Instead, we become enmeshed in a network of long-distance and potentially insecure interdependencies.
19 Figures in "international dollars" based on purchasing power.
20 This often seems like a convenient way to avoid addressing inequity through policies to redistribute wealth.
21 Ironically, one of the effects of global restructuring under prevailing expansionist policies has been a marked *increase* in income disparity in many countries, including the United States (see *The Economist* November 5-11, 1994, for several articles on "slicing the cake").

References

Alexander, W. 1994. Humans Sharing the Bounty of the Earth: Hopeful Lessons from Kerala. Paper prepared for the International Congress on Kerala Studies, Kerala, India, 27-9 August.

Ayres, R.U. 1994. *Information, Entropy and Progress: A New Evolutionary Paradigm.* Woodbury, NY: AIP Press.

BCSD (Business Council for Sustainable Development). 1993. *Getting Eco-Efficient.* Report of the BCSD First Antwerp Eco-Efficiency Workshop, Geneva, November.

Beckerman, W. 1992. "Economic Growth and the Environment: Whose Growth? Whose Environment?" *World Development* 20,4: 481-96.

Berry, R.S. 1972. "Recycling, Thermodynamics, and Environmental Thrift." *Bulletin of the Atomic Scientists* 28: 8-15.

Caldwell, L.K. 1990. *Between Two Worlds: Science, the Environmental Movement, and Policy Choice.* Cambridge, UK: Cambridge University Press.

Catton, W. 1986. Carrying Capacity and the Limits to Freedom. Paper prepared for Social Ecology Session 1, Eleventh World Congress of Sociology, New Delhi, 18 August.

Costanza, R., and H. Daly. 1992. "Natural Capital and Sustainable Development." *Conservation Biology* 1: 37-45.

Daly, H. 1986. "Comments on 'Population Growth and Economic Development.'" *Population and Development Review* 12: 583-5.

–. 1990. "Sustainable Development: From Concept and Theory Towards Operational Principles." In H. Daly, *Steady State Economics.* 2nd ed. Washington: Island Press.

–. 1991. "From Empty World Economics to Full World Economics: Recognizing an Historic Turning Point in Economic Development." In R. Goodland, H. Daly, S. El Serafy, and B. von Droste, eds., *Environmentally Sustainable Economic Development: Building on Brundtland.* Paris: UNESCO.

–. 1992. "Steady-State Economics: Concepts, Questions, Policies." *Gaia* 6: 333-8.

Ecological Economics 15: 2. Special "Forum" on Economic Growth, Carrying Capacity, and the Environment.

Ehrlich, P., and J. Holdren. 1971. "Impact of Population Growth." *Science* 171: 1212.

Ekins, P. 1993. "'Limits to Growth' and 'Sustainable Development': Grappling with Ecological Realities." *Ecological Economics* 8: 269-88.

Folke, C., J. Larsson, and J. Sweitzer. 1994. Renewable Resource Appropriation by Cities. Paper presented at "Down To Earth: Practical Applications of Ecological Economics," third international meeting of the International Society for Ecological Economics, San José, Costa Rica, 24-8 October.

Folke, C., A. Jansson, J. Larsson, and R. Costanza. 1997. "Ecosystem Appropriation by Cities." *Ambio* 26: 167-72.

Georgescu-Roegen, N. 1971. "The Entropy Law and the Economic Problem." In K. Townsend and H. Daly, eds., *Valuing the Earth: Economics, Ecology, Ethics.* Cambridge, MA: MIT Press.

Goodland, R. 1991. "The Case that the World has Reached Limits." In R. Goodland, H. Daly, S. El Serafy and B. von Droste, eds., *Environmentally Sustainable Economic Development: Building on Brundtland.* Paris: UNESCO.

Gurr, T. 1985. "On the Political Consequences of Scarcity and Economic Decline." *International Studies Quarterly* 29: 58.

Haavelmo, T., and S. Hansen. 1991. "On the Strategy of Trying to Reduce Economic Inequality by Expanding the Scale of Human Activity." In R. Goodland, H. Daly, S. El Serafy, and B. von Droste, eds., *Environmentally Sustainable Ecological Development: Building on Brundtland.* Paris: UNESCO.

Holdren, J., and P. Ehrlich. 1974. "Human Population and the Global Environment." *American Science* 62: 282-92.

Homer-Dixon, T., J. Boutwell, and G. Rathjens. 1993. "Environmental Change and Violent Conflict." *Scientific American*, February.

Hornborg, A. 1992a. "Machine Fetishism, Value, and the Image of Unlimited Goods: Toward a Thermodynamics of Imperialism." *Man* 27,1: 1-18.

–. 1992b. Codifying Complexity: Towards an Economy of Incommensurable Values. Paper presented at "Investing in Natural Capital," the second meeting of the International Society for Ecological Economics, Stockholm, 3-6 August.

IIED (International Institute for Environment and Development). 1995. *Citizen Action to Lighten Britain's Ecological Footprint.* A report prepared by the International Institute for Environment and Development for the UK Department of the Environment. London: International Institute for Environment and Development.

McNeill, W. 1976. *Plagues and Peoples.* Garden City, NY: Anchor Books.

Mitlin, D., and D. Satterthwaite. 1994. Cities and Sustainable Development. Background paper prepared for Global Forum '94, Manchester, 24-8 June. London: International Institute for Environment and Development.

Neumann, I. 1995. (Department of Economics, Trier University, Germany). Personal communication.

Pauly, D., and V. Christensen. 1995. "Primary Production Required to Sustain Global Fisheries." *Nature* 374: 255-7.

Peacock, K. 1995. "Sustainability as Symbiosis: Why We Can't Be the Forehead Mites of Gaia." *Alternatives* 21,4: 16-22.

Pearce, D. 1994. Valuing the Environment: Past Practice, Future Prospect. CSERGE Working Paper PA 94-02. London: University College Centre for Social and Economic Research on the Global Environment.

Pearce, D., and G. Atkinson. 1993. "Capital Theory and the Measurement of Sustainable Development: An Indicator of Weak Sustainability." *Ecological Economics* 8: 103-8.

Pearce, D., A. Markandya, and E. Barbier. 1989. *Blueprint for a Green Economy.* London: Earthscan Publications.

Ratcliffe, J. 1978. "Social Justice and the Demographic Transition: Lessons from India's Kerala State." *International Journal of Health Services* 8: 1.

Rees, W.E. 1990. "Sustainable Development and the Biosphere." *The Ecologist* 20,1: 18-23.

–. 1992. "Ecological Footprints and Appropriated Carrying Capacity: What Urban Economics Leaves Out." *Environment and Urbanization* 4,2: 121-30.

–. 1995a. "More Jobs, Less Damage: A Framework for Sustainability, Growth and Employment." *Alternatives* 21,4: 24-30.

–. 1995b. "Achieving Sustainability: Reform or Transformation?" *Journal of Planning Literature* 9: 343-61.

–. 1996a. "Revisiting Carrying Capacity: Area-Based Indicators of Sustainability." *Population and Environment* 17,3: 195-215.

–. 1996b. "Ecological Footprints and the Imperative of Rural Sustainability." Chapter in preparation for I. Audirac, ed., *Rural Sustainability in America.* New York: John Wiley and Sons.

–. 1997a. "Is 'Sustainable City' an Oxymoron?" *Local Environment* 2: 303-10.

–. 1997b. "Urban Ecosystems: The Human Dimension." *Urban Ecosystems* 1: 63-75.

Rees, W.E., and M. Wackernagel. 1994. "Ecological Footprints and Appropriated Carrying Capacity: Measuring the Natural Capital Requirements of the Human Economy." In A.M. Jansson, M. Hammer, C. Folke, and R. Costanza, eds., *Investing in Natural Capital: The Ecological Economics Approach to Sustainability.* Washington, DC: Island Press.

–. 1996. "Urban Ecological Footprints: Why Cities Cannot Be Sustainable (and Why They Are a Key to Sustainability)." *Environmental Impact Assessment Review* 16: 223-48.

Schneider, E., and J. Kay. 1994. "Life as a Manifestation of the Second Law of Thermodynamics." *Mathematical and Computer Modeling* 19,6-8: 25-48.

Solow, R. 1986. "On the Intergenerational Allocation of Natural Resources." *Scandinavian Journal of Economics* 88: 1.

Sterrer, W. 1993. "Human Economics: A Non-Human Perspective." *Ecological Economics* 7: 183-202.

Victor, P. 1991. "Indicators of Sustainable Development: Some Lessons from Capital Theory." *Ecological Economics* 4: 191-213.

Victor, P., E. Hanna, and A. Kubursi. 1995. "How Strong is Weak Sustainability?" *Economie Appliquée* 48: 75-94.

Vitousek, P. 1994. "Beyond Global Warming: Ecology and Global Change." *Ecology* 75,7: 1861-76.

Vitousek, P., P. Ehrlich, A. Ehrlich, and P. Matson. 1986. "Human Appropriation of the Products of Photosynthesis." *BioScience* 36: 368-74.

Wackernagel, M., L. Onisto, P. Bello, A.C. Linares, I.S.L. Falfán, J.M. Garcia, A.I.S. Guerrero, and M.G.S. Guerrero. 1999. "National Natural Capital Accounting with the Ecological Footprint Concept." *Ecological Economics* 29: 375-90.

Wackernagel, M., and W.E. Rees. 1996. *Our Ecological Footprint: Reducing Human Impact on the Earth*. Philadelphia and Gabriola Island, BC: New Society Publishers.

Walker, L. 1995. *The Influence of Dwelling Type and Residential Density on the Appropriated Carrying Capacity of Canadian Households*. Unpublished MSc thesis. Vancouver: UBC School of Community and Regional Planning.

WCED (World Commission on Economy and Environment). 1987. *Our Common Future*. Oxford: Oxford University Press for the UN World Commission on Economy and Environment.

Wilson, E.O. 1988. "The Current State of Biological Diversity." In E.O. Wilson, ed., *Biodiversity*. Washington, DC: National Academy Press.

World Bank. 1993. *World Development Report 1993: Investing in Health*. New York: Oxford University Press.

World Resources Institute. 1992. *World Resources 1992-93*. New York: Oxford University Press.

Zürcher, D. 1995. (Infras Consulting, Switzerland). Personal communication.

2
Global Consumption from the Perspective of Population Health
Clyde Hertzman and Shona Kelly

Can wealthy societies maintain their health status while consuming less of the world's ecologically productive resources? There are reasons to be pessimistic about the answer to this question. It is well known that differences in per capita income among the countries of the world correlate positively with differences in longevity. Early in this century, the relationship was simple: life expectancy was longer in countries with higher per capita incomes. However, in recent decades, the relationship between health and wealth has become more complex as rich nations have grown richer. The specific character of this complexity forms a basis for a more encouraging answer to the question posed above.

By 1970, the world's richest nations had unprecedented levels of national wealth and a distinct "flat of the curve" emerged; increasing income among those countries with per capita incomes greater than $US 11,000 was no longer associated with further increases in life expectancy (Figure 2.1). By 1990, the world's wealthiest nations in the Organization of Economic Cooperation and Development found themselves on this flat of the curve (World Bank 1993). At the same time, the traditional monotonic relationship between health and wealth persisted among the world's poorer countries: a pattern referred to here as the "steep incline," to distinguish it from the "flat of the curve."

There are several ways to interpret these trends. One of the simplest is to assert that the material factors that limit health status in poor societies, such as food, clothing, shelter, and clean water, become relatively unimportant determinants of health when national income reaches a certain level. This is intuitively appealing because it is common sense to recognize that there is such a thing as an amount of food, clothing, shelter, and clean water, above which further consumption would not lead to further health benefit. It may be pleasant to have better food, clothing, and shelter, but they would not necessarily confer additional health benefits.

One simple conclusion, from the standpoint of economic development

Figure 2.1

Life expectancy and income per capita for selected countries and periods

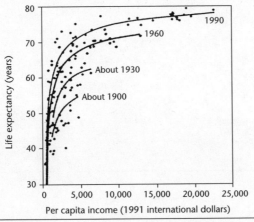

Source: World Bank (1993).

and health, is that poorer countries' attempting to match the rich and reach the flat of the curve is an essentially benign objective. In other words, the relationship between healthy and wealthy countries and poor and unhealthy countries ought to be one of imitation of the former by the latter. This interpretation assumes that economic growth, traditionally defined, is a laudable objective regardless of the forms that it takes. This view is increasingly challenged by new insights that show how differently rich and poor nations appropriate global resources. One such insight is found in the calculation of the ecological footprint, which is a measure of the area of the Earth's surface appropriated for its use by a given population in a given year (Chapter 1, this volume; Wackernagel and Rees 1996).

Consumption of ecologically productive land, that is, land appropriated for energy, agriculture, and forest products, as well as the area of the built environment per se, has grown rapidly across the globe in recent decades. Between 1950 and 1990, the appropriation of ecologically productive land by the worlds' richest countries increased from approximately 2 hectares to between 4 and 6 hectares per capita. Over the same period, the global supply of ecoproductive land declined from approximately 3.6 hectares to 1.7 hectares per capita, primarily as a result of population growth. In other words, over the last forty-five years, the fraction of the world's ecoproductive resources appropriated by the richest countries has exceeded a level that everyone can share for the first time in history. We are leaving the world's poorest nations with little room to increase consumption of those goods and services derived from ecologically productive land. In order to allow the rest of the world to reach the mean consumption levels of the

Figure 2.2

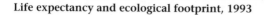

Life expectancy and ecological footprint, 1993

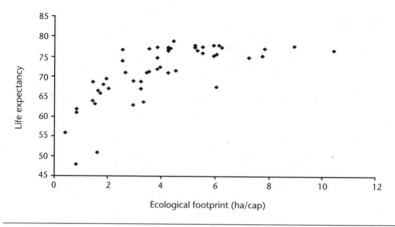

Ecological footprint (ha/cap)

Source: World Bank (1993) and Wackernagel (1997).

world's richest countries, the planet Earth would need to appropriate at least two more planets' worth of ecoproductive land (Wackernagel and Rees 1996). Despite the marginal efficiencies that could be achieved through technological innovation, this is clearly an impossible dream.

If this perspective is valid, then the relationship between the health and wealth of nations takes on a new character. To begin with, the seemingly benign construct of per capita income should be replaced in international comparisons with more stringent measures of ecologically productive land appropriation. Calculations of the size of various countries' ecological footprints have been carried out for the year 1993 (Wackernagel 1997). Figure 2.2 shows the relationship between life expectancy for 1993, or nearest year, by country, versus its ecological footprint. As ecological footprints rise from zero, life expectancy increases rapidly. Once again, however, there is a flattening of the curve wherein the vast differences in the size of the world's richest countries' ecological footprints do not correlate with further increases in life expectancy. Indeed, there are no improvements in life expectancy, on average, above an ecological footprint of 4 hectares per capita.

When this observation is considered alongside the evidence of limited global resources, the relationship between countries on the steep incline and those on the flat of the curve is transformed. The flat of the curve no longer seems benign but begins to look as though it exists at the expense of the steep incline. This, in turn, transforms the definition of success in national development and health. The most successful group of countries are those that maximize their health status while limiting increases in consumption. From the standpoint of global citizenship, these are the countries found at the left end of the flat of the curve, where the world's best health status coexists with the minimum necessary levels of consumption. Those countries found farther to the right are increasingly inefficient producers of health which, through competition for global resources, may well be limiting the health chances of countries on the steep incline. The prospect of richer countries playing the role of a global consumer to the poorer countries' global supplier raises obvious ethical issues, but a realist might suppose that these will not be decisive in determining the behaviour of nations in the future.

If success were measured by the ratio of life years produced to ecoproductive land consumed, the world's healthiest country would not be found on the flat of the curve. It would be Costa Rica. By 1991, Costa Rica delivered a life expectancy of seventy-six years to its citizens, compared with an average of seventy-seven years for the world's twenty-two richest countries. This was accomplished with a national income of $US 1,850 per capita, and an ecological footprint of 2.5 hectares per capita, compared with an average of $US 21,050, and an average ecological footprint of greater than 6 hectares per capita (Wackernagel 1996), for the twenty-two richest nations. In other words, Costa Rica would be found up, and to the left-hand corner, of both Figures 2.1 and 2.2.

Costa Rica is not the only poor, low-consuming society with world-class longevity, and recognition of this group of societies is not new. These countries are characterized by high levels of literacy and independence among the female population and high levels of spending on education and welfare compared with other countries in their income bracket (Caldwell 1986). In the case of Costa Rica, the most healthful choice was made in 1947, when a political decision was made to eliminate the army and concentrate government spending on education, social services, and health care. In general, the poor but healthy societies have come about because of longstanding cultural traditions and choices made by them, and not because of the effects of international aid.

The characteristics of poor but healthy societies may be useful to other developing countries striving to make the best use of scarce resources, but this knowledge provides little help to wealthy societies which, over time, will be pressured to reduce their current appropriation of global ecoproductive resources to make room for others. What will happen if the developing world decides that the products of ecoproductive land that are currently being exported to the developed world for cash ought to stay where they are? This circumstance raises an important question: Can wealthy societies maintain their health status while consuming less of the world's ecologically productive resources?

This question forces us to envision the pathway from how we live now to how it would be under conditions of globally sustainable consumption.

The flat of the curve, and the existence of countries like Costa Rica, demonstrate that low levels of consumption are compatible with high levels of health status. What is at issue is this: Can the highest consuming societies successfully become more like a Costa Rica in terms of consumption patterns without undermining social stability and sharply increasing inequality in the socioeconomic domain? Are we doomed to relearn the lessons from the fall of the Aztec empire as discussed in the Conclusion of this volume? This is a question about society's capacity to fairly distribute a smaller basket of consumables, and its capacity to replace excess consumption with a stronger psychosocial environment over time.

Can We Live as Well on Less?

A very indirect answer to the question, Can we live as well on less?, may be extracted from studies of the relationship between economic growth, income equity, and gains in life expectancy in wealthy societies (Wilkinson 1992) and jurisdictions within societies (Kaplan 1996). Information can also be derived from studies comparing the magnitude of socioeconomic gradients in mortality between a wealthy country with relatively high mortality, Britain, and another with relatively low mortality, Sweden (Vagero 1989). Wilkinson's and Kaplan's work suggests that equality of income distribution in wealthy societies is a predictor of relatively high life expectancy compared to wealthy societies with greater inequality in income distribution. Preservation of relative equality over time in the face of economic pressures toward increasing income inequality is a positive predictor of the rate of increase in life expectancy. Wealthy countries with wide income gradients do show increases in health status over time, but they are smaller than in wealthy countries with narrower income gradients. On the other hand, differing rates of economic growth over the past twenty years have not been predictive of growth rates in life expectancy in wealthy countries. Vagero's work suggests that societies that can minimize the socioeconomic gradient in life expectancy are able to maintain better health status for all social classes than are societies with large socioeconomic gradients.

An optimist might see in these findings evidence to promote the view that wealthy societies can maintain or improve their health status irrespective of income level and, presumably, their level of consumption, by addressing equity issues. This would be a premature conclusion. An adequate answer requires a more careful and detailed understanding of the determinants of health in whole societies than has been achieved so far.

Consider, for example, some rough calculations that have been made about the size of the ecological footprint of different classes of Canadian citizens. The rich leave a much larger footprint than the poor. Professional couples with two cars and no children leave a footprint approximately three times as large as an average-income Canadian family, and four times as large as a family living on social assistance. Indeed, consumption among those on social assistance approaches a level that is globally sustainable (Wackernagel 1993). Unfortunately, the health status of such families is not as good as those who consume more because life expectancy in Canada declines across the range of family income. Those families in the lower one-fifth of the Canadian income spectrum have life expectancies approximately six years shorter for men and two years shorter for women than those with the highest one-fifth of income (Wilkins et al. 1989). When we consider healthy life expectancy, by removing from consideration those periods of life in which individuals are disabled,[1] the differences across the income spectrum increase. In both sexes, healthy life expectancy is approximately ten years lower among those in the lowest one-fifth of the income spectrum compared with those in the highest one-fifth (Wilkins 1992).

Canadians who are consuming at a globally sustainable level appear to pay a price in terms of their health, and it is a price not paid by those in countries like Costa Rica who consume at the same or lower levels. It is unlikely that these international differences are tied to the material advantages of consumption. The most likely explanation is that individuals consuming at a globally sustainable level in a country like Costa Rica have, on average, higher social status within that country than their counterparts consuming at the same level in Canada. Moreover, there may be many elements of civil society that improve the psychosocial well-being of Costa Ricans in ways not found in Canada.

The role of the psychosocial environment as a determinant of health will be explored later in this chapter. Before that, this chapter will critically evaluate the notion that differences in consumption patterns are an integral part of social class differences in wealthy societies. In the absence of further evidence, consideration should be given to the prospect that trying to drive down the consumption of the wealthy to the level of those whose consumption is globally sustainable would disrupt society in ways that would drive down the health status of the whole population.

Central and Eastern Europe: A Cautionary Tale

Are there natural experiments that we can look to that might be informative about the pitfalls of forced reductions in consumption across societies as a whole? It is true that acute reductions in consumption during famine are a threat to life and limb, but no one would suggest that episodes of starvation share important characteristics with the problem at hand. More relevant are the experiences of middle-income societies where purchasing power has been sharply curtailed but where outright starvation has not resulted.

The best documented of these is the experience of Central and Eastern Europe since 1989. Within three years of the sudden political and economic changes, real wages in every country of the former Warsaw Pact fell between 15 and 35 percent (UNICEF 1993). These changes were accompanied by increases in the proportion of household income being spent on food in some countries in the region, especially Russia, Ukraine, Bulgaria, and Romania. Average per capita consumption of meat, fish, and dairy products declined in these countries, with an accompanying decline in the size of the ecological footprint. At the same time, there was marked disruption of the social environment, as demonstrated by declines between 19 and 35 percent in crude marriage rates and more modest reductions in preprimary school enrollment. The most significant change was the dramatic increase in the death rates in all the former Warsaw Pact countries except Hungary over the course of four years (ibid.). This is a startling finding that could not have been predicted by those who believe that socioeconomic influences on health status are effects with decades-long latent periods, or by those who believe that individual choices regarding smoking and diet have been the principal determinants of East-West differences in health status across Europe.

The abrupt increase in mortality raises yet another question: Was increased mortality an inevitable concomitant of sharp declines in disposable income, or could the outcome have been buffered somehow? In particular, was the disruption of the social environment a significant intermediate step? Thus far only the dilemmas have compounded and the evidence has not.

A Model of the Determinants of Health in Whole Societies
There are significant barriers to creating a comprehensive model of the determinants of health in whole populations. Human societies are complex, and the study of the determinants of health is limited by money, time, and the supply of useful natural experiments. These limitations, however, do not apply to studies of primate populations that show remarkable similarities to humans. By combining information from studies of free-ranging baboon populations (Sapolsky 1993) and rhesus monkey colonies (Suomi 1987), it is possible to create a preliminary model of social relations and human development that can serve as a leading hypothesis of how societies produce health.

Despite obvious differences, baboons and rhesus monkeys share many genetic and behavioural characteristics with humans and can serve as a rich source of hypotheses about the determinants of health and well-being in human societies. To generate hypotheses in this way is not to overindulge in reductionism. There is no reason to believe that hypotheses generated on the basis of observations of other species are any less likely to be valid than those based upon ad hoc observations in humans.

The health-determinant model that emerges from the study of baboons and rhesus monkeys can be expressed in population-based, person-specific terms. In other words, it incorporates characteristics of society as a whole and simultaneously deals with how these characteristics encrypt themselves within the individual. The model has four dimensions: position in the social hierarchy; the level of social stability and the nature of its enforcement; the individual experience of hierarchy, stability, and enforcement; and individual personality and coping styles.

With one eye on primates and the other on people, it is possible to identify the analogous elements of human society that determine health and well-being. It also becomes easier than it was in the absence of the primate model to create a preliminary model of the relationships between these elements. For instance, in contrast to existing models of health determinants, the primate model suggests that all levels of societal aggregation need to be considered simultaneously in order to explain inequalities in health and well-being. Hierarchy and social stability are, fundamentally, characteristics of whole societies, though they may be encrypted either within society as a whole (social stability) or in the individual (place in hierarchy). The experience of hierarchy, stability, and enforcement takes place, to a larger degree, at the individual and local levels. Personality and coping styles are primarily individual but have a social network aspect. Analogous human models would have to take simultaneous account of individuals, voluntary social networks, and local and national communities. Moreover, each relevant factor has both a cross-sectional and a longitudinal dimension to it, such that both time frames would need to be considered as well.

At the highest level of aggregation, the analogy to human society is straightforward. Hierarchy translates into socioeconomic status as a determinant of health in human societies. After all, social class gradients in health status closely parallel the findings of rank and well-being in baboon societies. The individual experience of rank, stability, and enforcement translates into the day-to-day stresses of good times, such as a positive work place and home life, and bad times, such as loss of control at work, layoffs, or long-term unemployment. Personality and coping styles need little translation, and speak to the role of social support, the value of good beginnings, and the role of personality styles and coping skills in dealing with an increasingly complex and difficult world.

The Whitehall Study, which is a longitudinal follow-up study of mortality by rank in the British Civil Service, supports the analogy most clearly (Marmot 1986, 1987). In this study, mortality from heart disease, and all other causes, was analyzed according to occupational rank within the civil service, as well as by each of the traditional cardiac risk factors, including smoking, blood pressure, and cholesterol level. The outcome was a large gradient in cardiac mortality. It was lowest for the administrative grades of the civil service, higher for the professional and executive group, higher still for the clerical grades, and highest for those in the unskilled grades. The traditional risk factors explained only a small fraction of the gradient. Instead, most of the gradient was a function of the attributes of occupational grade per se (Marmot 1987).

Further useful evidence comes from the World Health Organization's MONICA project, a multicentre follow-up study in fifty-two communities around the world that examined heart-disease risk factors and rates of heart disease. Specifically, it evaluated the significance of smoking, high-blood pressure, and high cholesterol in explaining international differences in heart disease and mortality from all causes. Table 2.1 shows that the explanatory power of these three risk factors is weaker in relation to heart disease mortality than to all-cause mortality (World Health Organization 1994). This observation reduces the validity of both associations, since, on biological grounds, the respective strengths of association should be reversed. In other words, the risk factors for heart disease ought to correlate more strongly with the risk of heart disease mortality than with all-cause mortality, since the latter includes many factors that are not thought to increase risk. This is not a surprising finding from the perspective of the baboon model. The simplest explanation for the reversal is that reductions in smoking, high-blood pressure, and cholesterol levels are characteristics of societies that are able collectively to mobilize energy in addressing health issues. In this model, ability to mobilize would be the real protective factor. The relationship between this idea and the concept of social carrying capacity is explored elsewhere in this volume.

There is a parallel between the association of increased well-being with low levels of violence and coercion in baboon communities and the findings described earlier, showing that relative income equality (Wilkinson 1992; Kaplan 1996) and shallow social class gradients in health (Vagero 1989) are determinants of longevity in human societies. In reality, income and health gradients may or may not be a function of how societies maintain order. A more careful analysis of the influence of social stability and methods of enforcing would have to take into account a wider array of factors. These should include government programs such as the social safety

Table 2.1

Explanatory power of smoking, high blood pressure, and high cholesterol in the MONICA study

	Men (%)	Women (%)
Heart disease mortality	23*	14*
All-causes mortality	40	34

* 95% confidence intervals include 0.0.
Source: World Health Organization (1994).

net; historical and cultural factors, such as the quality of civil society; and the political and economic situation, such as the political transformation of Central and Eastern Europe, the rise of ethnic nationalism, recession, or abrupt changes in trade.

Civil Society

Consider the concept of civil society, which, in terms of the model described above, is a label for the way that stable societies function on a day-to-day basis. Civil society encompasses voluntary aspects, such as those "features of social organization, such as networks, norms, and trust, that facilitate coordination and cooperation for mutual benefit" (Putnam 1993). It also encompasses structural aspects, such as institutional responsiveness to people's needs, neighbourhood safety and cohesion, and psychosocial conditions at work. From the standpoint of population health, civil society is an attractive concept because it has the potential to serve as a measure of society's capacity to buffer the stressors confronted by individuals and groups in modern life. It is feasible to use because it has been translated into a series of measurable constructs that are calculable using data routinely available at the regional and national levels in many countries. Furthermore, its use is illustrated in a series of worked examples comparing northern with southern Italy (Putnam et al. 1993).

The main objective of Putnam's work was to understand why devolution of many government responsibilities from the national to the regional level in Italy in 1970 seemed to function much better in the north of Italy than in the south. Measurable constructs that collectively represent social capital were defined. The most useful of these are institutional performance and civic community. Institutional performance is defined as how responsive representative government is to its constituents and its efficiency in conducting the public's business. In practice, it is composed of measures of the policy process and internal operations, the content of policy decisions, and the capacity to carry out policy. Civic communities are defined as those that value solidarity, civic participation, and integrity, and where social and political networks are organized horizontally, not hierarchically (Putnam 1993). The index is composed of measures of civic engagement, political equality, social structures of cooperation, and, finally, qualities of solidarity, trust, and tolerance.

Figures 2.3 and 2.4 show how the regions of Italy score on the indexes of institutional performance and civic community. They show that the northern regions of Tuscany and Lombardy, which have a 1,000-year tradition of civic society, score higher than the southern regions. The southern regions have a much weaker civic tradition but a stronger tradition of family loyalty. This loyalty has served as a sanctuary against forces of political and economic control, which were seen as alien, hostile, and threatening.

Figure 2.3

Institutional performance in Italian regions, 1978-85

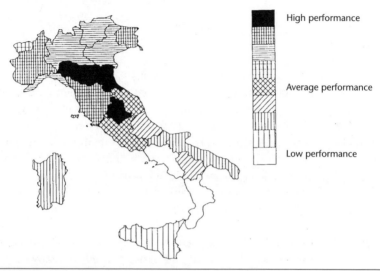

High performance

Average performance

Low performance

Source: Putnam et al. (1993).

Figure 2.4

The civic community in the Italian regions, 1978-85

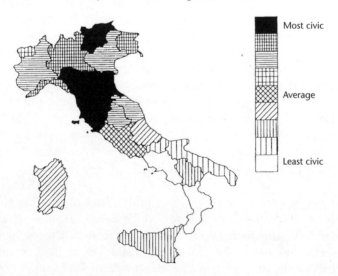

Most civic

Average

Least civic

Source: Putnam et al. (1993).

Table 2.2 summarizes available data on mortality and social capital formation in Italy. For each mortality variable, it presents the variation in rates across the regions of Italy, which is "explained" by the indexes of civic community and institutional performance. The table shows that there is a strong positive association between both institutional performance and civic community, on the one hand, and decreasing infant mortality rates, on the other. Child mortality, ages one to fourteen, as a proportion of total mortality, is also lower in regions with higher levels of social capital formation. There is no association with overall life expectancy (not shown); however, when life expectancy gains over time are disaggregated by sex, a startling pattern of sex differences emerges. The table shows a significant association with both measures for men between 1971 and 1986 and for women between 1961 and 1971. For women, there is essentially no correlation after 1970. This raises important questions about the relationship between sex and the determinants of health, in particular, the protective effects of women's traditional place at the centre of the family network.

The logic of the above analysis is that higher quality civil societies may lead to better health status. If so, this would support the notion that societies consciously trying to reduce their ecological footprints could maintain or improve health status by simultaneously strengthening civil society functions. If so, this logic should be reversible. That is, differences in health status among defined geographic regions within a broader economic zone should also suggest differences in the quality of civil society functions among them.

An examination of, for example, the twenty health regions of British Columbia (Figure 2.5) shows that life expectancy varies by more than four years, which is a large difference by the standards of wealthy countries (British Columbia 1996). What are the determinants of this difference? At the most macro level, socioeconomic status matters.

Figure 2.6 presents the correlation of age-standardized mortality for these regions with each region's rank on a socioeconomic indicator that includes the percent of the population on income assistance, the percent aged 25 to 34 with less than high-school graduation, and unemployment rates. The figure shows that there is a variation of approximately 50 percent across health regions on this scale, and a strong correlation with the indicator of socioeconomic status. This strong relationship may be seen to be in contradiction with what we would hope to see. However, none of these socioeconomic variables need change in negative ways with reductions in the size of the ecological footprint.

There is also a large off-diagonal component that does not correlate with the overall socioeconomic indicator. For instance, the South Okanagan region has approximately 25 percent lower mortality than would be

Table 2.2

Proportion of regional variation in mortality explained by social capital formation in Italy

	% of mortality 1-14 (1991)	Infant mortality rate (1951)	Infant mortality rate (1987)	Increase in male life expectancy (1961-71)	Increase in male life expectancy (1971-86)	Increase in female life expectancy (1961-71)	Increase in female life expectancy (1971-86)
Institutional performance	.49*	.66**	.78**	.54*	.54*	.65**	.02
Civic community	.36*	.73**	.83**	.43	.50*	.62*	.13

*p < 0.05
**p < 0.005
Sources: Putnam (1993); Istituto Nazionale di Statistica (1994).

Figure 2.5

Life expectancy in the health regions of British Columbia

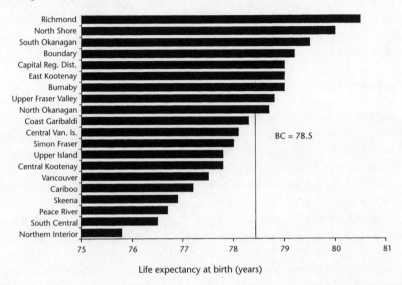

Life expectancy at birth (years)

Source: British Columbia, Ministry of Health (1996).

Figure 2.6

Overall rank on three socioeconomic variables and age standardized mortality rate in the health regions of British Columbia

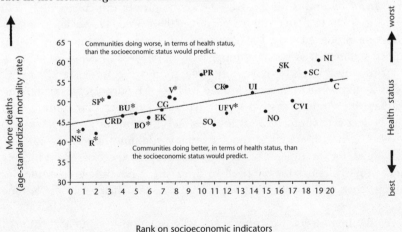

Rank on socioeconomic indicators

* The regions of the Lower Mainland are V (Vancouver), NS (North Shore), R (Richmond), SF (Simon Fraser), BU (Burnaby), BO (Boundary), and UFV (Upper Fraser Valley).
Source: British Columbia, Ministry of Health (1996).

predicted, while the Prince Rupert region is approximately 15 percent above expectation. Richmond, despite its high socioeconomic position, also falls on the positive side of the line, with approximately 15 percent less mortality than expected. The central question raised by these data is, Are those health regions that fall below the line better civil societies than those above the line?

Summing Up

Wealthy societies consume too much of the world's resources and need to cut back. In principle, this can be done without sacrificing human health; there are examples of societies that consume at globally sustainable levels and maintain a health status similar to ours. We know that the principal determinants of health in wealthy societies reside, broadly, in the social environment. But do we know how to reduce our levels of consumption without sacrificing those aspects of our social environment that are health-giving? At present, the answer is a qualified "yes," but we are steadily gaining insights that are changing the answer to an unqualified "yes."

There are four levels to consider: the macro level of socioeconomic factors, the meso level of civil society, the micro level of social networks, and the developmental trajectory of individuals across the life course. At each level, it is possible to imagine making a conscious effort to protect that which is health-giving and improve that which has not been given adequate attention. For instance, we already know that maintaining relative income equality within a society is important. Canada is one of the few countries whose social safety net has effectively prevented income inequalities from becoming wider over the economically difficult period from 1980 to 1995 (Canada 1996; Smeeding 1996). Canada's social programs must be protected, and the rhetoric of taxpayer resentment, which is aimed squarely at our social safety net, must be discounted.

At the meso level, we have done little to measure, understand, or consciously intervene to improve human welfare. Yet, our society is rich in initiatives that strengthen civil society. There is evidence that communities can collectively compensate at the meso level for misfortune at the macro level. The health status of those in many communities in the Atlantic provinces, for example, is better than one would expect based on income and employment data. We need to understand how these communities buffer stress, and ensure that we do not pursue policies that undermine these processes.

At the micro level, we know that social isolation is a threat to human health. We also know that adequate housing and the community context of housing are important for social connections and, surprisingly, for mental development in children. Measuring and increasing social support of communities is possible without invading individual privacy and needs to be a priority in a society where traditional support structures, such as the extended and nuclear family, are continuing to break down.

Finally, we need to understand and respond to the developmental needs of individuals throughout the life course. We know that human potential can be better realized by improving the quality of emotional and mental stimulation during sensitive periods in early child development. This can be accomplished through early intervention programs for children at high risk of delinquency and teen pregnancy; through programs of national service in early adulthood; through work environments where the individual has some measure of control over job demands and pacing; and through the provision of housing, community facilities, and flexible work arrangements for the elderly to keep them involved in community life as long as possible.

A society that successfully takes on these challenges can manage on less, and will be better for it.

Note

1 In practice, this means taking the average life expectancy and subtracting out the average number of years an individual can expect to live in a state of (greater or lesser) disability throughout life.

References

British Columbia. Ministry of Health. 1996. *A Report on the Health of British Columbians: Provincial Health Officer's Annual Report 1995.* Victoria: BC Ministry of Health and Ministry Responsible for Seniors.

Caldwell, J.C. 1986. "Routes to Low Mortality in Poor Countries." *Population and Development Review* 12: 171-220.

Canada. Statistics Canada. 1996. *Income after Tax, Distributions by Size in Canada 1994.* Ottawa, Minister of Industry.

Istituto Nazionale di Statistica. 1994. Statistical tables (provided on request).

Kaplan, G.A., E.R. Pamuk, J.W. Lynch, R.D. Cohen, and J.L. Balfour. 1996. "Inequality in Income and Mortality in the United States: Analysis of Mortality and Potential Pathways." *British Medical Journal* 312: 999-1003.

Marmot, M.G. 1986. "Social Inequalities in Mortality: The Social Environment." In R.G. Wilkinson, ed., *Class and Health: Research and Longitudinal Data,* 21-33. London: Tavistock Publications.

Marmot, M.G., G. Rose, M. Shipley, and P.J.S. Hamilton. 1987. "Employment Grade and Coronary Heart Disease in British Civil Servants." *Journal of Epidemiology and Community Health* 32: 244-9.

Putnam, R.D. 1993. "The Prosperous Community: Social Capital and Public Life." *The American Prospect* 13: 35-42.

Putnam, R.D., R. Leonardi, and R.Y. Nanetti. 1993. *Making Democracy Work. Civic Traditions in Modern Italy.* Princeton: Princeton University Press.

Sapolsky, R.M. 1993. "Endocrinology Alfresco: Psychoendocrine Studies of Wild Baboons." *Recent Progress in Hormone Research* 48: 437-68.

Smeeding, T.M., and P. Gottschalk. 1996. The International Evidence on Income Distribution in Modern Economies: Where Do We Stand? Paper presented at the annual meeting of the Population Association of America, New Orleans, May.

Suomi, S.J. 1987. "Genetic and Maternal Contributions to Individual Differences in Rhesus Monkey Biobehavioral Development." In N. Krasnegor, E. Blass, M. Hofer, and

W. Smotherman, ed., *Perinatal Development: A Psychobiological Perspective.* New York: Academic Press.

UNICEF. 1993. *Central and Eastern Europe in Transition. Public Policy and Social Conditions.* Regional Monitoring Report No. 1. United Nations Children's Fund. Florence: International Child Development Centre.

Vagero, D., and O. Lundberg. 1989. "Health Inequalities in Britain and Sweden." *Lancet* 2: 35-6.

Wackernagel, M. 1997. *Ecological Footprints 1993.* Mexico City: Centro de Estudios para la Sustentabilidad.

Wackernagel, M., and W.E. Rees. 1996. *Our Ecological Footprint: Reducing Human Impact on the Earth.* Philadelphia and Gabriola Island, BC: New Society Publishers.

Wilkins, R. 1992. Personal communication: telephone conversation with author, March.

Wilkins, R., O. Adams, and A. Brancker. 1989. "Changes in Mortality by Income in Urban Canada from 1971 to 1986." *Health Reports* 1,2: 137-74.

Wilkinson, R.G. 1992. "Income Distribution and Life Expectancy." *British Medical Journal* 304: 165-8.

World Bank. 1993. *World Development Report. Investing in Health. World Development Indicators.* New York: Oxford University Press.

World Health Organization MONICA Project. 1994. "Ecological Analysis of the Association Between Mortality and Major Risk Factors of Cardiovascular Disease." *International Journal of Epidemiology* 23,3: 505-16.

3
Social Capital, Civil Society, and Social Transformation
Michael Carr

The ecological footprint analysis of the Lower Fraser Basin shows that the human population of this region requires an area fourteen times larger than its home territory to maintain our present levels of consumption (Rees, this volume; Rees, 1996; Wackernagel and Rees 1996, 86-8). This revealing figure, which is typical of high-income regions, suggests that, in these regions at least, we are so far beyond ecological carrying capacity that major changes in our sociocultural and economic arrangements are needed if we are to be serious about sustainability.

The purpose of this chapter is to help us to begin thinking conceptually and broadly about the profound social transformation in both consumption *and* production that will be necessary to achieve sustainability. In order to sufficiently curtail consumption, we need to begin to understand it differently, breaking out of the narrow economic-growth vision of our industrial society. One tool to help us to do this is the notion of social capital, with its companion concept of cultural capital. Together, these concepts provide the conceptual basis for our social caring capacity tool, the measurement of and facilitator for a social sense of connectedness, belonging, and well-being characteristic of caring communities. Moreover, social and cultural capital, located in a civil society-based framework for analysis, can be directly applied to help us conceptualize broad, strategic social change possibilities at the local, regional, and interregional scales.

A Mode-of-Production-Consumption Framework
A conventional definition of mode of production includes four factors of production: land, labour, entrepreneurial skills, and capital. Capital is sometimes further subdivided into finance and physical capital. A conventional analytic framework regards these factors merely as inputs into the production process.

In my definition, the mode of production is viewed dialectically as a mode of production *and* consumption. Production and consumption are seen to be directly related aspects of an integrated human economic system. In this view, the link between production and consumption is explicitly recognized. As consumption grows, so does production, and as production grows, so generally does consumption. For example, when the industrial mode of mass production became so productively successful in the nineteenth century, it became necessary to create masses of consumers and national markets to supplant the great variety of small local and regional markets. This was done through the creation of advertising and a mass media industry (Ewen 1976). In turn, the rise in consumption stimulated further increases in production, in an endless positive feedback loop.

In my definition of a mode of production and consumption, I include six factors of production:

1   natural capital, including not only land but all nature's goods and services
2   human capital, including skills and knowledge of labour and management
3   physical capital, sometimes called human-made capital
4   finance capital
5   social capital (to be defined below)
6   cultural capital (to be defined below).

Since all human modes of production are actually modes of production and consumption, we cannot consider the various factors as merely inputs to production; we cannot ignore their role in consumption. For example, natural capital is a factor in production, but natural capital can only be a factor of production when a portion of it is consumed.

Defining Social Capital

In the simplest terms, James Coleman's social capital refers to those organizations, structures, and social relations that are built up by people themselves, independently of the state or large corporations. They could include anything from a choral society to a community bank. In Coleman's sociological view, social capital refers to relationships and is manifested in the structure of relations between and among persons (Coleman 1990, 300-18). Social capital is therefore a social-structural resource for people and can help them to enhance their human capital. This first point is crucial to understanding the potential of social capital to replace much of natural capital throughput. Second, social capital is a relational term: it is manifested in the relations between people, not in individuals, not in the implements of production, nor in the physical infrastructure. Social capital is a resource that has value only in the practice and expression of social relations and, therefore, unlike physical capital, it cannot be exchanged, nor can it be alienated like private property. It is a qualitatively different kind of capital from either financial or physical capital. Social capital has the potential to produce a stronger social fabric. It builds bonds of information, trust, and solidarity between people, most often as a by-product of other activities (Coleman 1990). For example, voluntary citizens organizations have many purposes, but whatever their particular purpose may be, a stronger social fabric, that is, greater stocks of social capital, is one outcome. This means that stocks of social capital increase with use; the more you use social capital, the more you have. In this, too, social capital is very unlike physical capital.

Because it is a relational term, social capital has an intangible nature that can perhaps be best understood through looking at its forms. There are three key forms of social capital:

1   dense horizontal networks and associations of community involvement
2   high levels of information about the trustworthiness of individuals involved in the networks
3   effective norms and sanctions (shared values) built up through past successes of collaboration in working to achieve common goals (Coleman 1990, 304-11).

These networks, associations, and norms promote strong local bonds of generalized reciprocity (Taylor 1982; Putnam 1993b). Generalized reciprocity represents the strongest form of solidarity possible, promoting the reconciliation of self-interest and social solidarity. There is a dialectical relationship among these forms of social capital that works to build up a system of mutual trust and shared values. In this process, the greater the levels of social capital, the stronger the norms of generalized reciprocity become. The use of social capital facilitates the further build up of even greater levels of social capital. The result of this process, as Robert Putnam has shown in his study of social capital in Italy, is a society where levels of trust are very high, lubricating social life, enhancing productivity, and facilitating action (Putnam 1993b).[1] The productivity of social capital is crucial to success in replacing natural capital throughput, as we shall see.

For the practice of general reciprocity to become profound, direct and many-sided relationships need to be nurtured in fairly small and stable communities. These small communities include the integration of both place and interest, a key integration that is too often ignored in debates about communities of place versus communities of interest (Boothroyd and Davis 1991).

The existence and use of social capital can perhaps be most clearly defined by looking at societies where small community was the predominant or sole form of social organization, communities where there was no state and where the economy was not seen as separate from, prior to, or above society.

Defining Cultural Capital

Cultural capital is the interface between natural capital and physical (often referred to as human-made) capital. This concept includes:

1   people's environmental philosophy, values, ethics, and religion
2   local or personal knowledge of the environment
3   traditional ecological knowledge
4   traditional resource-management institutions.

For Berkes and Folke (1994), there is a dynamic, dialectical relationship between natural capital, cultural capital, and physical capital. They argue convincingly that the dominant cultural capital of industrialism and the technologies that reflect it have masked societies' dependence on natural capital. Positive feedback between cultural capital and physical capital intensify this dynamic, reinforcing a monocultural technology and society that encourage people to see themselves as separate from or above nature (Berkes and Folke 1994).

In stark contrast, the cultural capital of societies based on small community is marked by ancient philosophical and spiritual traditions that include the "community of beings" ethic in their worldviews. Berkes and Folke argue that we need to transform modern cultural capital by restoring the ancient ethic of a life-community to help cure our modern, widespread alienation from nature (Berkes and Folke 1994). I call societies practising a community-of-beings ethic "earth-based societies."

In earth-based societies, the norm of reciprocity is not limited to the human community but is extended symbolically to the community of all beings. Humans are not seen as apart from or above nature but, rather, as part of the greater ecological community. One crucial result of this ethic has been a high level of de facto ecological knowledge and wisdom, a knowledge that is now being recognized as traditional ecological knowledge (Berkes et al. 1998; Pinkerton 1998; Lertzman 1999). In earth-based societies, the relationship between cultural capital and physical capital reveals rather than conceals human dependence on natural capital. Strong cultural norms, sanctions, and taboos exist to ensure that physical capital and human technology does not deplete or despoil natural capital. I will consider examples when looking at the domestic mode of production.

We can see that social capital, when informed by a community-of-beings ethic of cultural capital, can now be defined as ecologically informed (or oriented) social capital. Ecologically informed social capital is that qualitative, productive force that made it possible for earth-based societies to enjoy a high level of well-being that did not depend on the excessive throughput and destruction of natural capital. In other words, the productivity of social capital did, and potentially still can, enable humans to achieve healthy economic activity with a much-reduced use of natural capital. This dynamic occurs when the form of cultural capital – as in the community-of-beings ethic – reveals and places value upon human dependence on natural capital.

To illustrate and develop the foregoing analysis, it will be necessary to examine in some detail the domestic mode of production.

The Domestic Mode of Production

With its roots deep in the Paleolithic period, the domestic mode of production used by gathering and hunting societies was by far the longest-running production and consumption system humans have ever used, comprising about 99 percent of our time on earth. This fact alone speaks volumes for the sustainability of this system over the (very) long term. In the domestic mode of production, the household, and usually the extended family, is the management unit of production and of deployment and use of labour power. It is also where what we moderns would call "economic objectives" are determined. The principal relations of production are therefore the inner relations of the family or the domestic group. All these production decisions are domestic decisions for the purpose of domestic consumption, satisfaction, health, and happiness. Production, then, is attuned to the family's customary requirements. It is the means by which people lived, in terms of both biological and certain social needs, rather than being an end in itself. Thus, in the domestic mode of production, there is no split between producers and consumers. On the contrary, we find an economy that is ordered primarily by kinship relations.

Many different cultures are included within the domestic mode of production, but thanks to the comprehensive overview provided by the economic anthropology of Marshall Sahlins, we have a definition and an analytical framework that captures certain common features of the spectrum of cultures practising this form of "economic" production.

It is actually very difficult to speak of an economy as such in reference to the domestic mode of production. As Sahlins has pointed out, structurally, the economy does not exist in the domestic mode of production. More precisely, economy is something that generalized social or kinship groups *do,* rather than a distinct, specialized organization (Sahlins 1974, 76). Sahlins adds a revealing comparison: "The household is to the tribal economy as the manor to the medieval economy or the corporation to modern capitalism: each is the dominant production-institution of its time" (1974).

Production for Livelihood

In our consumer society, we tend to consider affluence in terms of the possession of things, the endless accumulation of material products. In contrast to modern affluent consumer civilization, Sahlins has counterposed the "original affluent societies" of Paleolithic gatherer-hunters and Neolithic agriculturists. Perhaps the most striking feature of such societies is what Sahlins has termed their "structure of underproduction" or production for livelihood (Sahlins 1974, 41). By this, Sahlins means that domestic mode of production societies used their own labour, their technological means, and their natural resources very conservatively. They simply did not exploit their labour, technology, or natural resources to the extent that they were capable of doing. We moderns have consistently seen these subsistence economies as materially impoverished, surviving only in a state of brutal hardship. This view is changing, but to regard such societies as affluent still shocks our sensibilities. Nevertheless, poverty is not merely a small amount of goods, nor simply a relation between means and ends, but, above all, a relation between people. Poverty has actually grown with civilization. Our global economy is synonymous with an era of mass starvation, associated with failing to meet most people's basic needs more massively and chronically than in any other era in the history of humanity. While Paleolithic and Neolithic communities had what we would call an objectively low standard of living, the material needs of peoples within a domestic mode of production were usually met. As Sahlins has put it, there is a Zen road to affluence. "Adopting the Zen strategy, a people can enjoy an unparalleled material plenty – with a low standard of living" (Sahlins 1974, 2). All the people's material wants could easily be satisfied, even with the economy running below its capacity, given their modest (by our inflated standards) ideas of material satisfaction. The modern state of Kerala in India provides us with a contemporary example of a basic need-meeting, production-for-livelihood strategy (see the discussion of Kerala in Chapter 1 of this volume). The point is that, in societies where the domestic mode of production is strong, the lives of people can be socially and spiritually rich while also meeting basic material needs.

Whether the domestic group was a single family or a group of families, production was primarily for the benefit of the producers, that is, for the domestic group itself. Sahlins points out that production for livelihood is essentially production-for-use value (1974, 84). Under these conditions, production is under no compulsion to advance to the physical or gainful capacity that it would if produced for exchange value on a market. On the contrary, production-for-use value is discontinuous, irregular, and sparing of labour power. Mere production-for-use value is production for livelihood only. Thus, the domestic mode of production's economic goals are limited to the self-defined needs of family groups. In this ancient system,

Sahlins explains, economics is a part-time activity only, or an activity of only part of the society. This point becomes obvious when we examine work in the domestic mode of production.

Work in the domestic mode of production has an entirely different character from work in our modern market economy. In the domestic mode of production there is what Sahlins calls an intrinsic discontinuity in the very way work is organized. "Work is accordingly unintensive: intermittent and susceptible to all manner of interruption by cultural alternatives and impediments ranging from heavy ritual to light rainfall" (1974, 86). The light use of labour power is well documented by Sahlins using many different ethnographies from a wide range of societies still practising the domestic mode of production in the twentieth century. Of course, reflected in the ethnographies reviewed by Sahlins, there is great variation indeed across such a broad range of time and space. As well, much work was seasonal and often required considerable effort over a concentrated period. Nevertheless, typically, the working week if averaged out was 15 to 20 hours in many of these societies (1974, 14-35). Generally, the individual working career in these societies tended to be much shorter and much more intermittent, leaving plenty of time for any number of other activities. Sahlins comments that this dimension of conservative production in the domestic mode of production conformed to European prejudices about "lazy Natives," suggesting that the more appropriate conclusion was that Europeans are overworked.

Interrelated with the light use of labour power was the conservative use of natural resources. Actual production was substantially less than what was possible. While the conservative use of resources was more difficult to measure than the light use of labour power in gatherer-hunter societies, Sahlins nevertheless has good anecdotal evidence for it. In addition, from a range of different studies on controlled burn cultivators, he reviews a range of quantitative research showing very low levels of resource use, that is, very low intensity of land use with long fallow periods typically several times the period of use (1974, 42-51). Since Sahlins published his economic anthropological overview of the domestic mode of production, a variety of other cultural and ecological anthropological literature confirms the conservative use of natural resources, at least in native North American societies (Brody 1981; Cronin 1983; Turner 1983; Tanner 1985; Sale 1990).

In the domestic mode of production, a ceiling is set by the capacity of household order to provide adequate forces and relations of production. Therefore, as long as this mode prevails, customary modest standards of livelihood will remain. Sahlins characterizes this dynamic of production as "the contentment of the household economy with its own self-appointed objective: livelihood" (1974, 82-7). In other words, production and consumption were not so much limited by technology as by the values of the societies practising the domestic mode of production.

Generalized Reciprocity and Redistribution
Let us examine more closely the claim of original affluence put forward on behalf of this structure of underproduction. First, I have mentioned that some households in domestic mode of production societies did not always meet even their own modest Zen standards of consumption requirements. These standards nevertheless fulfilled, but did not exceed, basic nutritional survival requirements. If some households did not meet even these modest standards, how can Sahlins defend the system as affluent? The answer lies, of course, in the system of generalized reciprocity that pertained at the level of the domestic group, whether gatherer-hunter band or Neolithic village, especially with the sharing of food. In the domestic mode of production, food sharing between haves and have-nots was the key to the success of generalized reciprocity (Sahlins 1974, 210-9).

For Sahlins, reciprocity represents a continuum from solidarity to balanced reciprocity. The most generalized reciprocity is solidarity, the end of the continuum where the material side of the exchange transaction is repressed by the social. In this form, the expectation of return is indefinite, not stipulated by time, quantity, or quality. This form takes place within close kinship relations. Failure of a recipient to reciprocate does not stop the giver from giving. From this extreme, the continuum moves out to less pure forms of kinship and chiefly dues, where there is definite expectation of commensurate return within a finite period. The continuum proceeds on to "balanced reciprocity," or direct exchange. This can take the form of either gift exchange or out-and-out trade, where the material side of the transaction is at least as critical as the social. At this extreme, transactions are conducted with those beyond immediate kinship relations. The distance between these poles of reciprocity is a social distance (Sahlins 1974, 191-5). It is important to clarify that actual kinds of reciprocity vary widely across the great array of societies practising the domestic mode of production as well as within any single society.

Reciprocity, then, whatever form it took on the continuum, was the cultural norm that governed redistribution in the domestic mode of production, ensuring nutritional adequacy for all families in a mode of production characterized by a structure of production for livelihood. From a variety of ethnographies as well as accounts of early explorers, Sahlins produces convincing evidence that, far from being undernourished, on the edge of starvation, and living lives that were "nasty, brutish, and short," gatherer-hunter peoples usually had an abundant and varied diet (Sahlins 1974, 9-32). Subsequent works on traditional Aboriginal gatherer-hunter-horticultural societies in North America echo the evidence from Sahlin's work, supporting a picture of domestic mode of production societies that have achieved a qualitatively different kind of affluence (Diamond 1974;

Tanner 1978; Brody 1981; Leacock and Lee 1982; Cronin 1983; Turner 1983; Sale 1990; Kew and Griggs 1991; Mander 1991; Clarkson, Morisette, and Regallet 1992).

Ecologies of Kinship and Social Capital in the Domestic Mode of Production

In the domestic mode of production, we see an economy thoroughly embedded in society. The economy exists only as a function and attribute of kinship relations. Production activity is a part-time affair. Extended kinship relations, that is to say society itself, are where economic direction is set and production decisions are made. In a very real sense, kinship relations set the pattern for and also embody the relations of production. The relations of production are therefore contained within society and are not part of a separate activity sphere.

In the domestic mode of production, the quality and extension of kinship relations are not limited to those who are strictly kin. Even within the most extensive clan organizations, people still behave toward each other as if they were kin. More than this though, all meaningful social, economic, and ideological relations have a kin or transfigured kin character. This personalism extends from the family outward to society and ultimately to all of nature (Diamond 1974, 144-5). In the domestic mode of production, there is no state. The political sphere is perhaps as embedded in society as the economic sphere. What then are the essential features of the relations of production embedded in kinship relations? Much has been written about this already, so I have merely composed a composite list of these features from a number of sources, both anthropological and First Nations, which I think we need to consider in order to analyze social and cultural capital in the domestic mode of production:

1 collective ownership of the means of production – the land or natural capital – at the level of the extended family or band
2 access to the technology – virtually everyone had knowledge and skills to make essential tools
3 reciprocal access beyond the band level to the means of production through marriage ties, visiting, and coproduction
4 little or no emphasis on accumulation
5 generalized reciprocity within the family, band, and clan
6 individual ownership of tools within a system of usufruct (the freedom of individuals within a community to use another's tools if a greater need is evident)
7 dense social networks in small communities
8 intensive and extensive nurturing of children

9   consideration of all social roles as equally significant
10   many-sided, engaging personal relationships throughout an individual's life cycle
11   a great deal of leisure time
12   cultural integration – sacred and secular united – all life sacred
13   oral laws and tradition – society operates through custom and by shared sanctions and taboos – history carried through memory (Diamond 1974; Leacock and Lee 1987; Mander 1991; Clarkson, Morisette, and Regallet 1992).

In summary, taking our definition of social capital and applying it to the above characteristics of the domestic mode of production, we can easily see that levels of social capital were extremely high in societies characterized by the domestic mode of production. Moreover, at the level of the family, band, or clan, social capital was ubiquitous in both production and consumption. Norms of reciprocity, cooperation, pooling, sharing, and mutual aid were everywhere associated with dense networks of intense horizontal interaction. Direct and many-sided personal and social relationships gave rise to very high levels of information about one another and deep bonds of trust based on this information. This process was enhanced by the sharing of oral histories through storytelling and by public ceremonies and ritual, bonding people to each other and to the ancestors (Eliade 1963, 1-38; Allen 1986; Abram 1997; Ywahoo 1987).

Of course, there were sometimes extreme variations in the seasonal productive capacity of a family or band. A bad winter could lead to excessive hardship, but even in these cases, the levels of social capital worked to encourage the sharing of hardships. Also, the above summary should not be read to mean there were no contradictions in domestic mode of production societies. Certainly, some individuals may have engaged in hoarding and even tyranny. However, the relations of production, given the high levels of social capital, including norms of generalized reciprocity, did not encourage such antisocial behaviour. Both norms and relations of production favoured the social individual, embedded in family, clan, and tribe. There is also good evidence that in these societies, mother-children groups worked together as gatherers and were the basis of the first human extended-family groups (Reiter 1975, 43; Mies 1986, 55-6).

Thus, the real questions for us moderns in reflecting on societies in the domestic mode of production are: What can we learn from the age-old norms of reciprocity? What use is learning from the domestic mode of production in working toward sustainable society in our contemporary mode of production? By comparing modes of production, we can avoid the exaggerated romantic view sometimes projected onto earth-based societies, while learning some lessons about our own consumption and production from their traditional ecological knowledge and wisdom.

Social capital in the *domestic* mode of production contrasts sharply with our modern mass system of production for the marketplace, the *capitalist* mode of production. Here, the economic sphere dominates society and, consequently, kinship relations as well. Not the family, but the impersonal corporation is the dominant institution of production in our time. This means that production is not geared to use value or the needs of kinship or society but, rather, to exchange value to the self-regulating market mechanism. Over the last 150 years or so, the market mechanism has worked to create – in sharp contrast to the structure of production for livelihood of the domestic mode of production – a structure of overproduction for conspicuous consumption. In this contrast we can begin to draw lessons from societies characterized by the domestic mode of production. The examination of cultural capital in the domestic mode of production will assist in deepening our inquiry.

Cultural Capital in the Domestic Mode of Production

Kinship relations were not considered to be limited to the human community in earth-based societies characterized by the domestic mode of production. The extension of transfigured kinship relations to all of nature provides the crucial link between social and cultural capital. Earth-based societies do not make the hard-and-fast distinctions that our modern industrial culture makes between human and nonhuman life, between the social and the natural. This simple fact has had enormous bearing on the use of natural capital in the domestic mode of production.

To understand how cultural capital, expressed in the community-of-beings ethic, informs behaviour in terms of the relationship between social capital and natural capital, I have relied on literature from a variety of First Nations writers. Given the postmodern crisis in Western anthropology, especially accusations of romanticizing Aboriginal cultures, I think it crucial to examine some views of First Nations thinkers themselves.

The following discussion will serve to illuminate the depth and rich quality of the social capital-cultural capital linkage in North American Aboriginal societies characterized by the domestic mode of production; provide an ethical understanding of the use of natural capital in these societies; and begin to identify those general features of the domestic mode of production we need to learn from so that we may adapt, adopt, and apply them to our contemporary crisis of sustainability.

The Haudenausanee or Iroquois Six Nations Confederacy is well known for its "Great Law," which provided both inspiration for, and many democratic ideas that were then embodied in, the United States Constitution. In

1977, the Six Nations Confederacy presented a series of position papers to the United Nations in Geneva on the global crisis facing all humanity, later published by the journal *Akwesasne Notes* as "a basic call to consciousness." It identifies Western civilization as the very process of abuse of both humanity and nature that is at the root of our global crisis. Their basic call is to reclaim consciousness of what the Haudenosaunee themselves conceptualize as "the sacred web of life of the universe." In their message, they assert that the Earth is a sacred place and that the role of humans, according to their own ancient traditions or "original instructions," is to be "the spiritual guardians of this place." For them, human relations were thoroughly integrated with and dependent on all life. The following captures this relationship:

> In the beginning, we were told that the human beings who walk about on the Earth have been provided with all the things necessary for life. We were instructed to carry a love for one another, and to show a great respect for all the beings of this Earth. We are shown that our life exists with the tree life, that our well-being depends on the well-being of the Vegetable Life, that we are close relatives of the four-legged beings ... We give a greeting and thanksgiving to the many supporters of our own lives – the corn, beans, squash, the winds, the sun. (Six Nations Confederacy 1978, 49)

This philosophy was not peculiar to the Six Nations. Similar sentiments can be found over and over again among the First Nations. In a report written by a team of First Nations people, the authors describe why, in Native traditions, respect for people and for the earth is linked together in order for people to survive and care for at least the next seven generations:

> When we begin to separate ourselves from that which sustains us, we immediately open up the possibility of losing understanding of our responsibility and our kinship to the earth. When we view the world simply through the eyes of human beings we create further distance between ourselves and our world. When the perceived needs of one spirit being is held above all others, equality disappears ... From this basic understanding, our ancestors assumed their role as the spiritual guardians of the earth. One of the most significant illustrations of this is the central belief that the whole of creation is a sacred place. (Clarkson, Morisette, and Regallet 1992, 5)

In this worldview, the sacred and the secular, the spiritual and the material, the human and the nonhuman are tightly fused. Another First Nations writer, Dennis Martinez, points out that this relationship between the people and the earth, expressed in the ceremonial phrase "all my relations," is really an indigenous concept of reciprocity. Reciprocity, in this sense, is a very powerful but straightforward concept that means helping our relatives so they will help us; in this case, all our relations – the plants, the animals, the birds, in short, all species and ecological relationships of our earth. Furthermore, this relationship takes the form of a "caretaking responsibility" associated with a subsistence livelihood (Martinez 1993). Reciprocity, expressed in the phrase "all my relations," is extended beyond the human as an ethic that includes the whole earth. The practice of this ethic informs both the use of social capital and the way that natural capital was used in the domestic mode of production.

When we then consider the meaning of these passages, we can understand that in the domestic mode of production, social capital was informed by a cultural capital infused with the profound and broad community-of-beings ethic. We can see why cultural capital played a key role in the underuse of natural capital in the domestic mode of production. More than this, it is evident that the ancient community-of-beings ethic was, in great part, responsible for the high quality of care practised in the use of natural capital. It was not only a matter of using less natural capital but also of using it with care and spiritual attention. We have seen that economic activity is only a part-time affair in the domestic mode of production. Now we can also see that the kinship ethic, the community-of-beings ethic central to the worldview of so many societies practising the domestic mode of production, supported and gave meaning to the careful way production was carried out, as it gave meaning to the whole way of life of domestic mode of production societies. Moreover, I think that this ethic reflects an eminently practical as well as spiritual approach to the use of both social and natural capital, rather than the naïve, romantic one that not a few Western thinkers have projected onto earth-based societies.

This analysis of the domestic mode of production has argued for breaking the bonds of a consumer mentality that would interpret the lessons from ecological footprint analysis of the modern human predicament with the narrow, pessimistic conclusion that cutting back sharply on conspicuous consumption and frenetic overproduction means cutting back on the quality of human life. On the contrary, social capital/cultural capital analysis of domestic mode of production societies suggests that cutting back sharply on consumption can be associated with a great, qualitative, and spiritual enrichment of human life in terms of both social and natural ecological relationships. These integrated social and natural spiritual ecological relationships form a single complex that I call an ecology of kinship.

Now, what can we learn about replacing natural capital with social capital in our modern mode of production by comparing social capital in the domestic mode of production with social capital in our industrial capitalist mode of production? In other words, what is the terrain or sphere of action of social capital in contemporary society?

Civil Society, Terrain of Social Capital, and the Analysis of Modern Social Relations

We need a theoretical basis for understanding the dynamics of modern economic, political, and social relationships to clarify just what terrain or sphere of action social capital operates primarily within. This is necessary before we can deepen our understanding of the potential of social capital, particularly ecologically informed social capital, to aid in the transformation of modern social relations and, ultimately perhaps, of the mode of production itself.

Political theorists concerned with the project of social, political, and economic transformation in the Western tradition from Hegel and Marx to contemporary neo-Marxists, neoliberals, and neoconservatives have generally used an analysis that differentiated between two analytical categories or spheres, namely civil society and the state (or, more broadly, political society). One common problem with all these models, however, is the lack of a third analytical category, the economic sphere. Focusing primarily on the relations between society (or civil society) and the state has tended to skew the theoretical analysis in favour of political transformation, to the detriment of theorization about projects in economic transformation. Of course, this has been reflected in practice, particularly in the attempts by the many revolutionary movements of the twentieth century that limited themselves to the narrow project of capturing state power. Consequently, once in power and without an adequate economic strategy embedded in their political strategy, they failed to institute a democratic transformation of the economic sphere. The unfortunate result was a series of revolutionary societies practising state capitalism and political dictatorship.

However, as Karl Polanyi so clearly pointed out half a century ago, nineteenth-century economic liberalism freed the market from its social and political fetters by establishing the self-regulating market through the mechanism of price. This "great transformation" was capitalist societies' response to the industrial revolution. The free-market economy established an entirely new type of society. The economic and productive system was now entrusted to a self-acting device, the market mechanism. For the first time in history, an economic sphere was created that was clearly delimited from other social institutions. Previously, human economic activity had been thoroughly embedded in social relations. Ultimately, the establishment of an autonomous economic sphere with its own self-acting mechanism had the effect of making the rest of society dependent on the economy. From this point on, instead of the economic system being embedded in social relationships, social relationships became submerged or embedded in the economic system (Polanyi 1957; Dalton 1968). Once the economy became a hegemonic force, it became easy to demonstrate on an ideological level the reality of *Homo economicus* and economic determinism as a general law for all human society in whatever historical period. The result was the hegemony of economic determinism in theory and in practice. For transformation theorists to deal analytically with such an overwhelming economic and ideological development, a new theoretical model was needed. It was for this reason that two contemporary theorists, Jean Cohen and Andrew Arato, have proposed a theoretical model that differentiates among three spheres: civil society, political society, *and* economic society (1992).

The Three Spheres

Cohen and Arato maintain that the industrial revolution produced an economic society, the market economy, that threatens to subsume and reduce autonomous social norms, relationships, and institutions (1992, 122). They also refer to the fact that, since the creation and expansion of the market economy, the state sector has likewise experienced enormous and complementary growth in tandem with the market sector, leading to the rise of the welfare state. The very success of the welfare state has created a great crisis of solidarity. The welfare state disorganizes social networks and replaces mutualist forms of association, self-help, and horizontal cooperation with vertical, functional, reified state-citizen relations in which the citizen is reduced to the role of a client. For Cohen and Arato, this development "fully matches the effects of the capitalist market economy," whose growth has also replaced horizontal with vertical relations (1992, 40). So, in sum, both the state and the economy have acted to subsume, fragment, and reduce the sphere of civil society.

All this is not to deny the obvious benefits of liberal-democratic society, such as freedom of expression, association, and information. We should not lose sight of "the utopian promise" of the liberal and democratic norms of modern society, nor should we reduce these to mere legitimation devices for capitalist industrialism as has so much of Marxist and neo-Marxist analysis. Regardless of this important caution, Cohen and Arato do adopt Habermas' theory of the colonization of civil society. Habermas emphasized that both the monetarization and bureaucratization of social relations have created a set of social benefits and securities at the cost of creating a new range of dependencies, while destroying or severely atrophying existing solidarities (Habermas 1975). This destructive process has served to undermine peoples' capacities for self-help and cooperative forms of horizontal communication for resolving problems at the base of society in civic communities. Cohen and Arato advance their three spheres as a society-centred model, unlike the state-centred model of Hegel or the economic-centred model of Marx. They point out that their model focuses on the empirical possibility of democratization in civil society, while also underlining the normative necessity of democratization, since civil society norms call precisely for democratization (1992, 411). Finally, they emphasize that their model lends itself to the defence and expansion of civil society against (1) the deleterious effects of a greatly expanded, dominant, corporate economic sphere; and (2) the overextension of the administrative apparatus of the interventionist state into the social realm (1992, 24).

Cohen and Arato credit the Italian Marxist Gramsci for first suggesting this "highly original" three-part conceptual framework. They also observe, however, that Gramsci's concept of civil society was presented in a confusing terminology, sometimes defined as the counterpart of the state, or as a part of the state along with and counterposed to political society, or as identical with the state (1992, 144-5).

In Cohen and Arato's revised model (see Figure 3.1), the civil society sphere is composed of both public and private elements: the intimate sphere or the family, the sphere of associations (especially voluntary associations), social movements, and institutions of culture and public communication. Within Cohen and Arato's framework, the primary locus for the building of social capital is in the sphere of civil society. This is the terrain where networks of intense horizontal interaction and self-organization, norms of reciprocity, and high levels of information and trust must be located to anchor the democratic revolution.

Moreover, differentiating analytically between civil and political society allows the conceptualization of a dual strategy based on rooting social capital horizontally in civil society, while also building a vertical public communication and bridging influence to the political sphere. Similarly, differentiating between civil and economic society allows us to conceptualize strategies of rooting social capital in civil society while also influencing the economic sphere.

Cohen and Arato's differentiation of the spheres calls for continuing and deepening the democratic revolution launched by the enlightenment, rather than suppressing it as have so many twentieth-century, narrow, class- and state-focused models of social revolution. The political sphere provides the theoretical space for the greatly increased influence of an expanded and democratized civil society on the state. At the same time, the political sphere shares a continuity with the civil society sphere.

The economic sphere in Cohen and Arato's model principally represents the formal, market-dominated sector. Cohen and Arato point out that, unlike the relations between civil society and the political sphere, the interface of civil society and market economy has not been adequately analyzed, an undertaking they say is a precondition for any serious conceptual alternative to the dangers of economic liberalism and the false promises of utopian socialism (1992, 77). Unfortunately, they too confine their own analysis primarily to the civil and political spheres and their interface. The undertheorization in the economic sphere represents a need

Figure 3.1

Three-sphere analytic framework (adapted from Cohen and Arato, 1992)

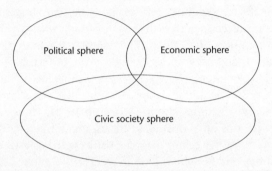

to advance the analysis of this sphere, and the relations between it and the sphere of civil society.

It is clear from the above that the primary locus of social capital is in the sphere of civil society. However, some caution is needed. Our modern industrial market society is the *only* society in history in which the economic sphere has not been embedded within social relationships and instead has come to dominate the sphere of civil society. Our current society, far from being the universal model we have been led to believe it is, is, in fact, quite atypical. Therefore, when we attempt to theorize norms for a future sustainable society without examining those social relations where the economic sphere *was* embedded within civil society, our models may be too narrowly restricted.

If we want to shed more light on the relationship of economic society with civil society in any potentially sustainable future society, we need to advance beyond the perceptual boundaries of our atypical market society. In domestic mode of production societies there was no separate economic sphere, nor was there any state. Civil society in the domestic mode of production was the dominant sphere of social, political, and economic relations; more, it was all of society. Domestic mode of production societies thus demonstrate a pure form of ecologically informed social capital that, by comparison, may help us to perceive its possibilities in our own society. To this task I now proceed.

The Mondragon Cooperative Movement:
Social Capital on a Regional Scale

There is perhaps no more successful example of social capital in an industrial context than that of the Mondragon Cooperatives in the now autonomous Basque region of northern Spain. Mondragon is the name of the town in Guipuzcoa province where the new industrial cooperative experiment, as its practitioners often describe it, was founded in 1956. Actually, the Mondragon Cooperative Movement (MCM) is a complex of industrial, agricultural, retailing, service, housing, banking, social insurance, and schooling cooperatives linked together, with a total of over 29,000 worker-members (IJPC 1998). The complex began, building on an old Basque industrial tradition, by founding an industrial cooperative, Ulgor. By 1991, there were 166 co-ops in the movement, including 86 industrial co-ops, 8 agricultural co-ops, 15 housing co-ops, a retail co-op with 270 stores, and 43 co-op schools (Morrison 1991). There are also several second-tier (co-ops of co-ops) institutions, including a bank, the *Caja Laboral Popular* (CLP) or working peoples bank, with over 180 branches, 500,000 depositors, and $US 4.8 billion in assets (IJPC 1998); a social security and medical co-op, *Lagun-Aro*; a technological research institute, *Ikerlan*; and the League of Education and Culture, *Hezibide Elkartea*, with 45,000 students and which includes a polytechnical college, a business school, and a professional college (Ellerman 1984; Morrison 1991).

All this began with a community-run training school founded in 1943 by a Catholic priest, Father Jose Arizmendiarrieta (who remains the movement's inspirational figure), with twenty pupils. Mondragon's schools were, along with the industrial co-ops, the foundation of the MCM. They provided technical training but also a social and ethical foundation that led eventually to the founding of the first industrial co-op in 1956 by some of Arizmendiarrieta's pupils, a core of young people well versed in the advantages of cooperativism (Morrison 1991, 46).

Over the four decades of their existence, the Mondragon co-ops have established a phenomenal record of social and entrepreneurial success. This growth was achieved at first under the hostile watch of the Franco dictatorship and later through the severe Spanish economic downturn of the early 1980s. While the MCM has undergone severe economic trials, there have been very few business failures during its entire history; this compares to a business failure rate for start-ups of 80 to 90 percent in the United States (Ellerman 1984; Whyte and Whyte 1988, 3). As various commentators have pointed out, there is no single reason for Mondragon's success, though some have tried to make the case for a Basque "exceptionalism" that, while giving credit to the Basque penchant for industrial initiative, would deny the movement's applicability to any other situation. When considered through a social capital analysis, the history of Basque industrial success and cultural cohesiveness does reveal historically high levels of social capital very similar to the case of northern Italy examined by Putnam and his associates (Putnam 1993a). The Basques have a long history of communalist and cooperativist traditions going back to the medieval guilds, which in the Basque region were health and welfare organizations as well as units of production (Whyte and Whyte 1988, 10-2). They also have a long history of metalworking, mining, shipbuilding, and integrated industrial and finance capitalism (Whyte and Whyte 1988, 9; Morrison 1991, 38-41). The Basque language, Euskera, is unrelated to any other (Whyte and Whyte 1988), and the Basque people have long fought for local autonomy under a distinctive Basque tradition of egalitarianism (Whyte and Whyte 1988, 10-1). In a real sense, then, the Mondragon Cooperative Movement is, in part, a flowering of repressed impulses for cultural self-expression coming out of the forty-year period of oppression and repression imposed by Franco's fascism (Morrison 1991, 38). It does, however, also represent a process of "social invention" (Ellerman 1984) that may have more general lessons.

An Overview of Mondragon

The Mondragon Cooperative Movement's process of social invention, captured in Father Arizmendiarrieta's slogan "We build the road as we travel," involves several important examples pertinent to the successful building of social capital on a regional scale. To appreciate these we need to examine the system at all three tiers of the movement.

The first tier is the individual co-ops that are autonomous organizations democratically controlled by the membership, based on the equality of owner-workers and one vote per member. This tier includes the cooperative principle of self-management, availability of information, and ongoing training of owner-workers, internal promotion for management positions, consultations and negotiations with all cooperators in organizational decisions, and pay solidarity with a factor of 6 to 1 between highest and lowest (this last compares to a differential of 100 to 1 in the United States). Each member must also, after a trial period, make a substantial, affordable, and equal financial investment in the co-op. The co-ops are built to human scale and rely on face-to-face relationships with an average of about 130 members.

Each co-op has its own general assembly that has ultimate authority for all co-op decisions and meets at least once per year. The governing council of each co-op, elected by the general assembly, meets monthly and is in charge of day-to-day implementation of policy. Each co-op also has a social council, elected by the members, usually as representatives of work groups that make decisions about personnel issues, pay, health benefits, and safety. The account control or watchdog group, elected by the general assembly, audits and monitors co-op operations. Member managers, hired by the governing council, are allowed to manage freely and are expected to show initiative in implementing the co-op business plan, but must remain effective to keep their managerial position. When fired, managers remain as full worker-owners of the co-op.

Here at the individual co-op level we see all the elements of Coleman's social capital in a small community. The structures described above evolved out of a profound commitment to basic cooperative principles of openness, solidarity, and social responsibility (Morrison 1991, 48-9).

Almost from the beginning, the industrial co-ops faced the problem all co-ops encounter in an economic system hostile to cooperation and worker control: access to finance capital. On the inspiration, encouragement, advice, and research of Father Arizmendiarrieta, they created a second tier co-op, the *Caja Laboral Popular* (CLP), or working people's bank. The *Caja* was a truly unique social invention, integrating a credit union, a cooperative social-insurance system, and a cooperative research and support structure for co-ops starting up or having business problems. Later, the social-insurance division hived off on its own to form another second-level co-op. The *Caja Laboral Popular* has been an important key to the huge success of the movement.

The *Caja Laboral Popular* is organized into two divisions, the Banking Division and the *Empresarial* Division. Its members are its own owner-workers, other Mondragon co-ops, and other members of the Basque public who use the Banking Division as a co-op credit union. Its financial resources are therefore based on the labour and savings of the co-ops, the owner-workers, and people in the communities in which it operates. The *Caja Laboral Popular* has been so successful in financial terms that its lending powers have been outstripping the needs of the associated co-ops for some time (Ellerman 1984). Its assets have continued to expand rapidly to the point where it can also lend funds to and invest in Basque government projects and even non-co-op firms (Morrison 1991, 90).

Equilibrio, or balance, is a watchword and working principle of the entire movement; it refers to the process of harmonizing and balancing the diversity of interests in the Mondragon system: between the individual and the co-op, the co-op and the support structures, and the co-op system and Basque communities in which the movement operates.

The Banking Division represents the consolidation and socialization of finance capital (the surpluses of the movement) in the Mondragon system itself and, to some degree, in the broader Basque community as well. However, the *Empresarial* Division of the *Caja* is the social invention most recognized by analysts of the Mondragon Cooperative Movement phenomenon as central to the success ratio of new co-ops and to their lasting effectiveness. *Empresarial* means entrepreneurial as well as management support. This reflects the dual role of aiding the start-up of new co-ops as well as supporting co-ops in business difficulties. For the *Caja*, an individual co-op is not merely an economic unit, as it usually is to a capitalist bank. Rather, a co-op is a structure for creating jobs as well as human values. What a co-op maximizes is not financial capital but human community (Morrison 1991, 118). In our terms, a movement co-op maximizes both human capital and social capital. The principle of *equilibrio* comes into play here, balancing human values with practical business acumen in the form of human and social capital concentrated in the experience and solidarity of the expert, cooperative entrepreneurs of the *Empresarial* Division who, as Ellerman has pointed out, represent the socialization of entrepreneurship (Ellerman 1984).

The *Caja Laboral Popular* staff of more than 120 experienced worker-owner management consultants provides a wide range of support services for the co-ops. This gives the *Caja* the capacity to foster new co-ops with market research, providing prefeasibility and feasibility studies, and to make a promotion loan to provide a salaried promoter/manager hired by the prospective new co-op, and an overseer supplied by the *Caja*, to assist in the development of the new business. The promoter/manager also has access to the socialized resources of the *Empresarial* Division.

Each member co-op of the *Caja* signs a contract of association with the bank. This contract leaves the co-op completely autonomous unless the co-op gets into difficulty. If this happens, the co-op is assigned an intervenor from the *Caja* and a contract of intervention is signed. The goal is not to save the funds of the bank as in "work-out" teams sent by capitalist banks and creditors to conventional firms in trouble. The goal in Mondragon is to save the jobs of the worker-owners and the co-op as a community resource (the social capital), as well as the socialized finance capital. The point is not short-term finance capital salvage but the long-term health of the co-op and the co-op system (Morrison 1991, 130).

Remarkably, the *Caja* has achieved the socialization of both finance capital and entrepreneurship (one form of human capital) on a system-wide, regional scale. Looked at in terms of social capital analysis, the *Caja Laboral Popular* represents the regional integration of socialized finance capital, socialized entrepreneurship (or human capital), and the interlinked community and regional power of social capital.

The evolution of the movement system at this second tier means that no Mondragon co-op is alone. Each co-op and co-op structure within this system may decide to associate voluntarily with other co-ops and co-op structures in response to their mutual needs. Each independent co-op, while remaining under the direct democratic control of its members, is also embedded in a support structure that provides financial, business, educational, philosophical, and social support (Morrison 1991, 16-7).

The third level of co-op institutions invented in 1987 is the Cooperative Congress and the General Council of the Mondragon Cooperative Group. The congress meets once every two years to consider system-wide issues within the movement. All co-ops send at least one democratically elected representative. The General Council, established to coordinate and implement the work of the congress, includes senior representatives of co-op groups and second tier co-ops; it is designed to improve operational planning, coordination, and cooperation among the co-ops. Its basic mission is to find mutually satisfactory solutions to problems the co-ops face in an increasingly complex political and economic environment and to promote cooperativism and technological advances that will expand employment in the region. In effect, the congress takes over some of the broad planning functions that had become part of the work of the *Caja Laboral Popular* and some of the other second-tier co-ops. More importantly, the congress represents the firm consolidation of democratic control, making it clear that even the powerful institution of the *Caja* is only a part of a democratically governed community (Morrison 1991, 160).

Social Capital in Mondragon
In the Mondragon Cooperative Movement, we can see the use of social capital over a much broader scale than that of the small face-to-face communities of the domestic mode of production previously considered. The social invention of these mutually supportive cooperative systems demonstrates that social capital can be effectively employed beyond the local community scale on a much broader, regional level, when it is manifested in multiple, democratic, organizational feedback links as described above. The use of social capital at an integrated community and regional scale can support human capital in the form of socialized entrepreneurship and social and business planning. The socialization of finance capital at the regional scale in the *Caja Laboral Popular* completes the circle. From the point of view of a civil society-based analysis, the economic sphere of human endeavour is effectively re-embedded into the civil society sphere, at least within the movement system itself.

This powerful combination obviously benefits everyone involved in the movement, but it also has positive effects on the public good of the Basque region. The movement reinvests the major portion of its surpluses in the Basque communities. This helps create new employment, community development, and the encouragement of Basque language and culture (taught in the movement's school system) beyond the movement itself. Cooperation, the use of social capital, is extended to other institutions in the Basque region as the movement collaborates with trade unions and the Basque government to promote even broader social capital growth.

What about the potential of replacing natural capital with ecologically informed social capital? At Mondragon, the building of human community does not appear to include much serious consideration of the natural environment. True, the movement has now instituted environmental impact statements as part of its planning process, but this is no more advanced than similar arrangements elsewhere in the industrial world. In addition, its research institute, *Ikerlan*, is researching new resources in wind and solar energy. However, Mondragon industrial co-ops currently tend to turn out consumer products and high-technology items that pose environmental problems (Morrison 1991, 162-3). Furthermore, Mondragon has deep roots in the heavy industrial orientation of Basque cultural capital and in the history of the Basque industrial region. In addition, much of the early theoretical development led by Father Arizmendiarrieta has been marked by an Adam Smith/Karl Marx-derived labour theory of value (Morrison 1991, 100-1), which completely ignores the contributions of natural capital to value and productivity. In this view, finance capital is regarded as accumulated labour, but natural capital is assigned a merely passive role. Moreover, the community-of-beings ethic evident in my examination of the domestic mode of production appears to be totally absent in the Mondragon Cooperative Movement. Cultural capital in the Mondragon system is purely human-centred. Consider the extreme orientation to technological progress evidenced both in Mondragon's roots in industrial manufacturing and to its current orientation to high-technology, especially in the context of the developing globalization of the marketplace. Given the movement's enormous financial success, which has outstripped the ability of the Mondragon system to use surplus capital, some in Mondragon already consider that there may be limits to self-development and are looking to joint ventures with the outside world (Morrison 1991, 207). Indeed, this problem of success has entailed the addition of a large number of workers into the Mondragon system who are not worker-owners to about 30 percent of the total work force (Whyte 1999). In the 1990s, private enterprises have been incorporated into the movement to aid the Basque region in creating more employment using more traditional market methods. The problem is that it now requires more investment to create a job than in the past. However, Mondragon leaders are exploring new ways to integrate workers into the movement as full worker-owners (Whyte 1999).

Toward an Ecologically Oriented Social Capital in Modern Civil Society: The Informal Economy

In terms of the three-sphere analysis of our modern industrial mode of production, what can we learn from the analysis of the domestic mode of production on the one hand and the Mondragon Cooperative Movement on the other? In our modern global system, the formerly all-embracing kinship/civil society sphere of the domestic mode of production has become atrophied and dominated by the economic and political spheres. From the perspective of replacing the need for natural capital with social capital, we have seen that social capital is most successful in the domestic mode of production where civil society, not the political or economic sphere, is the predominant sphere of social relations. In a contemporary industrial context, we also saw that in the Mondragon Cooperative Movement, the economic sphere is at least partially re-embedded on a regional scale within the Mondragon system itself, even though it remains part of the global system. This is achieved through the use of social capital with multiple, democratic, tiered linkages and feedback systems throughout the Basque region. Now, drawing on the civil society theory of Cohen and Arato, we can consider the potential of social capital in the contemporary informal economy in the light of what we know from our analysis of the domestic mode of production and the Mondragon Cooperative Movement.

Civil society theory encourages the eventual democratic transformation of the political and economic spheres. Cohen and Arato argue strongly that democracy can advance much farther on the level of civil society (1992, 417-91). My examination of the Mondragon Cooperative Movement illustrates and confirms this position. By building social capital based in the civil sphere at both the local community and regional scales, the movement was eventually able to influence, or bridge to, both the political sphere (the Basque government) and to the economic sphere (noncooperative firms), promoting cooperativism on an increasingly broad scale.

A brief examination of the sphere of civil society in our contemporary industrial era will help to clarify the actual size and potential for democratization in the civil society sphere. My examination of the domestic mode of production has revealed civil society in full flower, civil societies where ecologies of kinship were the prevailing way of life. Economic and political activity served kinship and kinship needs in this system. Kinship was extended to nature, which was used conservatively and with great care and spiritual respect. Our contemporary industrial mode of production provides an almost total contrast to the domestic mode of production. In our society, nature has become natural capital and is squandered. Meanwhile, civil society has been marginalized by the political and economic spheres. The hub of the domestic mode of production, the household, has been trivialized or ignored altogether as a factor in production. As many feminist analysts have pointed out, women's work in the home does not even count as productive labour. In our terms, it does not even qualify as human capital.

Marilyn Waring has given us a detailed analysis of the consistent omission of women's domestic labour in both the United Nations System of National Accounts and in many different systems of national accounting. In all these systems, the household is simply not counted as part of the economy. Women are invisible as producers in their capacities as housewives (Waring 1988). Of course, this applies also to men who do domestic work in the home, but as Waring and others have shown, the vast majority of the work done in the home is still done by women, even after twenty-five years of feminist organizing and education.

Relevant for our study is the question of the size of the household and community economy. There are several different names for this economy: the hidden economy, the informal economy, the dual economy, the grey (or black) economy, the barefoot economy, and the cooperative love economy. Hazel Henderson, who uses the term "love economy," refers to sociological studies (economists generally ignore the informal economy) in France, Sweden, Canada, and the United Kingdom, showing that about 50 percent of all productive work is unpaid (Henderson 1991, 120). The sheer size of this workforce gives it great potential to feed efforts at social change and transformation.

Another dimension of the love or caring economy is the volunteer sector, which itself is huge. Barbara Brandt, in *Whole Life Economics,* cites a study showing that 51 percent of all United States residents over age seventeen do volunteer work (1995, 20). While there remain difficulties with measuring the informal economy, it is clear that this sector is enormous.

As a contribution to the measurement problem and to clarifying the larger strategic picture, Brandt has made a very useful list of the various components of the informal economy that help us to characterize the size, importance, and potential of the informal economy for transformational analysis and action in the civil society sphere. She presents six major sources of informal human economic activity that have emerged to make this formerly invisible economy visible:

1   unpaid domestic activities for home and family, commonly known as women's work
2   women's biological activities of pregnancy, childbirth, and breast-feeding
3   household production and neighbourly exchanges of goods and services
4   volunteer activities for the community and public good
5   innovative new economic models and institutions, such as worker ownership, consumer cooperatives, land trusts, community money systems
6   economic forms from non-Western and nonindustrial cultures.

As Brandt points out, these informal activities are beginning to be recognized partly because of the efforts of women, partly because of changing values and the growing failure of the formal sector to meet people's needs (1995, 108-10). The great extent of all these activities taken together is impressive. Moreover, it is clear merely from examining the above list that these are all activities that take place in civil society. For Henderson, Brandt, and a number of feminist analysts, the homegrown economy functions as a support base for the formal economic sector. Equally, or perhaps more importantly, the love economy can provide a minimal social safety net from the GNP-dominated "world trade roller coaster" (Henderson 1991, 119). Civil society, then, in particular the informal economy, is the most appropriate sphere for the theoretical and practical effort to build ecologically oriented social capital in our times.

Conclusion

How can ecologically informed social capital grow in the Lower Fraser Basin to help us strengthen and enhance our ability to reduce our ecological footprint? This chapter has pointed to some critical social and cultural dimensions of our problem. As Chapter 1 (this volume) shows, our individual and collective ecological footprints are far beyond global averages. This heavily urbanized region is at or near the top of the global consumption hierarchy. Both our dominant cultural capital and the gap between our regional consumption and the globally diffused effects of our footprint work to prevent us from seeing the depth of our crisis. Indeed, a strong argument can be made that our affluence, manifested in commodity consumption, especially automobiles, and the consumption of mass advertising acts to alienate us as individuals from forming strong community ties.

As I have argued, cultural capital is a crucial determinant of the relationship between natural and physical capital. Clearly, the profound social, economic, and political changes needed to effectively address the dilemma of sustainability will not come about without cultural transformation. Civil society theory, informed by ecologically oriented social and cultural capital concepts, can aid us in thinking about and evaluating efforts of social transformation. Local efforts in a growing civil society base, networked regionally and interregionally, can increasingly operate to influence the formal political and economic spheres in the direction of greater democracy.

The benefits of greatly increased levels of social capital could, as in the domestic mode of production, provide a more spiritually fulfilling and richly rewarding social life – Sahlin's Zen road to affluence. Reduced consumption in these circumstances is more than paid back by the quality-of-life benefits of ecologically informed social and cultural capital. The modern, alienated, asocial individual consumer can begin to feel the immediate benefits of a sense of belonging, connectedness, and well-being in caring communities. Policy direction at the institutional level in the state sector as suggested in Boothroyd (this volume) and Green and Shoveller (this volume) can assist efforts in the sphere of civil society to make the democratic social, economic, political, and cultural changes toward living within ecological carrying capacity.

Much more needs to be done if we are to take ecological footprint analysis seriously. Our global crisis cannot be addressed adequately by policy changes alone. Social and cultural capital analysis highlights the need for broader and more profound cultural transformation. We do not have to accept globalization, which is just another socially constructed reality, but *not* an irrevocably fixed direction. Like those in the Mondragon Cooperative Movement, we in the Lower Fraser Basin and in other similar high-consumption, urbanized regions can choose to build social capital in civil society even in the face of corporate dominated global markets.

Building our own road as we travel will not be easy and will require prolonged effort and commitment. However, given the increasing cutbacks in both state and corporate sectors, as citizens, we may not have much choice but to build our own local and regional economic alternatives. Working together toward this accomplishment, even if forced by circumstances, we may find that social support networks, mutual aid, solidarity, and trust, informed by a reclaimed community-of-beings ecological ethic, are really just what is needed for sustainable human well-being after all.

Already hundreds of citizens organizations and fledgling networks exist in the Lower Fraser Basin and in many other urban regions in North America. These generally fall under broad categories of ecological sustainability, ecological restoration, social justice, community health promotion, antipoverty, neighbourhood improvement, and community economic development. Getting out of our cars and off our living-room couches to join these community efforts for the public good or starting new groups can make a difference to long-term ecological and social health and provide immediate relief for our individual feelings of alienation and powerlessness.

Note
1 Putnam's analysis of social capital focuses on norms and networks of civic engagement. It is based on a long-term comprehensive study of effective civic engagement and regional government in Italy from 1970 to 1990, as well as an historical analysis of civic society over the past 1,000 years (Putnam 1993a). At the heart of this civic heritage are dense networks of organized reciprocity and civic solidarity from medieval communes, religious fraternities, and guilds to contemporary cooperatives, mutual aid societies, neighbourhood associations, and choral societies.

References
Abram, D. 1997. *The Spell of the Sensuous: Perception and Language in a More-Than-Human World*. New York: Vintage Books.
Allen, P.G. 1986. *The Sacred Hoop: Recovering the Feminine in American Indian Traditions*. Boston: Beacon Press.
Berkes, F., and C. Folke. 1994. "Investing in Cultural Capital for Sustainable Use of Natural Capital." In A.M. Jansson, M. Hammer, C. Folke, and R. Costanza, eds., *Investing in Natural Capital: The Ecological Economics Approach to Sustainability*. Washington, DC: Island Press.
Berkes, F., M. Kislalioglu, C. Folke, and M. Gadgil. 1998. "Exploring the Basic Ecological Unit: Ecosystem-like Concepts in Traditional Societies." *Ecosystems* 1: 409-15.
Boothroyd, P., and C. Davis. 1991. "The Meaning of Community Economic Development." UBC Planning Papers. Vancouver: Centre for Human Settlement, University of British Columbia.

Brandt, B. 1995. *Whole Life Economics: Revaluing Daily Life*. Philadelphia: New Society Publishers.

Brody, H. 1983. *Maps and Dreams*. Vancouver: Douglas and McIntyre.

Clarkson, L., V. Morisette, and G. Regallet. 1992. *Our Responsibility to the Seventh Generation: Indigenous Peoples and Sustainable Development*. Winnipeg: International Institute for Sustainable Development.

Cohen, J., and A. Arato. 1992. *Civil Society and Political Theory*. Cambridge, MA: MIT Press.

Coleman, J. 1990. *Foundations of Social Theory*. Cambridge, MA: Harvard University Press.

Cronin, W. 1983. *Changes in the Land: Indians, Colonists, and the Ecology of New England*. New York: Hill and Wang.

Dalton, G., ed. 1968. *Primitive, Archaic, and Modern Economies: Essays of Karl Polanyi*. New York: Anchor Books.

Diamond, S. 1974. *In Search of the Primitive: A Critique of Civilization*. New Brunswick, NJ: Transaction Books.

Eliade, M. 1963. *Myth and Reality*. New York: Harper and Row.

Ellerman, D. 1984. "Entrepreneurship in the Mondragon Cooperative." *Review of Social Economy* 42,3.

Ewen, S. 1976. *Captains of Consciousness: Advertising and the Social Roots of the Consumer Culture*. New York: McGraw-Hill Book Co.

Habermas, J. 1975. *Legitimation Crisis*. Boston: Beacon Press.

Henderson, H. 1991. *Paradigms in Progress: Life Beyond Economics*. Indianapolis: Knowledge Systems Inc.

IJPC (Intercommunity Justice and Peace Center). 1998. "Mondragon is ... " Cincinnati: Intercommunity Justice and Peace Center. [website: http//www.members.aol.com/IJPCCinti/mondragon.html.]

Kew, M., and J. Griggs. 1991. "Native Indians of the Fraser Basin: Towards a Model of Sustainable Resource Use." In A.H.J. Dorey, ed., *Perspectives on Sustainable Development in Water Management*. Vancouver: Westwater Research.

Leacock, E., and R. Lee, eds. 1987. *Politics and History in Band Societies*. New York and London: Cambridge University Press.

Lertzman, D. 1999. "Planning Between Cultural Paradigms: Traditional Knowledge and the Transition to Ecological Sustainability." PhD thesis, University of British Columbia.

Mander, J. 1991. *In the Absence of the Sacred: The Failure of Technology and the Survival of the Indian Nations*. San Francisco: Sierra Club Books.

Martinez, D. 1993. "Managing a Precarious Balance: Wilderness Versus Sustainable Forestry." *Winds of Change,* summer.

Mies, M. 1986. *Patriarchy and Accumulation on a World Scale: Women in the International Division of Labour*. London: Zed Books.

Morrison, R. 1991. *We Build the Road as We Travel*. Philadelphia: New Society Publishers.

Pinkerton, E. 1998. "Integrated Management of a Temperate Montane Forest Ecosystem through Wholistic Forestry: A British Columbia Example." In F. Berkes, C. Folke, and J. Colding, eds., *Linking Social and Ecological Systems: Management Practices and Social Mechanisms for Building Resilience*. Cambridge, UK: Cambridge University Press.

Polanyi, K. 1957. *The Great Transformation*. Boston: Beacon Press.

Putnam, R. 1993a. *Making Democracy Work*. Princeton: Princeton University Press.

–. 1993b. "The Prosperous Community: Social Capital and Public Life." *The American Prospect,* spring: 35-42.

Reiter, R.R., ed. 1975. *Toward an Anthropology of Women*. New York: Monthly Review Press.

Sahlins, M. 1974. *Stone Age Economics*. London: Tavistock Publications.

Sale, K. 1990. *The Conquest of Paradise: Christopher Columbus and the Columbian Legacy*. New York: Penguin Books.

Six Nations Confederacy. 1986. *A Basic Call to Consciousness*. Rev. 3rd ed. New York: Akwesasne Notes.

Tanner, A. 1985. *Bringing Home Animals: Religious Ideology and Mode of Production of the Mistassini Cree Hunters*. St. John's: Institute of Social and Economic Research, University of Newfoundland.

Taylor, M. 1982. *Community, Anarchy and Liberty*. Cambridge, UK: Cambridge University Press.

Turner, F. 1983. *Beyond Geography: The Western Spirit Against the Wilderness*. New Brunswick, NJ: Rutgers University Press.

Wackernagel, M., and W.E. Rees. 1996. *Our Ecological Footprint: Reducing Human Impact on the Earth*. Philadelphia and Gabriola Island, BC: New Society Publishers.

Waring, M. 1988. *Counting For Nothing: What Men Value and What Women Are Worth*. Wellington, NZ: Allen and Unwin.

Whyte, W. 1999. "The Mondragon Cooperatives in 1976 and 1998." *Industrial and Labour Relations Review* 52,3: 478-81.

Whyte, W., and K. Whyte. 1988. *Making Mondragon*. Ithaca, NY: ILR Press.

Ywahoo, D. 1987. *Voices of Our Ancestors: Cherokee Teachings from the Wisdom Fire*. Boston: Shambala.

Part 2:
The Box We Are In
and Some Ways Out

This section of the volume builds upon the previous one by exploring in more detail how societies do or can respond to the imperatives for change demanded by the transformation to sustainability. Since public discourse routinely invokes the desirability of becoming more sustainable, the first question that must be asked is, What is stopping us? The case example of a large and prosperous North American city is explored in detail in Chapter 4. This provides both an understanding and a taxonomy of the many ways in which the movement toward sustainability can be thwarted by our collective actions or inactions. To understand how we might avoid this outcome, we must understand both the theory and practice of policy development and social change. The evolving intellectual base for understanding this very complex arena where concerns get translated into collective action is outlined in Chapters 5 and 6. It is clear from our studies that effective adaptation to change takes place only when grassroots concern and action is combined with thoughtful leadership and policy development. This section of the volume explores the elements necessary for such a conjunction to occur.

4

What Is Stopping Sustainability? Examining the Barriers to Implementation of *Clouds of Change*

Jennie L. Moore

Why do we talk one way and act another? As societies around the planet move closer to understanding the issues surrounding human impact on the ecosphere, it is becoming increasingly clear to many community activists that there is disjunction between what citizens and local governments say they want in terms of securing a sustainable future and what they are willing to do to achieve it. Understanding this dilemma is a crucial focus of this volume.

This chapter demonstrates an attempt to understand how things break down in the space that exists between knowledge and action. It is not about finding villains or culpable parties. It is too simple a response to point fingers at politicians and lay the blame on lack of political will. The onus of responsibility is on all of us. We must shift blame from the political to the societal realm in order to recognize the responsibility each of us shares in creating a sustainable world. There are barriers that prevent taking action in support of sustainability; by understanding how the barriers operate, I hope that readers will become better equipped to assess situations in which barriers are operating in their own communities and to devise strategies for overcoming them.

This chapter addresses political and institutional barriers to sustainability. Its goal is to identify what inhibits local government from implementing policies that support sustainable development.[1] The 1990 *Clouds of Change* report prepared by the City of Vancouver Task Force on Atmospheric Change is used as a case study to examine how barriers function to impede policy implementation efforts. The report defines a framework for action to (1) protect public health, (2) phase out uses of ozone depleting chemicals, (3) reduce emissions of sulphur dioxide and methane, and (4) address the challenge of carbon dioxide (CO_2) reduction. Unanimously endorsed by City of Vancouver Council, it makes recommendations for transportation planning, land-use planning, energy conservation, City demonstration of leadership, lobbying of senior governments, and networking with other municipalities. Most of the recommendations were to be implemented by 1991, with a few requiring a longer time frame. However, as of 1994, many of the recommendations had not been fully implemented.[2] By 1999, although further progress has been made, some recommendations have still not been implemented and several more remain only partially addressed (Losito 1999).

Fifty-six people representing Vancouver Council members, civic staff, Task Force on Atmospheric Change members, and citizens involved with the task force's public participation process were asked to identify the barriers impeding efforts to implement the *Clouds of Change* report recommendations. The primary barriers identified by all groups were lack of understanding about the issues, perceived lack of empowerment, competing issues, inadequate funds, fear of losing constituent support, and limitation of jurisdiction. These barriers represent all three categories of barriers established in the research: (1) perceptual and behavioural, (2) institutional and structural, and (3) economic and financial. The barriers seem to operate in a mutually reinforcing way. Perceptual barriers, such as perceived lack of empowerment and competing issues, are reinforced by institutional barriers, such as limitation of jurisdiction. Financial considerations and economic realities, such as inadequate funds, further influence perceptions of what is and, perhaps more importantly, what is not feasible.

Research Methods
Information for the research was gathered in two ways: through a review of relevant literature and through interviews. The literature search focused primarily on changes within democratic societies and institutional structures, and barriers to action-taking within this context. From the literature search, a framework for analyzing barriers was established, using a three-tiered model that reflects how barriers operate at the level of the individual, the organized group, and the larger society. A list of potential barriers was also generated. Interviews were then conducted with key informants, who were also asked to complete a brief questionnaire. Four target groups were selected, all of which have played a role in implementing the recommendations: City of Vancouver Members of Council, civic employees, Task Force on Atmospheric Change members, and participants in the task force's public participation process and other individuals who had written letters to the *Vancouver Sun* newspaper expressing an interest in the outcome of the report's implementation. All interviews were either audio recorded and then transcribed, or transcribed directly during the interview.

Interviewees were asked to identify the barriers they had experienced in their efforts to implement the recommendations. They were also asked to make suggestions regarding how barriers might be overcome. The barriers they identified were then matched to the list. Not only did the barriers identified by interviewees match those found through the literature search, but additional barriers were also identified. In addition, two interviews were conducted with people involved in the creation of the *Healthy Atmosphere 2000* report to test whether similar barriers impeded implementation of that report's recommendations.[3] A frequency table was used to identify which barriers were perceived by research participants to be the most common.

Action-Taking and Barriers

At the 1990 Conference on Climate Change and Global Security sponsored by the Canadian Institute for International Peace and Security, some of the world's leading authorities on atmospheric change reached the following conclusion: "While the scope for possible action may grow with technological developments, it is very clear that the obstacles to sustainability are not technical or even economic: they are social, institutional and political" (Bush 1990, 1). Many cultural values, government regulations, and financial accounting systems ignore the importance of taking responsibility for the environmental consequences of need-meeting activities. As a result, they contribute to a society structured to encourage actions that do not support sustainability and a population that demonstrates emergent behaviour patterns that are not conducive to its own long-term survival. Social behaviour and institutional structures are determined in part by the desire to meet human needs. To this end, the perception of which needs are to be met and what priority they should take becomes crucial. Thus, attention is paid to the role of perceptions because perceptions guide behaviour (Stein 1984, 122) and determine consent to operate within existing political and institutional structures. Furthermore, perceptions condition acceptance of the economic constructs that heavily influence the operations of institutions.

The set of ideas an individual or society has about the way the world works is the paradigm through which that person or society operates. In today's world, a particular paradigm operates at the global level; this scientific materialist paradigm drives the global economic system. It rests on the tenets of neoclassical economic theory and scientific reductionism. Neoclassical economics embodies such familiar beliefs as "the invisible hand of the market" and the "trickle down effect" work to the benefit of all in society. Thus, consumer sovereignty must not be compromised. In fact, the economy satisfies only the demand that is supported by an ability to pay (Keynes in Heilbroner 1980, 268). Witness the fact that hunger among the poor is common, yet so is the sight of heaps of food being destroyed or stored because of inadequate market demand. A second belief is that market-pricing mechanisms are the most accurate and efficient way to determine resource values (Heilbroner 1980, 52-65; Samuelson and Scott 1980, 51-2). However, this overlooks the point that most natural life-support systems and their products, such as clean air, are not commodities in a market system, and thus, no pricing cues exist for them. Furthermore, price is determined at the margin, meaning that the inherent value of something is not reflected, only its current status of availability. Such a system is better suited to the pricing of finite, or nonrenewable, resources, rather than renewables whose status of availability can be difficult to predict. Pricing at the margin sends false signals to society, overemphasizing the value of certain things, such as oil and platinum, and undermining others, such as air and water.

The market-pricing mechanism is further influenced by scientific reductionist theory, which fails to appreciate biological relationships and nonreversible chemical reactions common in natural systems. Thus, the market system also assumes reversibility. If it is discovered that society's pricing mechanism has erred and a resource such as clean air has been underpriced, economic decisions can be adjusted and actions reversed to respond to its newly realized scarcity. Unfortunately, society's actions can be reversed, but the impact of those actions in many cases cannot. The impacts leave the sphere of human influence and enter the realm of environmental consequences, an area where humanity has often proven ineffectual.

Finally, since the scientific materialist paradigm considers natural and human-made capital to be interchangeable (Simon 1981), it does not accept the argument of limits to growth (Daly and Cobb 1989; Christensen 1991, 78). The scientific materialist paradigm argues that human ingenuity gives rise to technology, a form of capital input that is able to circumvent the restrictions placed on production by scarce resources. Thus, resources are no longer considered a limiting factor, either to production or to human survival (Simon 1981). It is interesting to note, however, that although technology has been able to temporarily overcome trends of resource depletion, it has not been able to reverse these trends in the long term. For example, while fertilizers and hybrid seeds mask problems of land degradation in the short term, the natural productivity of agricultural land continues to decline (Smith 1986, 9), causing the global loss of twenty-four billion tons of topsoil and six million hectares of land annually (Postel 1989, 21; Brown 1990, 3).

Current dominant economic paradigms may not be compatible with present biophysical realities (Rees and Wackernagel 1992, 5). Continued action in accordance with these paradigms may prevent the adoption of alternative actions that would place society on a sustainable track.

Given the scientific materialist paradigm's dominance in twentieth-century society, it becomes very difficult to act in a manner that favours sustainable development. Governments that have co-evolved with scientific materialist beliefs unwittingly become its defenders. Thus, defensive actions used to bypass embarrassment and threats prevent opportunities for learning and change in government (Argyris 1993, 20). As a result, the status quo is maintained. We see the accumulation of knowledge and the conceptualization of ideas and initiatives to promote sustainability, only to have them stymied and prevented from being translated into actions.

It is important, therefore, to track the specific point at which such initiatives are blocked. The analysis of barriers is broken down into three tiers: the first tier examines perceptual and behavioural barriers that affect the individuals who make up an organization; the second tier examines institutional and structural barriers that affect the organization itself; the third tier examines economic and financial barriers that affect the organization's ability to function within a larger societal context, in this case, the market system in which the organization is embedded (Weiss 1972, 311; Robbinson 1993, 44). Because the role of perception is so extremely pervasive, it should be noted that behaviours observed in response to institutionalized systems of governance or economic pressures will be listed under the categories focusing on those issues.

The research participants identified forty-eight barriers in total. While it

Table 4.1

Perceptual and behavioural barriers

Barrier	Council	Civic staff	Task force	Citizen	Total
Number of citations from a possible total of:	6	21	11	18	56
Lack of understanding about the issues	4	6	8	5	23
Perceived lack of empowerment	3	6	7	6	22
Competing issues	3	11	3	3	20
Lack of buy-in by civic staff	3	8	2	2	15
Differences in perception	2	7	3	2	14
Citizens disunited or not supportive	5	4	1	3	13
Lack of choices	3	3	–	5	11
Disjunction between verbal support and willingness to take action	1	8	–	2	11
Uncertainty	2	3	2	3	10
Perceived inequity	1	3	1	4	9
Overwhelming complexity	–	3	3	1	7
Prestige motive	–	3	1	3	7
Media's presentation of information	1	1	–	4	6

Table 4.2

Institutional and structural barriers

Barrier	Council	Civic staff	Task force	Citizen	Total
Number of citations from a possible total of:	6	21	11	18	56
Fear of losing constituent support	3	7	3	6	19
Limitation of jurisdiction	5	10	2	1	18
Weak link between government and constituents	4	3	4	4	15
Weak link among policies of civic and senior levels of government	2	6	1	6	15
Inappropriate structure of government	1	7	4	3	15
Fear of losing control and power	2	6	3	2	13
Lack of understanding about action roles	2	3	4	1	10
Lack of an environmental nongovernment organization	1	1	3	2	7
Lack of information sharing	1	2	–	4	7
Existing contractual agreements	1	4	–	1	6

Table 4.3

Economic and financial barriers

Barrier	Council	Civic staff	Task force	Citizen	Total
Number of citations from a possible total of:	6	21	11	18	56
Inadequate funds	4	9	2	4	19
Inadequate resources	3	6	3	3	15
Financial gain motive	2	1	4	4	11
Failure to guarantee results	2	5	2	1	10
Marginal pricing and economic valuation	2	1	3	3	9
Lack of prioritizing mechanism	1	6	1	–	8
Unwillingness to pay more taxes	3	3	–	1	7
Fear of disadvantaging the poor	3	1	3	–	7
Existing funds preallocated	–	3	1	1	5

is not possible to discuss each one in detail in this work,[4] the most significant barriers appear in the following tables. Table 4.1 identifies perceptual and behavioural barriers. Table 4.2 identifies institutional and structural barriers. Table 4.3 identifies economic and financial barriers.

The tables reveal that different interview groups perceived different barriers as most relevant. Vancouver City councillors identified the primary barriers as citizens disunited or not supportive and limitation of jurisdiction. Civic employees cited competing issues and limitation of jurisdiction. Task Force on Atmospheric Change members identified lack of understanding about the issues and perceived lack of empowerment as the greatest impediments. Citizens who participated in *Clouds of Change* public processes identified perceived lack of empowerment and fear of losing constituent support.

Perceptual and Behavioural Barriers

Perceptual and behavioural barriers affect cognition of circumstances related to sustainability and interfere with action-taking. They operate predominantly at the level of the individual but can permeate an entire society.

Lack of understanding about the issues is a perceptual or behavioural barrier that refers primarily to incomprehension of the relationship between cause and effect in terms of individual decisions and their cumulative impact on the ecosphere. Because the links between cause and effect are not always clear, there is an incomplete feedback loop.[5] By failing to understand how decisions contribute directly to unsustainable existence, individuals and municipal governments are not stimulated to change behaviours that maintain the status quo. Thus, decisions continue to be made that undermine the long-term objectives that individuals and their local governments may espouse as being desirable.

An illustration of this point can be found in municipal decisions to approve subdivision proposals on agricultural land or on land adjacent to wilderness areas despite regionally agreed-upon objectives to protect such resources.[6] These decisions are made on a case-by-case basis, often with the attitude that "this project is not going to have an impact in the big scheme of things." Councillors face compelling reasons to approve such developments. Examples include existing zoning that allows development to take place, improvements to services and community facilities, and expansion of the municipal tax base. However, these considerations do not include the long-term impacts of urban expansion on natural resource stocks. (An attempt to reconcile explicit policy, meaning that reflecting societal goals, with implicit policy, that resulting from day-to-day decisions, is explored further in Chapter 5.)

With respect to the impact of this barrier on efforts to implement *Clouds of Change* recommendations, the need for improved understanding of the environmental impacts of our actions is eloquently revealed by a civic employee:

> If you go back to the good farmer, what he understands is that his livelihood depends on what he has; that supports him. If he damages his land,

he damages his livelihood. It's a very close connection. Think about this in terms of Marx's theory of alienation: the farther away you get from this connection, the harder it is for you to understand it. Like me for instance, I get into my car in my carport and I get out in the underground parking at work. I don't even need a raincoat. I don't know what the environment is doing. I'm totally alienated from it, so how am I going to be concerned about it?

The scientific materialist paradigm of modern society does not reflect connections to sources of life. To understand issues linked to sustainability, we need improved education to re-establish this connection. This sentiment was supported by councillors, civic staff, task force members, and citizens alike. However, education alone will not be the solution. Other barriers prevent knowledge from turning into action.

One such barrier is perceived lack of empowerment, illustrating the way beliefs affect actions. Within the City of Vancouver municipal government, there are beliefs that (1) ability to affect consumptive behaviour is limited because it is entrenched in cultural values; (2) the City is able to implement symbolic measures, but actions that will result in meaningful change can be implemented only by senior levels of government; and (3) political attempts to bring about change are secondary in impact to those of technological improvement. These perceptions prevent dedicated action because people believe results will not be forthcoming. In this respect, perceived lack of empowerment contributes to lack of political will because municipal staff enthusiasm for implementing the recommendations wanes, especially in the face of obstacles. Perceived lack of empowerment, therefore, creates the paradoxical situation of a governing body that is not motivated to bring about the changes it desires. Thus, perceived lack of empowerment is a barrier that reinforces acceptance of the status quo.

From a citizen's perspective, perceived lack of empowerment is a learned perception. When asked whether concerned people had attempted to persuade government to move faster in implementing the *Clouds of Change* recommendations, the following sentiment typically defined citizens' responses: "You feel like you're beating your head against a stone wall. The City is not forthcoming in the rationale for the decisions they make ... Some public participation processes I've been to, you really get the feeling that the planners have already made their decision. They stare at you, don't respond, walk out while you're talking. The average citizen over time gets worn down and wonders what's the use." This comment illustrates how experiences build perceptions that then negatively affect citizen's behaviour, influencing many to opt out of participating in civic governance. (Chapter 6 discusses the challenges of public participation in more detail.)

Adding to the difficulty encountered by local government in its attempts to implement policies that support sustainability is the problem of competing issues. Limited municipal resources force councillors and civic staff to make value-based decisions on which issues are the most important to address. Comparing the urgency of a broad spectrum of issues such as housing, crime, and drinking water in addition to that of air quality, for example, is difficult. Competing issues can undermine action-taking if air quality is not perceived as a priority by some decision makers. In the case of the City of Vancouver, differences in perception among municipal department heads also proved to be a major impediment to implementation. It creates difficulty in organizing interdepartmental initiatives. If administrators see other issues as priorities, they direct staff's time to deal with those issues first. As a result, establishing funding, scheduling meetings, and coordinating people to do the work becomes difficult.

Uncertainty about future impacts of poor air quality biases decisions against the allocation of resources to address this issue. Accommodating new policy initiatives requires trade-offs that affect existing programs. Unless the benefits of reallocating the money are clearly visible, there is little incentive to do it. As a civic employee points out with regard to the implementation of *Clouds of Change* recommendations, "Sometimes when you get down to the actual decisions, you realize that clean air for police safety is not always an acceptable trade-off." This statement illustrates how short-term issues with complete feedback loops inhibit initiatives to deal with long-term sustainability issues. Government may want to pursue both types of issues in principle, but in practice, the issues of short term, that is, those whose impacts will be felt first, take precedence.

Because public opinion tends to observe policy initiatives in isolation, there is an expectation that policies will be implemented as outlined. When this does not happen, inaction is rationalized as being caused by lack of political will. However, citizens may not realize that conflicting policies slow the progress government can make in any one-policy direction. With regard to *Clouds of Change* implementation, a Vancouver Council member explains: "Debates arise over conflicting policies. One calls for keeping costs under control, the other calls for improving air quality which will add costs to the government's budget."

Given the frustrations that can arise from trying to implement a host of initiatives while simultaneously administering standard municipal services, it is important that civic staff and municipal councillors feel enthusiastic about implementing policies that support sustainability (Sabatier 1980, 547). In the City of Vancouver's case, a common theme among civic employees was frustration over the way the *Clouds of Change* report was handed down to them. Many civic staff members felt overwhelmed by the demands of the community and council. They felt the *Clouds of Change* report was simply "dumped on them." The pressures of competing issues, overwhelming complexity, perceived lack of empowerment, and inadequate funds contributed to lack of civic staff buy-in.[7]

An additional problem is that citizens do not always agree about how a recommendation should be implemented. If people do not share common bonds, philosophies, or interests, or if they do not face similar problems spatially, economically, or socially, it is difficult to reach consensus on which items are priorities. Alternatively, there may be agreement on certain values and disagreement on how they should be embodied in action. Fear of economic and social impacts motivates citizens to resist change in their neighbourhoods, regardless of an initiative's role in the greater context of urban planning. In these circumstances, information is not always an adequate tool for gaining citizen support.

An alternative to forcing change in the face of citizen resistance is to focus on providing choices. As governments grapple with the issue of influencing citizens' behaviour through policy implementation, it is very important to observe a key point. Some policies fail despite their inherent logic because they assume citizens have a greater range of choices available to them than may actually be the case. For example, creating town centres so that people have the opportunity to work close to home influences only those citizens who are in a position to choose either their work location or place of residence. Often citizens are in a position to choose neither; they may be locked into a mortgage, reside in an area for the benefit of their children, or be unable to leave their place of employment without incurring career setbacks. Such factors cause need-meeting behaviours that keep citizens commuting around town despite policies that facilitate centralized living.

A common criticism of *Clouds of Change* was that it "doesn't address the trade-offs, or offer adaptation strategies, or recognize choice restrictions of the people for whom the policy is being designed." Creating opportunities to live close to work is fundamental, but this must be supported by initiatives that enable people to meet their other daily needs in ways that support sustainability. The focus should be on creating supplemental policies that facilitate choice in the face of the restrictions cited above. By creating and facilitating choices, government begins to work at the tremendous task of shifting behaviour. Imposing penalties is one side of the coin; the more difficult task is making it easy for people to change in a world that has historically been designed for unsustainable living.

Many of the restrictions cited above serve as the penalties citizens endure if they choose to act in ecologically considerate ways. These penalties contribute to perceived inequity, a barrier that produces the "free rider" phenomenon seen in public good problems (Hardin 1968; Castells 1983, 293; Van Rees 1991, 100). Action that supports sustainability is usually not adopted in a society when the personal sacrifices required are per-ceived as greater than the benefits both to the community at large and to the individual. If one feels that one's own sacrifice will be taken advantage of by someone else, thereby nullifying any possible benefit, motivation to act is diminished. Thus, perceived inequity becomes a rationale for abdi-cating personal and civic responsibility to behave in ways that support sustainability.

By understanding how perceived inequity functions, we begin to gain insight into perhaps the most puzzling barrier: disjunction between verbal support and willingness to take action in support of sustainability. As Ken Hultman observed in *The Path of Least Resistance*, "values all tend to sound good and noble on the surface. Consequently, people can verbally state that they have a value, even though that value has no impact on their behaviour" (1979, 29). Research by the Organization for Economic Cooperation and Development further reveals that an individual's behav-iour is only partly due to her or his values and is heavily influenced by con-textual setting and tradition (Michaelis 1996). Disjunction between what people say and do exists primarily because there is a separation between what people believe to be a general good and what they need in an imme-diate, short-term context. Certain immediate needs may be fulfilled by behaviours that support sustainability, but others may not. A common frustration heard by City of Vancouver councillors and civic staff was that "everyone says they would support transit, carpooling, etc., but when it comes time to do it, or time to pay, they don't." There is a tendency to ver-bally support environmental initiatives without taking into consideration what will personally be required to implement them.

The impact of this barrier is that it creates cynicism among government employees, who feel that there is no widespread public support for their efforts. In turn, cynicism grows amongst the general public, who feel gov-ernment is not sincere about implementing environmental policies. A Task Force on Atmospheric Change member provides the following insight: "People blame politicians without recognizing their own responsibilities as lobbyists. They blame politicians out of laziness. They want someone else to tackle what is hard and complex to do."

This observation introduces yet another barrier, that of overwhelming complexity. An issue spanning many factors of cause and effect becomes very difficult to understand (Van Rees 1991, 100) and difficult to address (Tindal and Tindal 1984, 190). Often the complexity of an issue is so over-whelming that people avoid dealing with it. As described by Boothroyd in Chapter 5, society's current problem-solving models are very good for solv-ing linear problems, but not good for addressing complex systems. The feedback loops are incomplete in many cases, and there is uncertainty about outcomes of possible actions. Unless politicians feel threatened by not taking immediate action, they have a strong tendency toward avoidance. Observing how this barrier affects municipal staff, a City of Vancouver employee admits: "If we were trying something like *Clouds of Change* again, I would want to move in smaller increments. Moving in one big step towards a specific objective becomes overwhelming. This can lead to inertia. We don't know how to do it. Paralysis sets in; people ask 'how do I get there, it's so far away?' Big organizations change better in small steps."

When there is uncertainty about how to deal with an issue, the default is often to accept the status quo (Rees 1994, 19) or to move ahead at a very slow pace, taking only small steps. Without proof that negative ecological consequences will ensue if the status quo is maintained, there is little incentive to act in ways that will inconvenience certain segments of the population.

Increasing uncertainty in today's information era is not a result of lack of information. This observation raises an interesting issue regarding news media. The selection of media content creates a barrier to the implementation of policies. Failure to present information comprehensively leads to biasing of audiences, and issues that are omitted have less chance of becoming part of public consciousness (Rees and Wackernagel 1992). A majority of research participants representing citizens and civic staff felt the news media affected the implementation of the *Clouds of Change* report by not presenting information to the public in a comprehensive and thought-provoking manner. The results of this problem are summarized by a civic employee, who states: "As a society, we are moving away from talking about ideas. Now we talk in slogans. The media doesn't force us to think issues through in their full complexity. Thus, we are getting policies driven by slogan orientation." Complaints such as this reflect a dilemma regarding the business of information management. Precisely because it is a business, run for profit, the media tend to operate on a mandate that encourages public consumption preferences (Downs 1972, 42; Herman and Chomsky 1988). It thus serves as an instrument that reinforces scientific materialist values.

Finally, the influence of media plays an important role in the barrier identified as prestige motive. Cultural norms inherited from past decades of sanctified consumption continue to define the aspirations of many citizens (Rees 1994, 19). Activities that reduce personal consumption are resented. With respect to the *Clouds of Change* report, two civic employees summarize: "We are not a transit conditioned society. Taking the bus is seen as something negative, something you do because you cannot afford a car." "We are still psychologically and economically wedded to the car." As a result, civic employees feel their efforts to induce changes supporting sustainability are frustrated by public desires to maintain high levels of consumption in their daily lives.

Institutional and Structural Barriers

Institutional and structural barriers interfere with government's or politicians' ability to implement policies that support sustainability. They are present in organizational operations of public institutions (or their structures). Institutional and structural barriers can have perceptual dimensions, as revealed by the most commonly cited barrier in this category: fear of losing constituent support. Sensitivity to constituents' needs or desire for reelection can affect the decisions of councillors. In such circumstances, decisions that would upset a particular group of voters may be avoided.

The difficulty of balancing the tension that exists between local and regional concerns is well illustrated in Vancouver City Council's attempt to implement a *Clouds of Change* recommendation to reduce traffic in an area of the city that borders Richmond, a neighbouring municipality. An arterial road connecting the two municipalities is heavily used by commuters during peak hours. A high-occupancy vehicle (HOV) lane was proposed as a means of promoting more sustainable commuting alternatives by allowing buses and other vehicles carrying more than one person to move quickly through the area. To create the lane, street parking during peak hours would have had to be removed. However, merchants with businesses located along the artery were opposed to the proposal for fear of losing business because their shops would become inaccessible to customers unable to find parking.

The merchants organized an effective campaign to lobby Vancouver City Council against designation of the HOV lane. Many Richmond residents resented the outcome and accused City of Vancouver Council of lacking political will to uphold regional objectives for promoting high-occupancy use of vehicles. Richmond residents desired the lane because it would have provided improved access to the central business district located in downtown Vancouver.

This example demonstrates what several City of Vancouver councillors refer to as the "tyranny of small decisions." When asked how often localized interest groups, also known as NIMBY groups,[8] sway council decisions away from its long-term goals, a councillor answered, "often." A second councillor explained: "Merchants vote, greater causes don't ... The general public will forget this decision, but the merchants won't." This comment illustrates how need-meeting behaviours, pursued by individuals, can affect the outcome of government actions. It also demonstrates how several barriers function in combination. In addition to fear of losing constituent support, uncertainty played a role because councillors were not convinced the initiative would contribute significantly to reduced air pollution. Hesitation about implementing the HOV lane was further strengthened by citizens who were unsupportive of the recommendation. A councillor commenting on this issue points out that:

A further complication is the issue of values. You may ask yourself what is in the interest of the broader, general public, but your answer may vary according to your values and belief system. For example, some people may say implementing high-occupancy vehicle lanes is clearly in the public's best interest, and perhaps from an environmental perspective this is true. On the other hand, someone who is oriented around economic measures could argue that continuing to support local economic development, even in a very isolated case, somehow contributes to the benefit of the public. So it's a value decision, which leaves it wide open.

Several councillors acknowledged that had a nongovernment, environmental organization been present to lobby Vancouver City Council on behalf of the "greater causes," the decision could have been reversed, in favour of the HOV lane. Such acknowledgement substantiates Castells' observation that change is initiated by groups and that governments are simply the "instruments of social bargaining" between such groups (1983, 294).

In 1998, subsequent to the designation of Richmond as a regional growth-concentration centre, a rapid bus system was approved for the arterial. Again, the initiative was resisted by Vancouver merchants and residents located adjacent to the artery. However, a compromise was reached whereby street parking could be retained. What is interesting to note about this solution is that environmental groups participating in the decision-making process eventually agreed that the retention of street parking was a benefit. It was seen as a traffic-calming measure, restricting the amount of road space available to commuters in single-occupant vehicles. The evolution of a better result than the one originally anticipated reflects what Jane Jacobs identifies as the value of the NIMBY voice (1998). Rather than discount the complaints of residents who oppose an initiative because of what appears to be self-interest, Jacobs argues that their reactions are a sign that the liveability of a community may be threatened. Listening to their concerns and attempting to integrate what matters to these people into the final decision can produce a better solution than was originally conceived.

Another manifestation of fear of losing constituent support is the content of reports written by civic employees who are motivated by a need for acceptance. In this context, this barrier reinforces acceptance of the status quo. The need for acceptance is linked to prestige motive and shapes individual behaviour on a daily basis. One City of Vancouver department head explains, in the context of the *Clouds of Change* recommendations, that perceived public opinion often conditions the tone of reports: "Perceived opinions of the public have more impact on political decisions than reality. Bureaucrats are also sensitive to public opinion and take this into consideration when writing their reports. Politicians must be careful of data they receive from bureaucrats ... Bureaucrats should take positions, and politicians should challenge those positions. Too often politicians simply accept bureaucrats' words." A civic employee's dilemma, caused by fear of losing constituent support, is as follows: it is important that "people in the know be willing to speak out and not be cowed by contrary perceptions." However, "the fear comes from the backlash of displeasing people; it is easier to straddle the fence and try to please, or at least not offend anybody." As a result, policy recommendations that would introduce radical change, even if the interests of sustainability call for it, are avoided.

Yet, even when government is willing to take affirmative action, other barriers such as limitation of jurisdiction may stand in the way. When trying to implement the *Clouds of Change* report, limitation of jurisdiction was recognized as a fundamental barrier among Vancouver City councillors and civic staff. The general perception among these groups was that the City was making progress on most of the recommendations except those that lay outside its jurisdiction. When a recommendation exceeds the City's jurisdiction, the City must lobby senior levels of government to either delegate power so that it can take action or urge the senior government to use its authority to take action.

This type of lobbying follows strict protocol. For the most part, lobbying is reduced to letter writing or, at best, a personal meeting between the mayor and the provincial minister under whose jurisdiction the issue of concern lies. If the request is denied, the City is offered no recourse to appeal the decision; however, it may attempt the same request the following year. In the case of *Clouds of Change*, lobbying is described by a civic employee as follows:

> The lobbying role becomes very nominal. Somebody writes a letter, the mayor signs it, and off it goes to the appropriate minister. The minister replies with excuses and that's that. There is a "not my job" phenomenon when it comes to lobbying. Nobody will be re-elected or defeated based on their ability to lobby other jurisdictions. The municipal government must provide basic services to its constituents. Lobbying senior governments is not pursued with great conviction. The only time lobbying is effective is when the mayor has a personal conviction that something needs to be done. When government works with the appropriate ministers, then things get done. But, both sides of this equation have to be committed.

This statement illuminates the role of need-meeting behaviours that stimulate councillors and civic staff to operate in a narrowly defined capacity of delivering municipal services. A complete feedback loop exists for issues such as the supply of water and the maintenance of roads, sewers, and street lights. That is to say, citizens would immediately notice and complain if these things were not provided. However, whether the municipality lobbies senior governments goes unnoticed. Therefore, lobbying efforts can be undermined by fear of losing constituent support, competing issues, and lack of championing by mayor and council.

However, when the City is successful in having power delegated, a host of new problems may ensue. For example, the Province may not delegate enough power to allow the breadth of authority necessary to implement a policy effectively. In the case of *Clouds of Change*, the City of Vancouver was successful in gaining some power to regulate trees on private lots. However, when this authority was delegated, the terms under which regulation could take place were so restrictive that the City found its extended jurisdiction to be almost useless. A civic employee explains: "The City may now require replacement trees for ones that are over eight inches in diameter that have been cut for development purposes. However, this regulatory power does not address concern for the preservation of old trees. There is no regulatory power to ensure that replanted trees receive adequate bedding preparation, and once occupancy permits are issued, there is nothing stopping people from removing these trees for other reasons."

Because of the poor construction of this legislation, civic staff advised Vancouver City Council not to move forward on the initiative. The same employee had this comment to make about the role of perception and lack of understanding about the issues: "The Province may not appreciate the administration difficulties encountered by the municipality." The precise range of powers required by the City must be clearly understood by the delegating authority.

A second stumbling block relates to lack of jurisdiction at the regional level. Because many transportation issues involve neighbouring municipalities, and because the Greater Vancouver Regional District (GVRD) has authority over air quality, council passed the responsibility for implementing several *Clouds of Change* recommendations to the regional level. However, the GVRD has limited planning authority, and until 1999, it did not have authority over regional transportation services. As a result, it has been poorly equipped to implement many of the recommendations that seem appropriate to it. This aspect of limitation of jurisdiction is directly applicable to inappropriate structure of government.

Limitation of jurisdiction, when not understood by the public, contributes to public perception of lack of political will and adds to feelings of disempowerment. Improved communication between government and its constituents could diminish the role this barrier plays in generating public cynicism about government's willingness to adopt actions that support sustainability.

As outlined in Chapter 6, responsive action in the public sector is dependent on strong communication linkages between a governing body and its constituents. However, the effects of disjunction between verbal support and willingness to take action may keep some councillors and civic employees sceptical about the information they receive from citizens. Furthermore, negative experiences in poorly run public-participation processes diminish the efforts citizens are willing to make to communicate their desires.

Not only must communication be strengthened between governments and their constituents, it must also be improved among the different levels of government. Regardless of which level of government authors a policy, each requires the cooperation of the various agencies that have authority over different issues. These agencies do not always share the same priorities, yet their cooperation in implementing certain initiatives is crucial. Thus, emphasis must be placed on bringing the different authorities together to identify how each can help the other attain their goals. Unless a mechanism for such cooperation exists, initiatives get "lost in the cracks" or are undermined by the actions of agencies pursuing different, and often directly opposing, objectives.

The problems associated with weak linkages among the policies of civic and senior levels of government often compound upon structural problems within municipal governments. The city is an urban ecosystem. The relationships among human actions, infrastructure management, and ecological impacts are closely related. However, municipal departments are often highly segregated. Policies administered by one department may directly contradict the efforts of another. This problem is exacerbated by limitation of jurisdiction, because still other functions in the city, such as public transportation, may be administered by agencies outside the municipality. The segregated nature of municipal departments reinforces the barrier of differences in perception by reducing opportunities for staff from various departments to share their perspectives on issues confronting the city. Not only does it inhibit opportunities to prioritize competing issues from other departments vis-à-vis one's own, it also impedes the development of cooperative strategies for dealing with them.

Addressing these concerns in the context of implementing *Clouds of Change* recommendations, several Vancouver civic staff observed that although meetings at which senior department staff members come together to discuss their concerns and projects are regularly scheduled, and interdepartmental committees to address certain issues are formed, more communication and cooperation among departments is desirable.

Another observation is that the hierarchical nature of the departments stifles communication opportunities for staff. Several staff members explained that the attitude of senior management sets the tone for how the whole department operates. This can inhibit attempts to improve coordination among departments, as a civic employee observes: "Attitudes permeate out from the director and affect middle management and sometimes line staff as well. The director and middle management also set the tone for the way bureaucrats are expected to act and conduct business in their department." Thus, segregation of departments reinforces differences in perception, which in turn impedes attempts to implement council initiatives.

The pressure on councillors to contend with ever-expanding agendas creates additional problems. At the municipal level, departmental staff and councillors often find themselves catering to the demands of those concerned with minor issues. This creates a dilemma for many civic employees, who are confronted with the following question: What's more important, dealing with an outraged citizen screaming at your counter or dealing with the stack of reports you must review for a long-range plan? Yet the dilemma was documented nearly twenty years ago using this analogy: "'Like the urban policy maker, the shooting gallery player has far more targets than he can possibly hit.' ... Given the need to react quickly and to deal with such a variety of targets, the player is likely to rely on reflexes more than any considered plan of action" (Yates 1984, 191).

The problem is that municipal government structure has not adapted itself to deal with ecological problems that extend past the realm of specific, short-term issues. Ashby's law of requisite variety states that the administrational framework must mimic the structures or mechanisms of that which it is trying to manage (Beer 1979, 89). The institutional framework of government does not have the requisite variety necessary to meet the demands of an ecologically sustainable society.

Fear of losing control or power further undermines government's ability to achieve sustainable communities. This barrier plays an interesting role in the allocation of funds and is associated with weak linkages among the policies of civic and senior levels of government. In the context of *Clouds of Change*, one deputy director states: "Most logical answers are not pursued because of turf wars." Another director from a different department gives the following explanation:

> We cannot spend money in all areas so we begin to misallocate money based on who is there first, or who can go to court to get court actions, and in my opinion, we're just missing the boat. We're not looking at all of these issues and saying where can we best apply our resources to improve our quality of life and our public health ... We should set up priority committees to assess risks. These committees should include representatives from civic departments and different Federal and Provincial departments ... I think the political decision makers would be better served if we could get together and say here are all the risks ... and their assessment ... and their effect on public health and the environment. Based on that risk assessment, this is where we think the funding should be allocated ... Unfortunately, that's not happening because everybody is pursuing their special interest, and I don't think the public is well served, and I don't

think the decision makers are well served, and I think it·is an unfortunate state of affairs.

The barriers of inadequate funds, inadequate resources, differences in perception, and lack of awareness about the issues all play a factor in fear of losing control or power and are elaborated upon in Chapters 5 and 6. However, as cited by Carr in Chapter 3, improved social networks might successfully overcome these barriers, especially when they operate in an institutional context. Robust social connections make it less likely that narrow self-interest will prevail, making it important to establish these connections both between and within government organizations.

Unfortunately, a significant portion of the public believes that once a report is approved or adopted by council, the citizens' job is done and it is government's job to implement initiatives and bring about the desired changes. This perception is an example of lack of understanding about action roles, a barrier that undermines institutional ability to make progress on plans and initiatives. Citizens do not realize that their role involves taking part themselves and demanding or ensuring that these changes are in fact implemented (Ley 1983, 306). In the context of *Clouds of Change*, the need for citizens to understand their own responsibilities in activating the changes they desire is exemplified by a Vancouver City councillor, who states: "The most important thing we could do in terms of implementing the report is have the citizens realize that it isn't what government does that will solve the problem, it's what they do that will solve the problem." Citizens may complain about lack of political will without realizing that their own behaviours, such as acceptance of the status quo, disjunction between verbal support and willingness to take action, and continued pursuit of prestige demonstrated through consumption are in fact some of the biggest barriers to government action-taking.

Furthermore, the absence of an urban environmental group to advocate issues of concern leaves many policies vulnerable to manipulation by other special-interest groups. The complaints of local agencies that might be negatively affected by the implementation of a council initiative must be heeded and weighted into the final decision. However, examples exist where such weighting seems to heavily favour localized interest groups, at the expense of taking action that supports sustainability and the benefit of the general public.

The presence of a nongovernment, environmental organization to lobby council on issues affecting the general public helps overcome the barrier of attention pressure. It is difficult, in the face of direct pressure coming from a special-interest group, to stick to goals that benefit the greater majority in a mild way at the expense of severely affecting a localized group (Sabatier 1980, 551). A potential negative threat to a small group of people serves as adequate motivation for it to mobilize and bring its grievance to council. However, a potential benefit to a largely dispersed population does not provide the same incentive for members of this group to band together and lobby in the same way. Furthermore, it is difficult to adhere to long-term goals when confronted with short-term interests because there is more dissociation between actions and consequences the farther one moves into the future: the feedback loops become increasingly incomplete. That the consequences of a short-term initiative are immediately felt provides an element of concrete realism absent in the long-term initiatives. In the latter, cause and effect are separated not only by time but often also by beneficiaries; those who experience the consequences may not be those who take the actions. Nongovernment, environmental organizations can play a vital role in attempting to bind long-term cause and effect relationships closely together in decision-makers' minds.

There are many nongovernment, environmental organizations currently operating in the City of Vancouver.[9] However, what is lacking is a coordination of these groups' efforts to support issues of common interest.[10] Better networking among such organizations, both to improve cooperation and to provide a united front when addressing specific council initiatives, could have a tremendous impact in moving the City toward actions that support sustainability.

The need for improved networking is further revealed by the barrier of lack of cooperation and information-sharing among the "different agencies of knowledge" (Ley 1983, 365). These agencies consist of government council members and civic employees who have knowledge of the whole system (the city politic), academics who have knowledge of specific issues affecting the city, and citizens who have knowledge of how specific issues affect certain sectors of the city; other stakeholders might also be considered. Without integrative consultation among these agencies, policy making remains a process of applying incomplete knowledge to problems, or remaining ignorant of them altogether, and thus deriving rather ineffectual results.

Finally, predetermined contracts can inhibit opportunities for change (Altman, Valenzi, and Hodgetts 1985, 626). Adaptations that would support sustainability may not be implemented until contracts expire and opportunities for renegotiation occur. For example, a *Clouds of Change* initiative to provide free transit passes in lieu of free parking could not be implemented because it would contravene existing agreements with municipal unions regarding worksite conditions. The initiative can be introduced only at a time when union contracts are being renegotiated. Existing contractual agreements also prevented opportunities for changes to public transit that would have allowed small operators of mini buses to provide shuttle services in suburban areas to and from major transit routes. The respective unions involved in the delivery of transit services were against allowing nonunionized shuttle services, and thus, the initiative was dropped.

Economic and Financial Barriers

Economic and financial barriers deter the implementation of government initiatives to support sustainability because of monetary cost considerations. Limited financial resources make it difficult for civic employees to implement initiatives with the level of thoroughness originally intended. Lack of a prioritizing mechanism to indicate the importance of a new initiative relative to those existing can delay its implementation (Sabatier 1980, 545). Many City of Vancouver civic staff members felt that the process used to create and adopt the *Clouds of Change* report did not allow them adequate opportunity to make adjustments to their existing and forecasted work programs. Thus, when the recommendations were handed down to them, their department funding had already been allocated to other initiatives. Without a prioritizing mechanism that included guidelines from council indicating which existing projects were to be subordinated to the *Clouds of Change* recommendations, many staff members found themselves unable to reallocate funds without severely hampering existing projects.

In addition, councillors and civic staff expressed frustration with the amount of work they are required to do and the limited staff resources available to do it. Most of the councillors interviewed felt the city would be better served if either more councillors were elected, assistant staff were provided to councillors, or government structure was adapted to provide greater roles for citizens in decision making. When asked if the role of councillor should be a full-time employment position, one councillor replied: "My first response is yes because I see what goes on here, and it's really very minimal. It would contribute to a more effective council."

However, these kinds of improvements would increase government operating costs, and most councillors and civic employees were sensitive to citizens' unwillingness to pay more taxes. A councillor expresses the situation thus: "There is a basic cynicism in people. They don't trust the government to spend the money wisely ... They think: 'Our taxes are always going up and the deficit is never coming down. Give them more money and it won't help anyway.'" Weak communication links between government and its constituency, weak linkages among the policies of civic and senior levels of government, and lack of understanding about action roles contribute to citizens' cynicism about government's ability to effect change. As one department head explains, "We've hit the wall in terms of what taxpayers are willing to pay and yet they are constantly calling for more services. You look at a council package and how many reports are called for every week, and then you say, 'Well, who is going to pay for all of this?'"

Citizens seem conditioned to expect government to look after problems as they arise. As Vancouver continues to grow, so too do many of its problems. However, as identified in Chapter 3, focusing on improving social capital stocks within communities and expanding the resulting cooperative attitude to the political sphere holds great potential for overcoming these types of barriers. Chapters 5 and 6 explore further the notion that perhaps it is time for a re-examination of government's role as a service provider. It may indeed be time for government to take on an increasing role as educator and facilitator, helping citizens find local solutions.

In an effort to combat public cynicism, government tends to favour action on initiatives that will have visible results in the short term. If the desired impact of a policy recommendation cannot be guaranteed, the chances that it will be implemented are severely reduced (Sabatier 1980, 543). Chances are further limited if the results are expected to occur only in the long-term future, yet require financial inputs today. Unfortunately, most *Clouds of Change* recommendations and sustainability initiatives fall into this latter category.

The constant pressure of limited fiscal resources creates resistance to implementing initiatives that might negatively impact income-generating activities for the city.[11] Restricting the ease with which employees commute to work and increasing the cost of goods movement within Vancouver, through the application of a carbon tax for example, were concerns, in terms of negative impacts on business as a result of implementing *Clouds of Change* recommendations.

In the past, technologies such as the automobile, which now poses a threat to sustainability, became inextricably tied to work practices. Unknowingly, society began to trade sustainability for productivity. As long as this pattern persists, efforts to change remain limited to those means that do not inhibit production. As a civic employee explains, "market failure is what you have ... The externalities of pollution have to be internalized so that they become a part of business decisions."

However, a *Clouds of Change* recommendation to internalize the costs of motor vehicle emissions through the application of a carbon tax was not pursued by council for fear that it would disadvantage the poor. The dilemma created by this barrier is explained by a councillor: "The carbon tax was voted against ... because it was a regressive tax. It would have priced low-end income earners out of cars which they might need for a job. But, if we subsidize cars so that the poorest person can afford to drive, then you'll never get rid of cars ... Other forms of transit cannot compete with the car." Fear of unjustly disadvantaging the poor is reinforced by the existing car-oriented structure of Vancouver, which limits the viability of alternative transportation choices. Owning a motor vehicle is an expensive endeavour for most citizens, and many of the people interviewed felt frustrated that the City continues to cater to automobile traffic despite a policy that places priority on the movement of pedestrians. The following are samples of what citizens have to say about transportation options for people who do not drive cars: "We should create environments that don't limit people to the grids (that is, having to use the same routes as automobiles). The urban environment should be designed for the human body and not for the car body." "The City could have made a more serious commitment to bicycle use, but their bike paths are a joke. Except for paths around the waterfront, all they've done is put up signs on side streets. But, that's unsafe for cyclists; it's why I don't cycle." "I don't know how much influence the City has on public transit. Progress could be made on intermodal transport, for example, allowing bikes on buses and trains." Although these suggestions would greatly improve transportation options for pedestrians, readers can perhaps anticipate how the barriers listed in this research, such as limitation of jurisdiction, inadequate funds, competing issues, and others, will operate to prevent their implementation.

Prescriptions for Overcoming Barriers

Taking a closer look at how barriers operate reveals important clues about the inertia that seems to hold society on an unsustainable course. It also provides insight into opportunities for change. When asked to suggest strategies for overcoming the barriers that impeded implementation of *Clouds of Change* recommendations, research participants put forward the following:

1ʺ Limit the number of recommendations to two or three crucial initiatives, or approach implementation of the whole report by attaching priority to the three most important things that need to be done first. Work with civic staff and community groups to create an implementation strategy for the chosen initiatives. This may include indicating the priority of newly adopted initiatives vis-à-vis existing projects in order to assist staff in making decisions about the reallocation of funds in their department budgets. It also may include an assessment of existing policies or regulations that contravene the new initiatives.

2 Concentrate on developing a public-education program and demonstrate the advantages of implementing the initiatives. Attention must be paid not only to environmental improvements but to financial benefits as well. The opportunity to serve multiple objectives should be highlighted wherever possible. Furthermore, the advantages should be presented using detailed information. Vague promises are not persuasive in gaining the approval of sceptical decision makers. Therefore, the specific· cost benefits of implementing a recommendation should be presented.

3 Establish standards to help monitor progress. In some cases, recommendations could not be implemented because baseline standards, such as

1988 levels of carbon dioxide emissions for Vancouver, were not known. Because investments required to establish standards and monitor progress are often viewed as too costly for the City to bear alone, assistance from other organizations or other levels of government could be sought. There is tremendous opportunity for partnerships among governments, nongovernment organizations, and private sector groups in providing solutions to problems of limited resources.

4   Improve networking and cooperation among all groups. Continue active lobbying by nongovernment organizations and citizen groups and enhance communication and coordination among these groups when addressing common interests before council.

5   Work on partnership-building and improved communication between government and constituents. Several corporations expressed an interest in working with the City of Vancouver to achieve *Clouds of Change* goals. Programs designed to facilitate this kind of cooperation could establish solutions to overcoming barriers hindering implementation of some recommendations.

6   Identify lead agencies and coordinate policies appropriately. The problems associated with a segregated, departmentalized government structure sometimes result in lack of cooperation and lack of a designated lead agency. Lead agencies responsible for addressing various air-quality and atmospheric-change issues must be identified. Once designated, they must be held accountable for the coordination of government policies and implementation efforts among the various government agencies concerned.

7   Develop government structures that accommodate long-term decision making. Structures such as roundtables and community forums should be examined to provide consultation in decision making that is based on a longer time horizon than the three-year term of elected officials. Such a long-term focus could operate as an auxiliary to council in an attempt to balance the short-term feedback loops in which council must function.

8   Provide a means of decision making that gives a greater role to citizens than they currently have. In addition to roundtables and community forums, the ward system was put forward as a possible alternative. Such a system could contribute to social capital[12] and may engender an increased willingness to adapt behaviours that do not support sustainability.

9   Develop policies that improve choices. Implementing policies that support people's choices for self-help and sustainability must become a priority of council. Such policies provide the interim steps to reaching *Clouds of Change* objectives. For example, policies penalizing motorists are resisted for fear of unjustly disadvantaging the poor; however, policies facilitating transportation for the poor are neglected. For example,

improving intermodal transportation, such as accommodating bicycles on public transit vehicles, would benefit the poor and improve transportation options that do not require an automobile.

10 Follow up task-force initiatives with a public participation process. Both the task force that authored *Clouds of Change* and the Victoria-based task group that authored *Healthy Atmosphere 2000* felt that as their reports were nearing completion, public interest ran very high. Effort to utilize the momentum of interest was identified as a crucial element in social change toward support of sustainability initiatives. Had public participation processes begun at this time, they might have provided opportunities to build social capital by helping citizens to (1) identify the trade-offs required by the recommendations and (2) identify strategies to overcome the barriers to action-taking that such trade-offs might impose. Furthermore, such a process would indicate to council that a large section of the constituency wanted change, and that they were willing to grapple with the consequences of what that change might necessitate.

11 Promote self-help and citizen-initiated projects. Citizens have more rights than local governments, which are restricted to operating within the powers granted by a municipal act or special charter. Therefore, citizens have more freedom to take action and can initiate more projects than can a municipality. Emphasis on self-help contributes to a norm of personal responsibility among social networks. It draws attention to need-meeting behaviours that do not support sustainability and identifies the individual, as well as the community, as a major source of power for change. In this respect, self-help creates opportunities for citizens to apply their own creativity to initiating local experiments and pilot projects. Where self-help initiatives are blocked by municipal regulations, a new and much-needed debate can arise on how regulations should be changed so as to encourage rather than hinder efforts to support sustainability.

Conclusion

By examining the barriers to implementation of *Clouds of Change*, it becomes apparent that the concept of lack of political will is composed of a number of factors operating both within the governance structure and outside of it. Laying blame on any one sector of society prevents a full understanding of why knowledge is not being turned into action, and conveniently externalizes the responsibilities we must all share if we are to realize a sustainable world.

Many of the strategies for overcoming barriers focus on ways to prioritize issues, adapt government structure, include ecological and social costs in financial considerations, and improve civic morale. This last point in particular bears further comment.

The research reveals that perceived lack of empowerment is fundamentally a learned perception that is often based on citizens' experiences in government-run, public-participation processes. Current public-participation processes seem to weaken the relationship between citizens and their government, creating a sense of alienation and cynicism that undermines government's effectiveness and ability to implement initiatives.[13]

In a national study about what factors contribute to effective regional government in Italy, it was determined that the degree of "civicness," or civic morale, of a community has more to do with successful implementation of policy initiatives than education level of the populace, economic development, demographic and social changes, urbanization, and personal stability (Putnam, Leonardi, and Nanetti 1993, 118). A civic community is characterized by interdependent relationships, trust, reciprocity and cooperation, closely interwoven associations and social networks, diversity among elected officials' backgrounds, and a belief that citizens can and should make decisions about issues affecting them. In short, citizens do not feel alienated and powerless against their government. They recognize that they have both a right and a responsibility to participate in public affairs.

A high degree of civic morale operates in several ways to improve government performance. A belief in government integrity, coupled with the belief that other citizens will obey the rules and regulations established by the government, sets a norm of compliance in a community. In a highly integrated social network, noncompliance is feared not so much for possible punitive measures as for negative social consequences, such as ostracism by peers or the loss of advantages gained by being a part of a social network. The denser the social networks in a community, the higher the possibility of cooperation in self-help initiatives. Thus, the social fabric of the community encourages compliance and cooperation. This point is crucial to understanding how management of public resources might be effectively carried out.

A civic community provides the contextual situation to act according to conscience despite economic and immediate, need-meeting motivations that encourage one to do otherwise. Thus, civic morale provides a means of completing the feedback loops that encourage actions that support sustainability, when such loops are not being completed by other social stimuli. Therefore, civicness can help overcome barriers to implementation of government initiatives to support sustainability.

At the heart of civicness is what might be referred to as social capital. Described in detail in Chapters 2 and 3, social capital stocks include those things that encourage individuals to participate in activities where they meet other members of the community and discuss common interests and concerns. Examples are sport clubs, social clubs, volunteer organizations, and business associations. The amount of social capital present in a community can be measured by assessing the number of such organizations and their level of activity. The longevity of such organizations as well as their size indicate the health of these stocks.

Putnam's findings reveal that government effectiveness is highly dependent on the informal, social connections of the populace, stimulated by their involvement in local activities. It is in this area that local agents can most effectively work together to promote behaviour among community members that is cooperative and adaptive to the changes that may result from policy implementation. Supporting community organizations and community events, encouraging membership in local organizations, and seeking ways to increase social networks help build social capital and over time can help improve the civic morale of a community.

Thus, it is important to improve our understanding of how civic responsibility and participation is engendered and how institutional reforms or adaptations can contribute to this process. It may be the case that self-organizing and self-help initiatives stem completely from outside the institutionalized government structure. Nevertheless, the factors that motivate them should be well understood. Government roles for facilitating their occurrence might be identified.

Finally, the scientific materialist paradigm lends itself to short-term thinking, and as a result, decision makers may mistakenly perceive actions that support sustainability as increasing the costs of government. However, taking a long-term view and considering the ecological and social costs presently ignored (i.e., internalizing the externalities) quickly corrects this fault and reveals that actions to support sustainability are cost-effective. Ecological economics provides guidance in adopting a long-term perspective and accounting for the costs that are presently overlooked by most decision makers. However, research into the potential uses of social capital as a means to reduce reliance on monetary capital for implementing sustainability initiatives may also prove to be very useful. For example, communities that enjoy dense social networks often display a high rate of self-sufficiency because amenities and social services such as daycare are provided on a volunteer basis (Howe Sound Round Table 1996, 53). Cooperation and trust encourage observance of regulations, thereby reducing the need for paid regulatory enforcement. Sense of place and community spirit enable participation in local initiatives such as stream stewardship projects, waste reduction and recycling campaigns, neighbourhood clean-up days, and community gardening and urban agriculture experiments. These activities reduce the need for government spending on similarly focused programs.

In the quest for healthy and sustainable communities, social capital appears to be an important key for turning knowledge into action. Fortunately, each of us can be a catalyst for change to foster social capital in our own communities. Conversing with a neighbour, working with other individuals and organizations on projects of shared interest, and participating in local politics builds social networks and increases opportunities for community self-determination.

Notes

1 Sustainable development in this research is defined as positive socioeconomic change that does not undermine the ecological and social systems upon which communities and society are dependent (see W.E. Rees, *Sustainability, Growth and Employment: Toward an Ecologically Stable, Economically Secure, and Socially Satisfying Future* for a comprehensive description of this definition). (See Rees 1994 for complete reference.)
2 A comprehensive table recording each recommendation, its status of implementation, and associated barriers is provided in the master's thesis *What's Stopping Sustainability? Examining the Barriers to Implementation of Clouds of Change* (see Moore 1994 for complete reference).
3 *Healthy Atmosphere 2000* was commissioned by the Capital Regional District to address Victoria's atmospheric concerns. It was initiated in direct follow-up to *Clouds of Change*.
4 See Moore 1994 for a complete assessment.
5 A feedback loop exists when an individual is (1) capable of assessing an initial state, (2) taking action, and (3) sensing the consequences of that action and its effects on the initial state. Such feedback may be positive, encouraging further action, or negative, suppressing further action.
6 Regional, in this context, refers to a partnership of several municipalities.
7 Interviews with people involved in the creation of the *Healthy Atmosphere 2000* report reveal that lack of early involvement of politicians and civic staff was believed to be the primary reason for political rejection of that report. This underscores the importance of early and intense involvement of the bureaucracy as essential to implementation success.
8 The acronym NIMBY stands for Not In My Back Yard.
9 Examples include Better Environmentally Sound Transportation, Farm Folk/City Folk, Neighbour to Neighbour, the Permaculture Network, the Society Promoting Environmental Conservation, and Stop Legislated Poverty.
10 The BC Environmental Network and Eco-city Network represent two local initiatives that attempt to facilitate this level of coordination.
11 Desire for financial gain can be a barrier to adopting actions that support sustainability at the individual level as well.
12 The concept of social capital is elaborated upon later in this and other chapters.
13 An exception to this observation is the CityPlan public-participation process which was used to develop a new Official Community Plan for Vancouver. It is the largest public-participation process ever undertaken by the City, lasting several years. Citizens and civic employees expressed hope that this process would begin to create a more positive relationship between the municipal government and its residents.

References

Altman, S., E. Valenzi, and R. Hodgetts. 1985. *Organizational Behaviour: Theory and Practice.* New York: Academic Press.
Argyris, C. 1993. *Knowledge for Action: A Guide to Overcoming Barriers to Organizational Change.* San Francisco: Jossey-Bass.
Beer, S. 1979. *The Heart of Enterprise.* New York: John Wiley and Sons.
Brown, L. 1990. *State of the World.* Washington, DC: Worldwatch Institute.
Bush, K. 1990. *Climate Change, Global Security and International Governance.* Ottawa: Canadian Institute for International Peace and Security.
Castells, M. 1983. *The City and the Grassroots: A Cross-Cultural Theory of Urban Social Movements.* London: Edward Alan Ltd.
Christensen, P. 1991. "Driving Forces, Increasing Returns and Ecological Sustainability." In R. Costanza, ed., *Ecological Economics: The Science and Management of Sustainability,* 75-87. New York: Columbia University Press.

City of Vancouver Task Force on Atmospheric Change. 1990. *Clouds of Change: Final Report*. Vancouver: The Task Force.

Daly, H., and J. Cobb. 1989. *For the Common Good*. Boston: Beacon Press.

Downs, A. 1972. "Up and Down with Ecology: the Issue Attention Cycle." *The Public Interest* 28: 38-50.

Hardin, G. 1968. "The Tragedy of the Commons." *Science* 162: 1243-8.

Heilbroner, R.L. 1980. *The Worldly Philosophers*. New York: Simon and Schuster.

Herman, E., and N. Chomsky. 1988. *Manufacturing Consent: The Political Economy of Mass Media*. New York: Random House.

Howe Sound Round Table. 1996. *Howe Sound 20/20: Issues and Initiatives in Growth and Sustainability, A Watershed-Wide Perspective*. Vancouver: Howe Sound Round Table.

Hultman, K. 1979. *The Path of Least Resistance: Preparing Employees for Change*. Austin: Learning Concept Publishers.

Jacobs, J. 1998. Presentation at the Community Development Institute, Town Hall meeting (sponsored by the Social Planning and Research Council), Vancouver, 28 July.

Ley, D. 1983. *A Social Geography of the City*. New York: Harper and Row.

Losito, D. 1999. Interview by author with D. Losito, chair, Special Office of the Environment, City of Vancouver, Vancouver, 30 July.

Michaelis, L. 1996. Greenhouse Gas Abatement in the Transportation Sector. Paper presented at "Towards Sustainable Transportation," International OECD Conference, Vancouver, 26 March.

Moore, J. 1994. *What's Stopping Sustainability? Examining the Barriers to Implementation of Clouds of Change*. Vancouver: School of Community and Regional Planning, University of British Columbia.

Postel, S. 1989. "Halting Land Degradation." In L. Brown, A. Durning, C. Flavin, L. Heise, J. Jacobson, S. Postel, M. Renner, C. Pollock Shea, L. Starke, eds., *State of the World*, 21-40. New York: W.W. Norton and Company.

Putnam, R., R. Leonardi, and R.Y. Nanetti. 1993. *Making Democracy Work: Civic Traditions in Modern Italy*. Princeton: Princeton University Press.

Rees, W.E. 1994. *Sustainability, Growth and Employment: Toward an Ecologically Stable, Economically Secure, and Socially Satisfying Future*. Vancouver: School of Community and Regional Planning, University of British Columbia.

Rees, W.E., and M. Wackernagel. 1992. Perceptual and Structural Barriers to Investing in Natural Capital. Paper presented at the second meeting of the International Society for Ecological Economics, Stockholm, August.

Robbinson, S.P. 1993. *Organizational Behaviour: Concepts, Controversies and Applications*. Englewood Cliffs, NJ: Prentice Hall.

Sabatier, P. 1980. "The Implementation of Public Policy: A Framework Analysis." *Public Studies Journal* 8,4: 538-60.

Samuelson, P.A., and A. Scott. 1980. *Economics: Fifth Canadian Edition*. Toronto: McGraw-Hill Ryerson.

Simon, J. 1981. *The Ultimate Resource*. Princeton: Princeton University Press.

Smith, S.L. 1986. *A Growing Concern: Soil Degradation in Canada*. Ottawa: Science Council of Canada.

Stein, J., ed. 1984. *The Random House College Dictionary*. Rev. ed. New York: Random House.

Task Group on Atmospheric Change. 1992. *CRD Healthy Atmosphere 2000: Final Report*. Victoria: Capital Regional District.

Tindal, C.R., and S.N. Tindal, eds. 1984. *Local Government in Canada*. Toronto: McGraw-Hill Ryerson.

Van Rees, W. 1991. "Neighbourhoods, the State and Collective Action." *Community Development Journal* 26,2: 96-102.

Weiss, C.H. 1972. *Evaluating Action Programs: Readings in Social Action and Education*. Boston: Allyn and Bacon Press.

Yates, D. 1984. "The Ungovernable City." In C.R. Tindal and S.N. Tindal, eds., *Local Government in Canada*, 191. Toronto: McGraw-Hill Ryerson.

5
Integrating Economy, Society, and Environment through Policy Assessment
Peter Boothroyd

The challenge in creating healthy and sustainable communities is twofold: first, the vision of what they would look like and how they would function needs to be clarified; and second, effective processes to move communities toward the vision need to be developed.

While much specific visioning work remains, those who write about healthy and sustainable communities share a common view on the general directions communities should be heading. Communities should become more ecologically responsible by appropriating less of the globe's carrying capacity; simultaneously, they should become more caring so that everyone's health is protected.

The practicable, mutually reinforcing implications of this vision for each policy sector are also commonly understood:

- preserve biologically productive land, maintain biodiversity, and do not overharvest
- use considerably less land for the highly consumptive, injurious, segregating automobile
- encourage a fine grain of domestic, productive, commercial, and recreational land uses to reduce travel and promote neighbourly interaction
- build infrastructure and design buildings to promote walking, cycling, and transit
- reduce, reuse, recycle
- replace ecologically damaging use of fossil fuels and electricity with solar energy
- produce locally to reduce energy-consuming trade where possible, and develop a stable economic base
- ensure distributive justice through legislation on resource access and taxation, and through full employment and service delivery
- develop a life-long education system that not only provides skills training but also education for citizens

- foster mutual aid
- encourage participation in governance to broaden the knowledge base for decisions and to heighten social learning
- safeguard the dignity of individuals and minority cultures.

In every community, there is an abundance of ideas on how to translate these policy implications into specific changes to land use, buildings, infrastructure, legislation, budgets, and service delivery. The problem is that the changes are not being made fast enough and widely enough. Indeed, in most communities, on many fronts, we seem to be moving away from sustainability and health. Fish stocks, old-growth forests, and prairie topsoils continue to be destroyed; fossil fuel consumption is rising and giant hydroelectric projects are still built; trade is increasingly promoted and industrial practices deregulated; unemployment, poverty, and crime rates increase while the safety nets get bigger holes; professional health care and education are privatized and thus less available to the poor; growing cities continue to sprawl onto productive land; car driving is promoted by new freeways and "street improvements" while transit systems stagnate.

Thus, the challenge in moving toward sustainability and health seems to be less of a problem in determining what communities need to do and more of a problem in determining how to get our collective selves to do it. There is abundant literature on what is desirable, and on isolated cases that prove that what is desirable can work. But there is a paucity of literature on the community and societal dynamics that continue to lead us away from sustainability and health, and the implications of these dynamics for action.

Liberals and Marxists offer limited help, as their theories of social order and change are based on ecologically illiterate and technocratically arrogant assumptions. On the other hand, development theorists who adopt sustainability and health as goals often seem to avoid tough social change questions, preferring refinement of dreams to strategic analysis of reasons for the current nightmare.

This chapter is intended to encourage more attention to the processes that lead to community sustainability and health. The focus of the chapter is on the potential of policy assessment as a conceptual tool for evaluating public institutional decisions in terms of their effect on health and sustainability.

Policy Assessment: An Overview

Public-sector policy making draws on advice from two traditions: policy analysis and impact assessment.

Policy analysis is intrinsic to design. It continuously analyzes and evaluates policies as they are planned and implemented in order to determine whether the objectives will be, or have been, met. Impact assessment is additive to design. Through impact assessment, plans are assessed in terms of their unintended consequences. Impact assessment asks, Regardless of whether the motivating objectives are met, what else occurs?

Policy assessment is best defined as an emerging synthesis of policy analysis and impact assessment. It is a process concerned with assessing *all* intended and unintended outcomes of policies being planned, proposed, implemented, or reviewed.

Policy Analysis
This section discusses the evolution of policy analysis as a progressive articulation and broadening of the social goals that frame it.

Particularistic Goals: Generic Tools
In its unsystematic form, policy analysis is as old as the state. Unsystematic policy analysis was limited to those in power, adding some rationality to their intuition in analyzing the political, physical, and financial feasibility of schemes, and in evaluating the effectiveness of schemes in terms of the powerholder's particular goals. State, societal, and personal goals were seen as synonymous.

Although unsystematic policy analysis still seems to dominate policy planning and decision making, especially at the highest levels and on the most important matters, modern governments have also systematized policy analysis by civil servants. Some systematic policy analysis tools are generic; that is, they are applicable to any goals, including particularistic goals, of any government. Others are specific to one or more universalistic goals; that is, they are applicable to goals assumed to transcend the interests of the government of the day.

Generic systematic approaches serving particularistic ends include those inappropriately adopted by government from business, such as the "management by objectives" theory from the 1950s, which attempted to make performance targets and outputs the basis for personnel evaluation. Management by objectives was based on the assumption that there can be a clear strategic hierarchy of objectives. Corporations do have a common, all-important particularistic goal, the bottom line of profit, to lead the hierarchy; governments, on the other hand, wrestle with a fluid mix of often-conflicting universal and particular goals.

Generic systematic policy analysis that is more indigenous to the public sector included program planning and budgeting systems, which emerged in the 1960s, and evaluation research, which became a specialty practice in the 1970s. Both were designed to help governments define and meet their current objectives. Under program planning and budgeting systems, plans and budgets were to be formulated in terms of program objectives instead of input line items. Evaluation research in its most basic form involved evaluating program outcomes solely in terms of immediate quantifiable targets (ignoring ultimate social goals and unplanned outcomes) in an attempt to ensure value for government money.

Generic systematic policy analysis tools for particularistic ends mark a pragmatic advance over the romantic adventurism and moral absolutism supported by unsystematic policy analysis. But they are amenable only to in-house technocratic practice. What is worse, those tools rested on a simplistic conception of the relationship between ends and means. Decisions were assumed to have a small number of directly traceable effects, and effects assumed to be attributable to specific decisions. Ignored was the complexity of dynamic social and natural systems that are affected by a multitude of decisions.

To serve the information needs of a turbulent democratic society seeking to manage itself, policy analysis has had to deal not only with the feasibility and effectiveness of schemes designed to meet the objectives of the powerful but also with the relations of these schemes to the broadly held goals of society. To determine these relations requires articulation of social goals and formulation of success measures. Going beyond generic tools serving particularistic ends, policy analysis has become a social-learning process through which a broadening range of universalistic goals has been recognized as necessary for government to serve. The following sections describe this process.

Efficiency Goals: Utilitarianism, and Welfare Economics Tools
Policy analysis took its first universal step with the beginnings of liberalism and the goals it articulated. The test of a good policy became its potential for contributing to the real wealth of whole nations (as Adam Smith clearly put it), not just its potential to serve the interests of the powerful. Since liberalism argued that laissez-faire policies are in the best interest of all society, basic liberal policy analysis consisted simply of subjecting policies to the laissez-faire test.

The liberal ethical philosophy that established the basis for a systematic and comprehensive policy analysis was the utilitarianism of Jeremy Bentham. Bentham's starting assumption was that individuals' happiness, and the utilities of actions for creating happiness, can be not only determined but also added and compared, because people are morally equal. Thus, policy should, as it is commonly put, create the greatest good for the greatest numbers.

Utilitarianism provides the philosophical basis for liberal economics which, in its explicitly normative guise, is known as "welfare economics." Welfare economics is concerned with the mathematics and logic of determining the relative merits of various policies, beginning with the assumption that merit can be equated to efficiency (productivity) of economic systems. Efficiency, in turn, is reduced to being a dollar-denominated ratio of all individuals' benefits to all individuals' costs. To the surprise of non-economists, the mainstream of welfare economics does not deal with equity issues.

Cost-Benefit Analysis   By the late 1930s, the paradigm shift to Keynesianism justified state intervention in the economy to tame business cycles and ensure steady growth. It also allowed technological and bureaucratic expansion and the full flowering of political liberalism, which recognized the equal rights of all to vote and pay taxes. This instigated water-resource management agencies in the United States to begin developing cost-benefit analysis as a welfare economics tool for evaluating dam and reservoir options. By the mid-1960s, the main conceptual issues in cost-benefit analysis had been defined (Prest and Turvey 1965). Attempts were then made to subject it to a wide range of investment policies and programs, such as transportation, mining, and defence. Cost-benefit analysis became an increasingly esoteric, quantitative policy analysis tool concerned with issues such as social discount rates, shadow prices, and risk.

Cost-benefit analysis offers a broader and harder-headed approach to policy analysis than do generic tools serving particularistic ends. Net aggregate economic benefits to the *whole* of society are now not ignored, taken for granted, or guessed at, but, rather, are systematically calculated and, presumably, considered.

Cost-benefit analysis is viewed by many as both superbly rational because of its quantification based on the common metric of money, and truly democratic because it considers equally all monetized costs and benefits, no matter to whom they accrue. No longer is the worth of a policy judged by its value to the powerful regardless of its cost to the small producer, the consumer, the taxpayer, or the indigenous person. The financial welfare of the poor is weighted equally with that of the rich; a dollar is counted as a dollar regardless of whether it is a rich person's or a poor person's.

Cost-benefit analysis' nominal equality is also its weakness. Social distributions of costs and benefits are not considered. An initiative is judged sound if it maximizes net benefits, even if all the benefits go to one group and the costs to another. Cost-benefit analysis does not consider whether some citizens have a superior claim on benefits (or reduced costs) owing to prior residency (e.g., Aboriginal peoples), differing cultural values,[1] relative need,[2] or for that matter, social status.[3] Nor does it consider costs or benefits to noncitizens, that is to say, jurisdictional externalities.

The only distributions cost-benefit analysis considers are those over time. Future costs and benefits are discounted to take into account human preference for present benefits over promises.

Macroeconomic Policy Analysis   The paradigm shift to Keynesianism and the devising of national accounts in the 1930s provided the rationale and tools for analysis and evaluation of fiscal and monetary policies. With the simple laissez-faire yardstick no longer sufficing as a policy analysis tool, new, apparently precise (at least quantitative) indicators, such as gross national product, were invented. These indicators were to measure utilitarian progress and, therefore, potentially, the efficiency of policies. As is widely known but ignored, these indicators have the same limitations as cost-benefit analysis.

Pareto-Optimality   Welfare economics has addressed distribution, or rather, tried to avoid it, by adopting and adapting Vilfredo Pareto's principle for determining optimality of a social decision. The principle holds that the best policy is that which creates the most efficiency without reducing anyone's economic welfare in the process. It reflects the optimism and the myopia underlying our unsustainable state. It implies economic growth need never be zero-sum, that progress for all is possible without redistribution.

The Pareto principle is difficult to apply as a policy analysis tool. Methodologically, it is impossible to determine the effects of a decision on every individual. Substantively, it is difficult to design policies that create no losers – a difficulty economists tend to deal with by interpreting the principle as allowing policies that create enough overall gains that winners could potentially compensate losers.

Equity Goals: Social Policy Tools
The post-Second World War welfare states, formed to care for each citizen, not just the aggregate citizenry, required a policy analysis focus on equity to complement, though not necessarily to balance, welfare economics' single-minded focus on growth. They required systematic policy analysis that could address distribution questions related to a growing range of social programs. Such policy analysis was entrusted to "social" policy analysts.

Such analysts have had some success in broadening policy analysis beyond the utilitarian fixation on aggregate economic welfare. For example, domestic poverty lines were drawn in the 1960s, and in the 1970s, a basic-needs approach to international development was instigated by criticisms of aid programs simplistically dedicated to fostering aggregate growth.

But social policy analysis has also tended to implicitly accept current distributions. The solution to the conundrum of how to alleviate poverty without redistribution is seen to lie in the magic of growth-with-trickle-down. Social policy analysis has devoted little attention to problems caused by affluence, or to the reasons for the highly skewed distribution of wealth. Finally, social policy analysis has focused only on "social" programs, such as welfare-state programs whose goals are to directly increase people's welfare, as opposed to programs that indirectly affect equity, for example, those related to infrastructure, resource management, economic development, trade, or defence.

Quality-of-Life Goals: Social Indicators and Urban Planning Tools
Through this century, policy analysts have increasingly recognized that better efficiency and even distribution do not necessarily translate into improved quality of life. This recognition has led to attempts to define and measure quality of life, and to evaluate policies in terms of this elusive goal.

Quality-of-life analysis can be said to have begun with governments' first concerns about public health, especially the needs created by city-building to manage waste and contain communicable diseases. Policy analysis related to health has continued to absorb significant energies. From the 1970s into the 1990s, policy analysis has become increasingly sophisticated in considering health as more than absence of disease, and the determinants of health as more than physical vectors. Policy analysis oriented to holistic health and quality of life (as promoted by the healthy communities movement) now encompasses such formerly discrete categories as quality of working life.

Social Indicators   In the 1960s, efforts began to develop meaningful "social indicators." At its most ambitious, this effort sought to create a comprehensive index of quality of life comparable in its influence to GNP and other money-based production and efficiency indices. This futile attempt bogged down in the problems of finding a consensus on values, societal goals, and linkages between observable traits and happiness. There were also methodological problems involved in weighting index components and defining a common metric to replace welfare economics calculations based on money exchange. In effect, the effort was a utilitarian atavism.

Efforts to develop indices of quality of life are now less ambitious. These efforts can produce useful heuristic tools that broaden the social goals of concern to policy analysis beyond production/efficiency and distribution/equity. They will be useful so long as they are seen as stimulating thought and inquiry rather than as empirically based valuations.

Urban Planning   Politicians and planners at local levels have been experimenting in recent decades with techniques to enhance policy analysis as both a systematic and participatory practice.

Among the better known of the techniques developed by and for local-level planners are Hill's (1968) goals-achievement matrix, which compares options in terms of how well they meet the full range of planning (usually quality of life) goals; the planning balance sheet of Lichfield et al. (1975), which compares options in terms of how interests (usually defined in terms of quality of life) are differentially impacted; and cross-impact analysis, which compares policies and policy goals in terms of how well they reinforce each other.

Senior governments are beginning to explore the potential of such urban-planning techniques to enhance the comprehensiveness, clarity, and collaborative capacity of their own policy analysis and impact assessment. The techniques can be used either technocratically or democratically. They can be used either pseudoscientifically to identify and support putative best solutions, or heuristically to provide insight into the nature of social and ecological systems and policy choices.

Limitation   While quality-of-life policy analysis concepts and techniques have significantly and systematically broadened the range of goals to be considered in government planning, they have not been applied to fundamental policies that ultimately determine quality of life, those related to the quality, quantity, and distribution of consumption. Hence the evolution in the 1980s of policy analysis oriented to sustainable development.

Sustainability Goals: Scientific and Heuristic Tools
The ecological sustainability focus for policy analysis can be traced back to the resource conservation measures taken about a century ago. Besides the famous designation of vast national parks, these measures provided for soil conservation, regulation of fisheries, and protection of wildlife, forests, and hydrological regimes.

Public concern in the 1950s about local pollution caused by inadequate waste management, especially urban smog and polluted-to-death rivers, followed by acute awareness in the 1960s of the toxic effects of radiation and modern chemicals such as pesticides (Carson 1962), led to a broadly based environmentalism. Though the movement tended to parochialize issues, it also forced policy analysis to pay more attention to ecological goals.

In the 1970s, local habitat and pollution concerns were augmented with concerns that mineral deposits, particularly petroleum, would soon be exhausted.[4] Awareness in the 1980s of threats to whole biological regions/ river basins (because of hydroelectric projects), forests, and fishing banks (because of overharvesting), and, indeed, to global, particularly atmospheric, systems (because of ozone-layer holes and global warming), has led to a more comprehensive view of sustainable development. It forced governments to make sustainable development (WCED 1987) the explicit object of proactive policies oriented to ecosystem rehabilitation, industrial and urban efficiency, and individual reducing, reusing, and recycling behaviour.

Traditional Tools   From the beginning of sustainable development policy analysis, its basic research tools have essentially been those of the natural sciences: for example, geological, chemical, and habitat analysis, resource mapping, and monitoring of species. Research findings have become increasingly accessible to policy analysis through state-of-the-environment reports. These offer information to spur sustainable development policy analysis, but they do not clearly delineate the causal relationships between policy and ecological change: like all indicator work, they tell us much more about effects than causes.

More actively, policy analysis methods have included computing maximum mineral production methods and rates, sustained yields for renewable resources, and sources of waste and pollution. These have resulted in some successes. For example, mineral high-grading has been curtailed, and in rich countries, at least, some dangerous chemicals, such as DDT, CFCs, and PCBs, are being eliminated.

More problematic has been the application of sustained-yield analysis to policy making for forests and fisheries, whose systems are governed by uncertain natural cycles, diseases, climate, species relationships, and actual, as opposed to approved, harvesting practices and rates.

Adaptive Management   The difficulty in making policies that sustain yields has led to calls for "adaptive management" (Holling 1978) of resource systems. Adaptive management attempts to deal with uncertainty. It does so less by scientifically reducing uncertainty prior to decisions (the traditional policy analysis approach) and more by retaining flexibility to respond quickly and appropriately to unexpected outcomes as they are observed. This dynamic approach to policy analysis is problematic when policies have potentially high-cost irreversible outcomes.

The Challenge
Knowledge generated by sustainable development policy analysis has not necessarily influenced policy making. When the costs of implementing a sustainable development policy have seemed low in terms of other goals, especially efficiency, the policy has had a good chance of being adopted. Easing in consumer recycling of paper and bottles is a good example of such a low-cost policy. Where the costs of a policy are perceived to be high, immediate, and broadly based, and the sustainability benefits diffuse or deferred, the policy has little chance of being adopted, especially in a liberal democracy. For example, unrealistic but popular perceptions of personal benefit to cost ratios have, until the unmistakable disasters of the last few years, blocked broad sustainable forest-, fisheries-, and soil-management policies. Such perceptions still inhibit sustainable transportation policies. Automobile reduction faces a continuous uphill battle, and reduction of air travel is not on any policy agenda.

The sustainable development challenge is now less, How to govern corporate production methods with good policies? and more, How to limit aggregate consumption and production which ultimately exhaust resource pools and pollution sinks? The intractability of the problem lies in what biologist Garrett Hardin (1968) calls "the tragedy of the commons" (more accurately called "the tragedy of open access"). By this, Hardin means the phenomenon that occurs when, in the absence of moral or legal restraint, individuals reinforce each other's competitiveness in maximizing immediate personal gains from a common resource (e.g., a community pasture or a fishery), and thereby, over time, exhaust that resource and their own welfare.[5]

New Tools
Recent sustainable development policy analysis approaches that attempt to address the aggregate consumption/production problem are concerned less with technical rigour than with heuristic value, for example, value for helping publics, planners, and decision makers understand systemic outcomes of policies affecting consumption and individual-collective relationships.

These approaches include introducing biodiversity as a crucial criterion of ecosystem health, revising national accounts, such as GDP, to incorporate net changes to natural capital stocks and nonmaterial, nonmonetary production flows (e.g., the work of homecare givers), and identifying impacts on global carrying capacity of local activities. For example, Rees (1992) and Wackernagel et al. (1993) provide tools for estimating the ecological footprint, or appropriated carrying capacity, induced by policy. These tools examine the percentage of global carrying capacity (renewable and nonrenewable resources), appropriated by consumption activities that are influenced by policies ranging from taxation to trade to urban transportation. These tools can also be used to assess equity by comparing gross consumption across regions or classes.

Fundamental questions about the cultural bases for, and antidotes to, excessive material consumption are also being addressed under the rubric of sustainable development. Relationships between fiscal crises and ecological crises, such as the collapse of Canada's East Coast fisheries, are becoming evident. Indeed, the sustainable development imperative is increasingly seen as requiring holistic policy analysis that simultaneously addresses efficiency, equity, quality of life, and sustainability.

Inherent Policy Analysis Tensions[6]
Throughout its evolution, policy analysis has been suspended by a basic methodological tension between positivistic and heuristic conceptions of how policy-relevant knowledge should be acquired and applied. The tension is not over the worth of science or the importance of rigour, but over the nature and role of science and the meaning of rigour.

Positivists seek ever more precision and replicability in their explanations and predictions, and seem prepared to sacrifice, if necessary, holistic understanding. At worst, they seek to know more and more about less and less. Trusting only well-validated information, they attempt to restrict judgments to those that are scientifically supportable. The result is that technical issues come to dominate their policy analysis. Complex issues are avoided or improperly simplified. Method determines question, tool becomes master.

Those favouring heuristic analysis seek policy analysis methods that give insight into the most important systemic processes influenceable by policy. Science is employed but does not limit inquiry. In addition to deductive logic and empirical research, policy analysis is informed by metaphor, reflection, and moral judgment. Arbitrariness is checked not only by the numbers of objective science but also by collaborative intersubjectivity. Good questions are rigorously developed and answered the best they can be.

Very much secondary in policy analysis is procedural tension over how much the timing and responsibility for analysis and evaluation activities (setting questions, answering, and reporting) should be formalized. It is generally assumed that policy analysis is a fluid art internal to government, and that, to the extent the public is involved at all, it should be through well-contained consultation processes.

Impact Assessment
This section traces the evolution of impact assessment in terms of its expansion in three dimensions: substantive breadth, systemic depth, and hierarchical range.

Broadening the Substance of Impacts Assessed
In terms of the goal-related substance of impacts assessed, impact assessment's evolution has roughly paralleled the evolution of policy analysis. The difference between the two at each stage is that policy analysis has involved analyzing and evaluating the effectiveness of political choices directed to the dominant goal at the time, while impact assessment has involved assessing the impacts on that goal of initiatives directed to other goals. Thus, impact assessment in practice, if not always in name, can be seen as evolving through the following stages.

Particularistic Impact Assessment   The most basic and continuously influential form of impact assessment (though not called such), has, from the beginning of the state, been the assessment of decision implications for the powerholders' own interests. It is essentially assessment of impacts on the maintenance of power and wealth distributions. In its current forms, particularistic impact assessment relies on lawyers to assess legal subtleties and precedents, media experts to assess images, and pollsters to assess political "fall-out."

Efficiency Impact Assessment The modern epoch in de facto impact assessment, for example, systematic assessment of impacts relative to assumed universal criteria, was initiated by liberals calling for *all* decisions to be accountable to the utilitarian principle of welfare efficiency, not just those initially designed to be so. What we may call "efficiency impact assessment" questioned subsidies, for example, and even created a name for self-serving inefficient policies: pork barrelling.

Efficiency impact assessment, still unnamed, is also still very influential. With the rise of the welfare state and equity-oriented policies, and the strengthening of special-interest (e.g., neighbourhood) groups fighting to protect quality of life and environmentalism, efficiency impact assessment became a reactionary force. It is now concerned with drawing attention to the impacts on productivity, and putatively gross consumption or decisions related to other goals, for example, the negative impacts of minimum-wage laws, community stabilizing local-hire preferences, or environmental regulations.

Through efficiency impact assessment, weaker interests are kept on the defensive, being required to prove that their policy choices for equity, quality of life, or sustainable development will not weaken productive efficiency of ostensible universal benefit. Efficiency impact assessment's continuous influence derives from its simultaneous pandering to the powerful and its mystifying use of liberal cant, esoteric utilitarian concepts, and quantitative techniques.

Equity Impact Assessment and Socioeconomic Impact Assessment   Impact assessment oriented to equity complements proactive social policy analysis. The bread and butter of socialists, this form of de facto impact assessment became respectable in liberal circles with the recognition by welfare economists in the 1950s that efficiency-oriented decisions can have "externalities," for example, public costs and costs to other individuals, or what most people would now call "impacts." Early equity impact assessment focused on society-wide impacts of efficiency-oriented decisions. The influence of impact assessment with this focus peaked about 1970; its steady decline since is one manifestation of the dying welfare state.

From the 1970s, equity impact assessment has thrived as "socioeconomic" impact assessment. It is the component of project social impact assessment (socioeconomic impact assessment) concerned with the distribution of economic benefits, such as jobs and costs (such as price inflation).

Equity impact assessment is also increasingly concerned with the impacts of policies to enhance quality of life (such as neighbourhood preservation) or sustainable development (such as forest protection).

Quality of Life Impact Assessment, Social Impact Assessment, and Health Impact Assessment   Assessment of impacts on quality of life stemming from land use and infrastructure decisions has been a central feature of urban planning for decades. For example, Patrick Geddes (1949) and others highlighted the health, social, and aesthetic impacts of emerging industrial cities and "conurbations" which, if planned at all, considered only production efficiency. Jane Jacobs (1961) showed that planning's modernistic conception of quality of life as cleanliness, predictability, and good services had its own negative impacts on urban vitality and civility. More recently, neighbourhood groups have succeeded in dramatically reshaping city plans by assessing the quality-of-life impacts of urban freeways.

With the institutionalization of environmental impact assessment and concern that the burgeoning environmental impact assessment industry was overlooking quality-of-life impacts, social impact assessment was developed and named (Wolf 1974) as a field of practice (Burdge and Vanclay 1995).

Although social impact assessment has broad application, for the most part, it has been practised as an adjunct to biophysical, project environmental impact assessment. In this role, social impact assessment has extended quality-of-life concerns, from urban design to resource management. At the same time, impact assessment's focus on individual sensory life, for example, safety, health, and aesthetics, has been broadened to illuminate changes in cultural life such as experiences that provide identity, meaning, joy, and security, including sharing knowledge, mutual caring, and organizing. At its best, social impact assessment has shown the links among well-being, economy, and environment.

As social impact assessment deals with people who, unlike the beings or things that concern biophysical impact assessment, are capable of speaking for themselves, it faces distinct methodological and procedural challenges. The studied have become part of the studying processes, sometimes directing them. They influence the procedures that determine when impact assessment is done, with what scope, on what initiatives, and with what products. Furthermore, social impact assessment must address fundamental conflict in lifestyle values. When environmental impact assessment is apart from it, social impact assessment primarily addresses trade-offs between sustainability and efficiency values, both of which almost everyone claims to hold. Social impact assessment has become a more transparently political process. Most recently, interest has been paid to the development of health impact assessment concepts and methods (Frankish et al. 1996).

Sustainability Impact Assessment and Environmental Impact Assessment   Recognition of environmental hazards and ecological stresses in the 1960s provided the impetus and rationale for institutionalizing environmental impact assessment. The United States National Environmental Policy Act (NEPA) of 1969 marked a resurgence of American interest in conservation and a growing awareness that efficiency-oriented, cost-benefit analysis does not address all social goals and needs. It also meant a major conceptual breakthrough in explicating the relationship of ends and means, and a major procedural innovation in planning and decision making.

The conceptual breakthrough was the realization that planning to serve one goal at a time can lead to net negative consequences when *all goals are taken into account*. It became apparent that the abstract decision-tree, through which linear hierarchies are deduced (as in a bureaucratic organizational chart, in which a subordinate reports only to one person), does not reflect the reality of complex governed or governing systems. It also does not reflect the relationship between the two. While previously it had been realized that working to one goal can impinge on others, this realization had not been conceptually systematized in planning and decision making. Before the National Environmental Policy Act, predecision impact assessment was intuitive and casual.

The National Environmental Policy Act's procedural innovation was its action-forcing mechanism. This was the requirement that, prior to a federal government decision on a potentially environmentally significant proposal before it, an environmental impact statement be prepared and publicly vetted. Formalized procedures, for example, on preparation responsibility, were established to implement the mechanism.

The tough-looking, and sometimes tough-acting, environmental impact statement mechanism was accepted by a society still fixated on economic growth. This was because the mechanism seemed concerned with production methods, particularly site-specific development projects and their local impacts, rather than with impacts on natural capital of aggregate consumption and production. Environmental impact assessment was saleable as a mitigation or design tool that need not threaten increasing throughput (harvesting, mining, burning) of natural resources. The global ecological impacts of policies were scarcely considered, and if they were, then judged or claimed too difficult to assess.

Environmental impact statements and related court cases somewhat democratized impact assessment. It was no longer left to politicians, bureaucrats, and, occasionally, lawyers fighting over property rights to assess impacts and determine their weight in decision making. Now all manner of interest groups, including groups caring for the public interest, such as "environmentalists," could become involved. Project planners were forced to pay attention to the fact that an effective project in terms of certain objectives may be dysfunctional from the perspective of others.

In each jurisdiction, the way environmental impact assessment has been institutionalized is the outcome of pressure and deliberation by many actors from government, industry, the courts, and citizens organizations who shape the process to fit their various needs and interests. The result, in many jurisdictions, is a highly systematic, step-by-step procedure, intricate in its internal checks and balances. It provides for much technical and consultative activity but has little direct impact on well-developed project designs.

At its best, the immediate output is mitigation, and in the longer term, social learning and preventative work at future design stages. At worst, environmental impact assessment procedures obfuscate the fundamental sustainable development issues. This can lull people into a complacent belief that costly technical environmental impact assessment activity is guarding against deleterious development.

Deepening the Systemic Awareness of Impact Chains
The substantive broadening of impact assessment has not just meant impact assessors have to consider longer checklists.[7] Increasing substantive breadth through and within the stages identified above has also led to a deeper awareness of the relationships within and among the various natural, social, and constructed systems and subsystems that mediate decisions and their impacts. The result of this awareness is that the horizon of impacts assessed has been progressively extended from the systemically immediate to the systemically distant. Or, in the usual impact assessment language, from the direct, isolated, local, and certain, to the indirect, cumulative/synergistic, global, and uncertain.

Efficiency impact assessment, for example, deepened systemic thought by adding consideration of indirect costs and benefits. Equity impact assessment has begun questioning whether, in real socioeconomic systems, the poor actually do gain from development following the simplistically efficient growth-with-trickle-down paradigm.

Further broadening of impact assessment, to a consideration of ecological relationships and quality of social life in the 1970s, roughly coincided with an intense period in the development of systems theory and its application to social issues.

General system theory and cybernetics, in their heuristic forms (as opposed to mathematical operations research), have provided impact assessment with potentially powerful conceptual tools for analyzing complex and uncertain impact chains – though the potential seems hardly recognized. The concepts include positive and negative feedback, homeostasis and entropy, open and closed boundaries, hierarchy and recursion, and control and variety (Beer 1975; Heylighen et al. 1990; Wolf 1990; Boothroyd 1994).

Systems theory not only enables more accurate impact assessment by lengthening, and therefore broadening, the identification of chains of impacts, it also enables impact assessment to consider cultural and ecological systems holistically. It allows consideration of their vitality, stability, and fragility, and therefore determines which decisions make them healthy, sick, or dead. For example, some impact assessments have shown the impact of northern Canadian dams, pipelines, and other resource megaprojects on the viability of Aboriginal peoples' "way of life," a holistic concept connoting the organic nature of ecology, economy, culture, and their linkages.

Increasing systems-sensitivity of impact assessment will affect not only what is studied and how, but by whom. The more we realize that impact assessment faces complexity and uncertainty, the more we realize that different kinds of knowledge must be brought to bear if we are to understand and respond appropriately to the full rippling of impacts. This is the systems theory rationale for impact assessment to be broadly participatory, or, what amounts to the same thing, politicized.

Stretching the Application of Social Impact Assessment and Environmental Impact Assessment

While environmental impact assessment is theoretically, and legally in many jurisdictions, as applicable to policies as physical projects, it has traditionally been applied primarily to the latter for several reasons:

- Projects are tangible, dramatic, highly organized, discrete geographically and temporally, and for all these reasons amenable to systematic impact assessment.
- Localized negative impacts of individual projects often appear mitigable or insignificant in comparison to project benefits, thus environmental impact assessment can be applied rigorously on a case-by-case basis without threatening the current unsustainable development path and those most benefiting from it.
- Policy making is secretive, or at least guarded. Powerholders feel threatened by increasing explicit systematization and the public accountability it produces or seems to imply. Rejection of a well-defined policy proposal because of an environmental impact statement would be regarded as causing loss of public confidence in the proponent – the higher the proponent, the more serious this loss.
- The most important policies are unspoken, certainly not reviewed, and therefore, not assessable.

In the last five years or so, however, there has been increasing interest in stretching the application of social impact assessment and environmental impact assessment to higher, and therefore more general, decisions relating to programs and policy.

The Evolution of Impact Assessment in Summary

Impact assessment has become increasingly comprehensive in three respects: kinds of impacts assessed, systemic depth to which assessment is taken, and level of decision to which impact assessment is applied. Taken together, these changes have meant that impact assessment, though still reactive in nature, is increasingly overlapping proactive, ever-broadening, policy analysis.

Inherent Impact Assessment Tensions

The relative importance of the methodological and procedural tensions in impact assessment is the reverse of that in policy analysis.

The fundamental tension in impact assessment, as it has culminated in environmental impact assessment, is procedural. The tension is created by the polar answers to this question: To what degree of detail and with how much authority should impact assessment procedures be explicitly prescribed so that impact assessment fulfils its current mandate as a public, accountable, and transparent scrutinizing process interposed between design and decision making to ensure proponents and decision makers consider externalities as they plan to meet specific sectoral objectives? In short, the question is, How formal should impact assessment be?

Highly formal impact assessment has three characteristics. Its procedures are explicit in their prescriptions, detailed in the accountability requirements imposed on those responsible for conducting the procedures, and fully enforceable. Informal impact assessment is vague and flexible, requiring little or no accountability, and offering no legal or specified administrative basis for enforcement. Formality-informality is a continuum rather than a dichotomy.

Legislation formalizes impact assessment because it enhances accountability and enforceability. Procedures that prescribe consulting and informing the public about planning designs, assessments, research, or case-specific processes are more formal than procedures that govern only internal government processes. Public involvement expands accountability and the likelihood of enforcement. For this reason, procedures that maximally empower the hitherto least powerful publics can be regarded as the most formal. Of course, public involvement in impact assessment can occur without procedures requiring it, that is, it can be informal.

Methodological tension is secondary in impact assessment. In impact assessment generally and environmental impact assessment especially, positivism reigns.

The need to rely on scientific laws and empirical research to give as precise quantitative predictions as possible is assumed in impact assessment. Accuracy of prediction or explanation is sought, rather than full systemic insight. Since accuracy is most attainable when only spatially and temporally immediate systems are considered, impact assessment avoids the big questions. For example, it does not deal with global warming or development paradigms, and finds it difficult to deal with cumulative effects.

Environmental impact assessment has favoured technical science over conceptual wisdom, not only because of a predisposition to positivism but also as an almost inevitable outcome of common environmental impact assessment procedures:

- The environmental impact statement, which has to be defended to the public, encourages assessors to limit speculation and to stick to "hard," verifiable data.
- Proponents, who are responsible for environmental impact statements, find it in their interest to focus on details over big questions.
- It is conceptually difficult for the environmental impact statement, because it is an add-on to the design process, to return to first principles. Technical mitigation, rather than systemic assessment, is the de facto focus of the environmental impact statement.
- Consideration of objectives is not really seen as within the purview of impact assessment (whether or not there is an injunction to consider project "need").
- A project orientation virtually precludes consideration of fundamental, as opposed to technical, issues.

The limitations to fundamental relevance posed by the technicality of impact assessment are rarely overcome by public involvement. Public groups find it difficult to raise fundamental issues in impact assessment because of the way issues are framed by proponents or regulators (who tend to see the world the same way). Indeed, technicality inhibits public involvement: the more technical the studies and impact statements, the greater their credibility, but the less opportunity for average people to participate and learn.

But to the extent public involvement is mandated and occurs, it does make asking timely, big questions possible (even if officials declare their substance outside the mandated process). Thus, formal procedures that require public involvement help promote fundamental debate and heuristic thought, despite impact assessment's proclivity for technical analysis.

Policy Impact Assessment

In this chapter, the term "policy impact assessment" is reserved for assessment of unintended outcomes only. (Policy assessment is discussed later as the integration of policy impact assessment with policy analysis.) Under policy impact assessment, a policy proposal is first formulated to meet certain social goals, then assessed in terms of its impacts on others. To make sure assessments are as efficient, objective, and useful to decision makers as possible, procedures are established to guide or regulate the assessment process.

The Need

Awareness of the need for systematic assessment of policy's impacts results from experience in project environmental impact assessment and social impact assessment, along with a deepening understanding of the sustainable development imperative. Impact assessment's potential to enhance decision making has been shown, but so has its inability at the project level to deal with the big issues.

While the need for systematic assessment of policy impacts is increasingly recognized, such assessment is conceptually and practically inchoate.

Conceptually, there is no agreement on what assessment of policy impacts should or could be in a systematized form – whether the application should be to policies of environmental impact assessment-like procedures or something entirely different; whether the process should be public or closed, centrally controlled or independent, environmentally focused or holistic, applied only to legislation or broadly to all executive decisions including budgets, programs, and regulations. Coherent and consistently named bodies of concepts are only beginning to be developed and accepted.

Institutionally, although the practice of assessing policy impacts is growing, it is diffuse, being undertaken in any given jurisdiction by a number of actors following a variety of fluid metapolicy procedures unique to that jurisdiction. This is unlike project-focused environmental impact assessment, which is often legislated under a specific act following one of a limited set of models (e.g., NEPA) and administered or overseen by a specific bureaucracy. There are not yet clear, essential bodies of practice to be commonly named.

Politically, because powerholding is threatened by explicit systematization, there is not a strong demand from the top for, and there is often resistance to, creating policy-making approaches with well-articulated identities.

Despite the difficulties facing the conceptualization and practical application of policy impact assessment, support for its development comes from both the impact assessment and policy analysis traditions. While policy impact assessment as an extension of project impact assessment (especially environmental impact assessment) is being proposed by impact assessment theorists, policy impact assessment is in fact already being practised as an adjunct to policy analysis. The differences between what the impact assessment tradition proposes and what policy analysis is producing reflect their different approaches to scientific method and planning procedure.

Policy Impact Assessment as an Adjunct to Policy Analysis: Policy-Vetting

De facto policy impact assessment oriented to equity, quality of life, and sustainability was introduced about two decades ago by governments elaborating on their internal proposal-writing procedures. This was in response to increasing awareness of the complex and significant consequences (e.g., for gender equity) of what, not so long ago, were regarded as fairly straightforward decisions in any given sector (e.g., transportation). Policy analysts, in both design and assessment roles, began to be required to vet high-level, in-house proposals for projects, programs, or policies – the distinctions among these often unclear in practice – against a growing checklist of policy desiderata reflecting usually overlooked social goals. The Canadian government, for example, has required departments presenting proposals to cabinet to note the likely impacts of a proposal on the environment, federal-provincial relations, Aboriginal people, and other areas of concern. In this form, which may be called policy-vetting, policy impact assessment was initiated as an adjunct to policy analysis initially oriented to particularisms or economic efficiency.

Policy impact assessment, conceived as an extension of policy analysis, automatically tends, like policy analysis itself, to be informal. Little attention is given to devising procedural checks and balances to ensure public accountability. It is assumed the public would preempt legitimate power, would not map well with the complex reality of policy making where sources of initiative and assessment are diffuse and continuous, and would compromise the presumed need for confidentiality.

The only requirement is for policy analysts to address, explicitly and tersely, the full checklist of specified impact categories. How they come to their conclusions is left to them. In contrast to environmental impact assessment, there are no policy-vetting rules governing whom to consult, when, in what form, and with what product.

Because of its low degree of procedural formality, policy-vetting, in practice, has been slow in living up to the spirit of its requirements. At its worst, the practice has been a cynical process in which departments ritualistically and perfunctorily predict no negative impacts. Even then, however, policy-vetting does represent a step in the in-house formalization of policy analysis. As it has matured, moreover, policy-vetting has encouraged departments and agencies to broadly and heuristically consider impacts when formulating policy proposals. Increasingly, policies are vetted against a checklist of thought-provoking questions, and conceptual assistance is provided to help with the answers.

Limitations of Policy-Vetting
Despite the policy impact assessment progress made in and through relatively informal policy-vetting, it still seems that this approach gives insufficient attention to methodological rigour in either the positivistic or heuristic sense. As a result, it is rarely as informative for assessors or readers as it could be. When making and stating required impact predictions, proponents rarely reference systems theory, state-of-the art substantive concepts, or empirical data. There is nowhere near the effort that is put into project cost-benefit analysis or environmental impact assessment/social impact assessment. Also, because it is in-house, it offers no public accountability or social learning.

Policy Impact Assessment as Environmental Impact Assessment Extension: Strategic Environmental Assessment
Since the 1980s, impact assessors have been frustrated with the inefficiency and limited effectiveness of project-focused environmental impact assessment. They have been calling for formal, publicly accountable environmental impact assessment to be extended "upstream" to the policy level, where generic impacts can be considered. Advocates of policy impact assessment formalization see this as an advance over the in-house, often confidential, ritualistic checklist approach of policy-vetting.

The arguments in favour of using environmental impact assessment or similar procedures at the policy level include those for the project level (i.e., procedures force good environmental information into the decision-making process) plus the added points that using procedures upstream will make environmental impact assessment more effective (by forcing even better information for more comprehensive, long-term predictions) and efficient (by assessing general decisions before specifics).

Strategic environmental assessment is the increasingly common term for environmental impact assessment at the program, plan, and policy levels (Wood and Dejeddour 1992; Buckley 1998). A positivistic bias to strategic environmental assessment seems implicit, or at least not rejected, by its promoters, who look to the environmental impact assessment tradition with its emphasis on science-informed impact statements.

The central policy impact assessment issues that the strategic environmental assessment perspective raises relate to the level and nature of procedural formalization. How detailed, strict, and enforceable should procedures be? Calls for strategic environmental assessment are calls for much more formality of policy impact assessment than policy-vetting offers, though few suggest strategic environmental assessment should have as much formality as environmental impact assessment of projects.[8]

Proponents of strategic environmental assessment are not opposed to policy-vetting but, rather, champion allocations of more energy and power to that process. They point to the history and promise of better decisions resulting from intensive public vetting, or the threat of same, pursuant to NEPA, its clones, or look-alikes. They are concerned that the vetting vets, that policy impact assessment as a policing function be incorruptible, that checks and balances ensure that assessment of a proposed policy does not become captured by its proponent.

The putative upside of strategic environmental assessment is the objectivity it induces. The downside is that it may settle for politically effete technical analysis.

Policy Assessment

The Need

Despite the policy-planning advances made through policy analysis, impact assessment, and the two forms of policy impact assessment they have spawned, there are still three major shortcomings in policy making as a rational, democratic process. There is still a need for the following:

- *Comprehensive assessment of outcomes.* That is, simultaneous assessment in terms of objectives, higher goals, and externalities.
- *Assessment of implicit fundamental policies as well as explicit policies.* This includes existing, as well as proposed, policies.
- *Assessment that is both integrated with policy design and scrutinizes designs.*

Together, the needed types of assessment constitute policy assessment which can be defined as the process by which fundamental policy options are continuously identified and assessed in terms of all highest-level societal goals.[9] Policy assessment as comprehensive fundamental continuous assessment thus fuses and goes beyond policy analysis and impact assessment (Table 5.1).

Through policy assessment, equity, health, and sustainable development, which are highlighted but still marginalized in policy *impact* assessment, become defining goals equal to economic efficiency and growth. The breadth of policy assessment requires not just breaking new conceptual ground but also developing appropriate procedures and methods. Just what procedures and methods are appropriate is a function of how formalized and positivistic policy assessment is conceived to be.

Evolving Forms of Policy Assessment

Policy assessment, as a synthesis of policy analysis and impact assessment, could be shaped by four possible polar resolutions of the methodological

Table 5.1

Policy assessment compared with policy analysis and impact assessment

	Policy analysis	Impact assessment	Policy assessment
Outcomes assessed	Intended	Externalities	All
Policies assessed	Proposed	Proposed	All
Relationship to design	Intrinsic	Scrutinizing	Both

tension in policy analysis and the procedural tension in impact assessment. On one end of the procedural tension would be those, often fully within government, who would favour informal policy assessment because it is more in tune with the informal technocratic policy analysis tradition. Informal proponents would call it "pragmatic" and would emphasize flexibility over rules, trust over accountability, and education over sanction. At the extreme, informality would mean no rules for either in-house procedures or public involvement: the proponent agency retains total control of the process and content of assessment. At the other end would be many impact assessment theorists who, focusing on the assessment, would see it like project environmental impact assessment, as best governed by formal procedures that include provision for public involvement.

On one end of the methodological tension would be those who see policy assessment as ideally technical and positivistic in the cost-benefit analysis and environmental impact assessment traditions; on the other would be those who look to more heuristic approaches that trade off precision for insight.

Combined, the procedural and methodological tensions give rise to four possible forms (Table 5.2). The three forms currently evolving are (1) informal positivistic policy assessment, from cost-benefit analysis; (2) informal heuristic policy assessment, from policy-vetting; and (3) formal positivistic policy assessment, from strategic environmental assessment. (Of course, actual policy assessment in any given jurisdiction may be some combination of these types.)

All three of these forms go beyond their respective practice bases by combining the substantive concerns of both impact assessment and policy analysis – objectives and externalities – to produce comprehensive assessment as part of policy design and as scrutiny of near-finished and existing policies. Informal positivistic policy assessment broadens the focus of cost-benefit analysis to incorporate as criteria what were previously externalities. Informal heuristic policy assessment broadens policy-vetting to address a wider range of externalities and to incorporate these as goals in design. Formal positivistic policy assessment broadens strategic environmental assessment's application to a wider range of policies and goals.

Table 5.2

Forms of policy assessment

	Informal	Formalized
Positivistic	Based on cost-benefit analysis	Based on strategic environmental assessment
Heuristic	Based on policy-vetting	No model yet

The fourth possible form, formal heuristic policy assessment, has no basis in existing practice. This is because formality was introduced to policy planning by environmental impact assessment – policy analysis has no such tradition – and environmental impact assessment is strongly positivistic because of its historical project-orientation, sponsorship, mandate, timing, and response to formality itself. But formal heuristic policy assessment could have the greatest potential to be the continuous, comprehensive, influential, educational, efficient, and democratic, informational support that is required for good decision making in a complex society.

Ideal Policy Assessment: Heuristic and Appropriately Formal

The Need

Considering the forms policy assessment can take, its potential can founder on the shoals of positivism and its dangerous promise of certainty, or the shoals of informality and its dangerous promise of flexibility. It can also be seen that just avoiding these shoals is insufficient. Policy assessment must aim for powerful heuristics, not nonchalance, and for formality that supports meaningful public involvement, not ritualism.

The starting point to the ideal is to break away from the limitations posed by simply extending policy assessment from either policy analysis or impact assessment alone. Starting fresh, policy assessment could synergize strategic environmental assessment's concept of formality (not its specific procedures) with policy-vetting's heuristic potential (not its checklists). This would create policy assessment formalized enough to safeguard against its becoming window-dressing for done deals or dead paradigms, and heuristic enough that the insights it yields are widely understood and useful in making crucial decisions. At the same time, ideal policy assessment, while formalized, would be efficient and fluid enough to meet the political and administrative realities of policy making, and while heuristic, empirical enough to reflect reality rather than cant.

The role of appropriately formal heuristic policy assessment would be to promote comprehensive discussion on fundamental issues in policy realms, ranging from trade to transportation to taxation. It would be integrative: substantively, by addressing the systemic links among goals, policy realms, and decision-levels from implicit policy to day-to-day work planning; methodologically, by combining empiricism with systems theory at once sophisticated and accessible; procedurally, by informationally linking publics and governments throughout the flux of policy making and review.

Formal heuristic policy assessment would be quite different than adaptive management, despite some seeming similarities. Recognizing the fact that uncertainty increases with complexity, adaptive management adds to planning, in complex situations, a capacity for monitoring action outcomes and for responding quickly to surprises. It confronts positivistic science's inability to provide accurate predictions, but it is an inadequate solution. It does not obviate the need to reduce uncertainty before making policy decisions.

Reduction of uncertainty is especially important in situations where bad decisions can have serious irreversible consequences. Putting lifeboats on ships is not a substitute for building safer ships and setting safer courses. When interventions are being considered into fragile, or self-regulating, systems such as ecologies or cultures, the proper response to uncertainty is not to wade in, intending to deal with problems as they arise, which adaptive management purists propose, but to hold back and get better information and understanding.

Thus, building adaptive management capacity into policy assessment is necessary, but far from sufficient. The limits of positivism also need to be addressed by improving predictive methods. The adaptive management capacity needed by policy assessment can be provided through procedures that formally require monitoring and policy audits, and that suggest heuristically powerful concepts for framing questions and interpreting answers.

Participatory Heuristic Methods
A heuristic approach to prediction would focus on the big picture over details, direction of change over quantity of change, and systems processes over systems states. It would favour insight over rigour. It would use soft systems concepts of, for example, feedback, entropy, variety, and recursion, to model cultural-institutional and biophysical systems affected by policy. Comparison of a system assuming the policy being assessed is in place (the with-policy scenario) with the system assuming the policy is not in place (the without-policy scenario) would acknowledge that in both cases the system is dynamic (even the without-policy system will not be the same tomorrow as today). This dynamism is often a function of human agency and choice; making and comparing movies of processes is better than comparing snapshots.

The widespread concern that a systems approach is necessarily authoritarian is understandable but is best dealt with not by abandoning systems thought but by emphasizing the heuristic potential of systems modelling for aiding thought and dialogue among policy analysts, decision makers, and the public. To realize this potential, procedures would need to be designed to ensure citizens participate in building the models rather than simply being (as they are in the positivistic conception) possessors of characteristics to be studied through the model. This would ensure, in short, that citizens are the predictors as well as the predicted. Participation on model-building would include identifying key variables and their relationships, as well as the intervention options whose if-then consequences are to be explored. This goes far beyond environmental impact assessment scoping. Computers could aid analysis of consequences, but they also pose dangers in distorting communication and by appearing to offer more clarity, precision, and certainty than is warranted. Electronic information networks could be used for information exchange and dialogue, again with caution. Felt pens could be the most useful hardware for heuristic policy assessment; analogies and meditations could be the most useful software.

Process and Procedures
A growing number of impact assessment theorists and practitioners are coming to the conclusion that policy assessment procedures should be developed from scratch rather than be adapted from those created for environmental impact assessment (Bailey and Renton 1997). Formal heuristic policy assessment, in contrast to policy assessment based on strategic environmental assessment, would follow these admonishments.

Rather than linear environmental impact assessment-like stages starting with screening by the initiating agency, formal heuristic policy assessment would be a continuous part of ongoing policy development. Discrete exercises would typically start with evaluation of existing policy (or what amounts to the same thing, with identification of problems or policy needs). Unlike strategic environmental assessment, which assumes hierarchical deductive decision making through logical decision-trees from policy to project, formal heuristic policy assessment would recognize the fluidity of decision making. It would also identify the complexity of relations among decisions by encouraging assessment at any time, at any policy level, at any point in the stream of causes and effects, in any policy sphere, by any party.

Formal heuristic policy assessment procedures, collectively indicating what outcomes of what policies should be assessed how, when, with what products for whom, fall into two categories: mechanisms to ensure meaningful public involvement in all aspects of policy assessment, and guidelines on policy assessment methods and products.

Table 5.3

Possible procedural mechanisms for involving publics in heuristic policy assessment

Public needs to be informed of:
- Explicit policies in place and outcomes relative to societal goals
- Consistency of policies with each and major goals
- Implicit policies in place and outcomes relative to major societal goals
- Major emerging or latent societal problems
- Policies being reviewed or generated, issues being worked on
- New policies being considered
- Thinking behind policy decisions taken
- Policy-making process
- Consistency of plans and day-to-day decisions

Agencies could be required to:
- Explicate and assess existing policies
- Conduct policy audits; initiate participatory policy reviews
- Do class audits of project EISs to show cumulative effects ignored; adhere to freedom-of-information laws
- Sponsor and disseminate state-of-society reports comparing trends
- Issue disclosure statements (as for conflict of interest)
- Prepare policy outcome statements
- Trace policy assessment history of decisions with explicit policy
- Publicize internal procedures
- Report decisions/plans in useful format

Publics need to be able to:
- Initiate policy audits
- Conduct policy audits
- Initiate policy design/redesign
- Contribute to policy design (including policy on policymaking)
- Scrutinize policy proposals

Agencies could be required to:
- Respond to petitions
- Adhere to freedom-of-information-laws
- Respond to petitions
- Facilitate public input to framing problems and options; allow public servants to consult with publics; devolve power to locally accessible governments; mediate conflict to get win-win situation
- Enable public assessments before final decisions; fund intervenors in method

Mechanisms to Facilitate Public Involvement

Rather than the environmental impact assessment and strategic environmental assessment procedures, which give publics only the roles of attempting to make sure scientists do their job right and of putting values on their findings, formal heuristic policy assessment would incorporate citizen values and knowledge throughout. Procedural mechanisms would ensure publics receive policy-relevant information in useful forms and have structured opportunities to use it.

Though policy assessment would be continuously open to public input, specific mechanisms would mandate proactive involvement of publics in identifying needs for policy change, and in design, as well as scrutiny, of options. These could vary from public audits of existing policies, to structured participatory processes for policy design, to provisions for public systematic monitoring of day-to-day decision making as a revelation of implicit policy (Table 5.3.) This table can be looked at in light of the more detailed consideration of public engagement explored in Chapter 6.

Existing Procedures

Environmental impact assessment procedures relating to screening, scoping, impact statements, public review, and so on, would be rigorously applied to the design scrutiny component of policy assessment. The content of assessment pursuant to these procedures would be expanded to become more holistic in scope.

Procedures governing impact assessment of projects will also continue to be necessary to monitor the consistency of projects with explicit policies and to reveal the unstated or lingering policies that initiate and encourage projects contradictory to current rhetorical goals.[10]

Annual Public and Participatory Transportation-Policy Audit: An Example

Consider the possibilities for an annual public and participatory transportation-policy audit. Planners and policy analysts describe policy contexts now when providing background recommendations to decision makers. The new procedural possibility would regularize the timing of this work, bring it from the background to the foreground, and enrich it by analyzing compatibility of explicit policy with societal goals, for example, sustainability. Implicit policy, as revealed by day-to-day decisions, would be made accountable to publics by facilitating public scrutiny. Selected information- and insight-rich literature on key transportation issues (e.g., Goodland et al. 1993) would aid analysis and scrutiny. Such audits would replace futile exercises in simplistically surveying people to identify their wish-lists without regard for trade-offs, systems dynamics, or radical options.[11]

Compliance with requirements for such audits could be ensured through legislation offering recourse to the courts, or watchdog agencies, such as the parliamentary auditor proposed for Canada by Bregha et al. (1990), who looked at the New Zealand experience. The introduction of some audit requirements could increase democratic expectations, which in turn could lead to further formalization.

Guidelines on Policy Assessment Substance and Methods

In addition to mandating public access to information and input to design and decision making, procedures for formal heuristic policy assessment could also take the form of guidelines. The guidelines could use methods, such as questions to be addressed and concepts to be employed in answering them,[12] as well as report contents. For example, guidelines could suggest that assessors:

- clarify the nature of policies being assessed, their context, objectives, and trade-offs intrinsic to the policy area
- identify the nature of systems (mechanical, natural, or cultural and human) impacted by the policy being assessed
- analyze systemic processes that would be or are being impacted, using such heuristically rich but easily explained and applied concepts as recursion, requisite variety, negative and positive feedback, entropy, throughput, and robustness
- consider critical sustainable development variables – for example, local and global natural capital, biodiversity, appropriated carrying capacity, social caring capacity, cultural survival, gender relations, personal and community health, aesthetic pleasure, spiritual development – and their relationships
- consider the usual environmental impact assessment list of impact qualities such as duration, intensity, reversibility, and mitigability.

The guidelines could be supplemented with information on a range of predictive or explanatory methods, providing various mixes of heuristic power, accuracy, completeness, and efficiency. The methods could be arrayed along a continuum from back-of-the-envelope to the highly sophisticated. The choices of where to enter the continuum, how often to iterate, and what trade-offs to make among assessment, transparency, efficiency, accuracy, and comprehensiveness should be left to the assessors and their case-by-case appraisals of their policy-making contexts. The appraisals would be rated in terms of urgency, apparent significance of impacts, open-mindedness of superiors, the integrity of assessors, and workload.

Menus of interpersonal and individual problem-solving techniques could be presented, including holistic methods such as scenario-building, black-box methods such as Delphi, and systematizing methods such as goals achievement matrices.

Guidelines could indicate the kinds of people to be considered for involvement, and how they would be involved, in various kinds of policy-assessment exercises. They could suggest the format and substance of reports. Guidelines for doing policy assessment through project impact assessment could be developed. These would show how to analyze project decisions, plans, and options presented by proponents to discover implicit policies and their consistency with explicit policies. Conversely, project impact assessment could be enriched with guidelines calling for analysis of project-policy consistency.

Education

Procedural steps will not be sufficient to produce good policy assessment of any kind. Popular education on policy issues and processes is necessary for tough collective choices to be supported and promoted. If participatory heuristic policy assessment, in particular, is to thrive, it is necessary that all those who practise it, including citizens, be versed in heuristic methods and be thoughtful about development paradigms.

Education to develop policy assessment motivation, knowledge, and skills can occur in the schools. It can result from meta-assessment of current policy assessment practice and can be built into future practice. Continuing education programs could introduce appropriate systems theory to elected and permanent officials, technical experts, and active citizens.

Teachers could develop heuristic policy assessment curricula that could include real, proactive activities. Pilot exercises could test the hypothesis that children quickly grasp general systems theory concepts and usefully apply them to unravelling "tragedy of open access" conundrums manifested in dynamics ranging from local littering to global warming.

Planners could show that community and regional public planning processes can usefully involve heuristic policy assessment. Instead of publics being asked to generate wish-lists or express opinions about pre-established policy options, they could be helped to analyze the dynamics of unsustainable social and ecological systems and to evolve good solutions.

Academics could sponsor national and international forums in which macroeconomic and social policies are not debated but, rather, analyzed and developed. The emphasis would be on sincere effective communication (Forester 1989) about systems dynamics, with technical information from experts available on request. Existing or potential policies would not just be espoused or denounced on the basis of different single goals but, rather, comprehensively and paradigmatically assessed in terms of agreed-upon sets of goals. Bases for agreement and unresolvable differences would be clarified.

Objections to Formal Heuristic Policy Assessment and Rejoinders

Some or all of the procedural mechanisms suggested for enhancing public involvement in heuristic policy assessment will dismay those who believe closed representative government equals efficient, and therefore, good government. The political and bureaucratic constraints to public predecision policy assessment are well identified by Bregha (1990) and Bregha et al. (1990).

The benefits of formalization, and therefore democratization of policy planning, are shown by the social learning and design benefits already resulting from environmental impact assessment (despite its many shortcomings) and, increasingly, from freedom-of-information laws. The possible formal public-involvement mechanisms identified above for heuristic policy assessment are intended to show that there is room for further democratization. Although they, like all democratization initiatives, could make policy making more cumbersome, they could also improve the overall efficiency of governance by producing better upstream decisions and downstream implementation in the short and long terms.

Specific objections to formal heuristic policy assessment are listed below in italic type, with rejoinders in normal type.

- *Ultimately, policy is about beliefs. We cannot resolve fundamental paradigmatic issues.* Beliefs change on the basis of new information and careful logic, both of which would be fostered by formal heuristic policy assessment.
- *People avoid fundamental issues. They fear conflict, difficult thinking, or the unbearability of conclusions.* Procedural mechanisms and guidelines can encourage assessment processes that are fun, satisfying, and redemptive.
- *Paradigmatic thought cannot be forced by procedures.* People do not need to be forced to think about and discuss major problems; they need the opportunity, useful information, concepts, and perhaps facilitation, all of which good policy assessment procedures could promote.
- *Paradigmatic thought cannot be directly applied to policy decisions; policies do not effect fundamental social change.* Policy reflects assumptions. Fundamental change to an equitable, high quality of life can happen through policy-by-policy decision making.
- *Policy is made continuously and fluidly by many decision centres; to formalize policy assessment is to ossify it.* Formalization could enliven policy assessment by increasing the variety of opportunities for initiating, applying, and conducting policy assessment.
- *Formal policy assessment is too slow; we need quick processes responsive to urgent issues, not more public consultation. Governments do not have enough time in policy making to engage in dialogue with publics about fundamental systems.* While formal heuristic policy assessment may slow some decisions, it will speed up the initiation and resolution of others. In any event, it is better to make a good decision slowly than a bad one quickly. Choosing not to dialogue can produce time-wasting problems and conflicts. A little time spent planning participatory policy assessment can significantly enhance the efficiency, quality, and continuity of information flows.

- *Formal impact assessment should be confined to technical environmental impact assessment of policies governing physical projects.* While environmental impact assessment is better than nothing, it will not lead to sustainable development so long as it operates within the growth-with-trickle-down development paradigm. Paradigm change can be achieved only through systemic analysis of the links among policy realms and levels of decision.

- *Social learning and better decision making, which formal heuristic policy assessment is to provide, are already being provided continuously, and more effectively and efficiently, through mass media and pluralistic politics.* Existing policy-making processes are not leading to sustainability, equity, and quality of life through the sharing of smaller, better pies. The growth-with-trickle-down paradigm, which is at the root of the problem, needs to be explicitly revealed and confronted, policy by policy, decision by decision.

- *Formalized processes should be saved for big issues.* Policy assessment has to be widespread and continuous because small decisions reflecting implicit policy produce cumulative effects.

- *Governments will use public policy assessment only to defuse hot issues, as they do with costly inconclusive commissions of inquiry.* Rhetoric-promoting public hearings can be replaced with processes designed to encourage mutual learning and collective problem solving (for an example, see Berger 1985).

- *Formalizing policy assessment may result in attention to procedures that overwhelm consideration of substantive issues; policy assessment could become ritualized but trivial.* The solution is to break the link between formality introduced to planning by environmental impact assessment, from environmental impact assessment's technicality, in order to combine public-involvement mechanisms with heuristic guidelines.

- *Heuristics equals soft-headed thinking; outcomes should be assessed using predictively powerful and precise quantitative techniques and detailed empirical data.* While technical scientific studies are often necessary, they are not sufficient for good assessment. For whole pictures to be kept in sight, technical findings must be put into context by systems concepts and knowledge of real systems. Some assessment resources need to be diverted from learning more and more about less and less to understanding the total implications of what is already well known. Formalized heuristic policy assessment is intended not only to generate information for decision makers but also to broaden public awareness of policy outcomes, limitations, and win-win options.

- *The interests of those who hold the ultimate power in society (the rich, the politicians, and the media) are not served by ensuring public assessment of important issues. They have the most to lose from public understanding, and therefore possible rejection, of growth-with-trickle-down development policies. Thus formal heuristic policy assessment, even if desirable to most, will never be implemented: those who can implement it, will not.* Heuristic policy assessment can start from the bottom. Increments of systemic awareness by publics, and even elites, can change conceptions of what constitutes self-interest, which in turn can lead to stronger support for effective policy assessment.

- *Participatory policy assessment will not work because most citizens are ignorant, mean spirited, or apathetic. Special-interest groups dominate participatory processes.* Formal heuristic policy assessment can be designed to overcome ignorance and to encourage the understanding of wider collective interests. Interest groups are part of the solution. Without groups, the individual is culturally bereft, politically impotent, and vulnerable to manipulation of information. Even parochial groups can facilitate learning.

Conclusion

Introducing impact assessment to the policy level, then combining it with policy analysis to create comprehensive policy assessment, and finally shaping policy assessment into a formal heuristic form, is a necessary progression if we are to have equitable sustainable development with high quality of life. It is a progression already underway. Policy analysts and impact assessors are grappling with the issues involved in creating a practicable, effective policy assessment. Many of them look forward to policy assessment that formalizes opportunities for meaningful public involvement and creates wide social learning of useful systemic knowledge. A simplified model of the cycle implied by this, and the role of the public in defining both direction and assessment of policy impacts, can be found in the concluding chapter of this volume. A detailed exploration of effective public engagement is considered in Chapter 6.

Notes

1 Cost-benefit analysis cannot value sacred or beautiful places, species prized for their very existence, or traditions. Assets highly valued for cultural reasons must either be ignored as outside the scope of cost-benefit analysis or inappropriately subjected to shadow pricing.
2 While it can be argued that redistribution, that is, favouring the poor, would cause the poor to gain in happiness more than the rich would lose, this line of thought has been avoided by welfare economics.
3 Superior legal claims to service, protection, or compensation – most notably property rights – are of course not compromised by cost-benefit analysis practice.
4 Technological improvements, conservation policies, but above all, the economic shock meted out by the central banks in 1980 and the continuing austerity and structural adjustment policies of powerful governments and international agencies (e.g., the International Monetary Fund and World Bank), have temporarily defused or disguised the mineral-supply crisis by reducing demand.
5 Economists are aware of the behavioural paradox that leads individual self-interest to reduce collective welfare, but not necessarily of the ecological limits to consumption. See Sen (1967), for example.
6 The remainder of this paper is adapted from Boothroyd (1995).

7 As outlined in Chapter 7, even longer checklists may have difficulty finding political acceptance.

8 Canada's in-house environmental review of the North American Free Trade Agreement (NAFTA), prepared pursuant to Canada's new (1990) highly informal environmental assessment (EA) process for policy and program proposals, provides one example of how, in the absence of formal procedures to ensure public involvement, proponent-conducted policy impact assessment can be the captive of the proponents. The review document (Canada 1992b), which finds no environmental problems with NAFTA, was prepared by the interdepartmental committee formed to ensure environmental considerations would be taken into account throughout the NAFTA negotiations. The document is deficient in information and systems sensitivity. It was released after it and the draft agreement had gone to cabinet. Even then, no process was established to encourage public comment. The review was a Canadian milestone in that EA of a crucial policy was supposedly integrated with design and the results were publicly reported, but it also shows that in the absence of procedural safeguards, policy assessment by proponents can be narrowly self-serving.

9 Under policy assessment, one goal could initiate the design process, but immediately others would be brought to bear on the formulation of the problem. Higher goals could be stated by the proponent, but they would be assessed against more universal values as interpreted by the assessor.

10 For example, comparison of major highway proposals and day-to-day road-widening decisions in the Vancouver area with provincial, regional, and municipal policy statements favouring transit and bicycles over cars reveals a major discrepancy between the intentions and the sustainable development rhetoric of politicians, bureaucrats, and voters. It reveals, in other words, the impotence of explicit general policies on transportation – those created with most public input and adopted with most fanfare – and the power of contrary mindsets, vested interests, and planning inertia that collectively conspire to entrench the real though unstated policy that roads should be continuously expanded to meet driver demand.

11 In Vancouver, policy decisions to build rapid transit or freeways in specific corridors are made by engineers; the public is either "consulted" (i.e., informed) about technical issues outside their competence or enjoined individually to state their transportation wishes without regard for fiscal trade-offs, ecosystem consequences, or compatibility.

12 An excellent Canadian government "sourcebook of helpful concepts and ideas" for informal environmental assessment of policies and programs (Canada 1992a) would be equally helpful in formal contexts. The sourcebook encourages early consideration of externalities in design, recognizes that assessments "should be rigorous but not necessarily laborious" and "*just sufficient* for informed decision-making;" that policy may be "relatively informal – even implicit;" and that "there are many [policy] areas where careful examination reveals very significant (though often subtle and/or indirect) environmental effects," for example, "loss of prime agricultural land due to urban sprawl accelerated by housing and mortgage policies." It offers a menu of heuristic techniques, criteria for selecting them in practice, substantive insights into specific impact categories, and key indicators. Summing up its environment-centred but comprehensive perspective of policy assessment, the sourcebook states: "Integration is the new norm: separation of social and economic analysis from environmental analysis is becoming an outmoded approach to public policy and program development." At the same time, it gives little attention to public involvement in its nine-step iterative process model, which begins with internal scoping and ends with public announcement "subject to any strictures of confidentiality."

References

Bailey, J., and S. Renton. 1997. "Redesigning EIA to Fit the Future: SEA and the Policy Process." *Impact Assessment* 15,4: 319-34.

Beer, S. 1975. *Platform for Change*. New York: John Wiley.

Berger, T.R. 1985. *Village Journey*. New York: Hill and Wang.

Boothroyd, P. 1995. "Policy Assessment." In F. Vanclay and D. Bronstein, eds., *Environmental and Social Impact Assessment*, 83-126. Chichester: Wiley.

–, ed. 1994. "Managing Population-Environment Linkages: A General Systems Theory Perspective." In P. Boothroyd, ed., *Population-Environment Linkages: Toward a Conceptual Framework*. Halifax and Jakarta: Environment Management Development in Indonesia Project.

Bregha, F. (rapporteur). 1990. "Report of the Workshop on Strengthening the Environmental Assessment of Policy." Ottawa: Canadian Environmental Research Assessment Council and National Roundtable on Environment and Economy.

Bregha, F., J. Benidickson, D. Gamble, T. Shillington, and E. Wieck. 1990. *The Integration of Environmental Considerations into Government Policy*. Ottawa: Canadian Environmental Assessment Research Council.

Buckley, R.C. 1998. "Strategic Environmental Assessment." In A.L. Porter and J.J. Fittipaldi, eds., *Environmental Methods Review: Retooling Impact Assessment for the Next Century*. Fargo: The Press Club.

Burdge, R.J., and F. Vanclay. 1995. "Social Impact Assessment." In F. Vanclay and D. Bronstein, eds., *Environmental and Social Impact Assessment*. Chichester: Wiley.

Canada. 1992a. "Developing Environmentally Responsible Policies and Programs: A Sourcebook on Environmental Assessment." Final draft. Ottawa: Federal Environmental Assessment Review Office (FEARO).

–. 1992b. *North American Free Trade Agreement: Canadian Environmental Review*. Ottawa: Federal Environmental Assessment Review Office.

Carson, R. 1962. *Silent Spring*. Boston: Houghton Mifflin.

Forester, J. 1989. *Planning in the Face of Power*. Berkeley: University of California Press.

Frankish, C.J., L.W. Green, P.A. Ratner, T. Chomik, and C. Larsen. 1996. *Health Impact Assessment as a Tool for Population Health Promotion and Public Policy* (draft). Vancouver: Institute of Health Promotion, University of British Columbia.

Geddes, P. 1949. *Cities in Evolution*. London: Williams and Norgate, 1915. Revised edition, London: Williams and Norgate.

Goodland, R., P. Guitink, and M. Phillips. 1993. "Environmental Priorities in Transport Policy." Informal Discussion Draft provided at Policy Impact Assessment Workshop, thirteenth annual meeting of the International Association for Impact Assessment, Shanghai, 11-5 June.

Hardin, G. 1968. "The Tragedy of the Commons." *Science* 162: 1243-8.

Heylighen, F., E. Rosseel, and F. Demeyere, eds. 1990. *Self Steering and Cognition in Complex Systems: Toward a New Cybernetics*. New York: Gordon and Breach.

Hill, M. 1968. "A Goals-Achievement Matrix for Evaluating Alternative Plans." *Journal of the American Institute of Planners* 34: 19-28.

Holling, C.S., ed. 1978. *Adaptive Environmental Assessment and Management*. New York: Wiley.

Jacobs, J. 1961. *The Death and Life of Great American Cities*. New York: Random House.

Lichfield, N., P. Kettle, and M. Whitbread. 1975. *Evaluation in the Planning Process*. Oxford: Pergamon.

Prest, A.R., and R. Turvey. 1965. "Cost-Benefit Analysis: A Survey." *Economic Journal* 75: 685-705.

Rees, W.E. 1992. "Ecological Footprints and the Appropriated Carrying Capacity: What Urban Economics Leaves Out." *Environment and Urbanization* 4,2: 121-30.

Sen, A.K. 1967. "Isolation, Assurance, and the Social Rate of Discount." *Quarterly Journal of Economics* 81: 112-24.

Therivel, R. 1993. "Systems of Strategic Environmental Assessment." *Environmental Impact Assessment Review* 13,3: 145-68.

Wackernagel, M., J. McIntosh, W.E. Rees, and R. Woollard. 1993. *How Big Is our Ecological Footprint? A Handbook for Estimating a Community's Appropriated Carrying Capacity*. Vancouver: Task Force on Planning Healthy and Sustainable Communities, University of British Columbia.

Wolf, C.P. 1974. *Social Impact Assessment: The State of the Art*. Milwaukee: Environmental Design Research Association.

–. 1990. "A Systems Approach to Impact Assessment." *Social Impact Assessment* 14,1: 3-16.

Wood, C., and M. Dejeddour. 1992. "Strategic Environmental Assessment: EA of Policies Plans and Programmes." *Impact Assessment* 10: 3-23.

WCED (World Commission on Economy and Development). 1987. *Our Common Future.* Oxford: Oxford University Press.

6
Local versus Central Influences in Planning for Community Health
Lawrence W. Green and Jean A. Shoveller[1]

The University of British Columbia Task Force on Healthy and Sustainable Communities has developed the concepts of appropriated carrying capacity and social caring capacity using an ecological approach. Ecological models portray a world of concentric circles that need to be analyzed and navigated in order to successfully plan and implement policies for environmental reforms and health promotion. At the centre of the concentric circles are individuals with personal histories that have conditioned their behaviour and lifestyles. Successive layers of social relationships, organizations, communities, cultures, economies, and regions surround these individuals. Community lies not at the centre, nor at the periphery, of the circles, but somewhere between individuals and societies.

This chapter examines the role of participation in decision making to promote healthful and sustainable living. We examine the issues of centralization and local control from the perspective of populations in various countries and their experience in planning and implementing public health and environmental programs. We review the conventional wisdom of planning in light of changing knowledge and circumstances about sustainability. We outline some of the forces that currently impact on decision making about public health and environmental issues. We conclude the chapter with suggestions for how individuals, communities, and our society can take positive steps toward the goal of participatory decision making to promote healthy and sustainable communities.

The Policy and Planning Context
Creating policy for population health and environmental reform is inherently interjurisdictional, interdisciplinary, and intersectoral. It depends on the science, methods, influence, and authority of multiple disciplines, from individuals to national government and multinational corporations. Consequently, some policies and plans, such as redesigning the nation's infrastructure, must be formulated centrally to coordinate and provide ade-

quate resources for efforts across many local jurisdictions. Simultaneously, other policies ultimately depend on individuals for their application, for example, decisions about transportation, housing, food, tobacco, alcohol; reproductive behaviours; and recycling practices. Some of these can be legislated centrally and implemented environmentally, but most depend on decisions and actions by individuals, families, and local groups. Even those legislated centrally rely on an informed electorate, a responsive government, and a system of delivery.

To operate effectively within the existing policy and planning context, a bifocal view of the world is required. A duality exists between the need for global goal-setting and central planning on one hand, and indigenous preferences and local implementation on the other. We must adjust the lens on social policy issues to examine both broad organizational and narrow personal forces in the etiology and solution of most health and environmental problems. Some can be handled with a dose of fluoride in the water supply or by banning the manufacture of an environmentally toxic chemical, but most require cooperation by lower levels of governments, organizations, or individuals. These forces operate at all levels of decision making: from the presidents of multinational corporations relating to their local branches, to provincial governments working through legislators and bureaucrats, to people in their everyday lives. Some of the influences flow up the chain (individuals influencing organizations) and some flow down (higher levels of organization influencing lower levels).

Examination of the community and lower-level components of a larger ecological reality has been the focus of the University of British Columbia Task Force on Healthy and Sustainable Communities. A focus at this level only could run the intellectual and analytical risks of reductionism. However, such selectivity and focus on the observable and manageable elements of the whole attends virtually any scientific study and most practical action. Our study of planning and implementation for healthy and sustainable communities has required an examination of the reciprocal impact among policies, people, and local environments. Our focus on community has been justified on several grounds. One is that policies designed to support or constrain some individuals often have unforeseen consequences for others. The public therefore demands local participation in those decisions. Similarly, the intended environmental or population health impact of a policy often spells short-term hardship or perceived sacrifice for some classes of individuals. Beyond these defensive reasons, we also have assumed that:

1 many policy levers affecting global environmental issues exist at the municipal level
2 the disjunction between international proclamation and action, for

example, less pollution by the reduced use of cars, takes place at the community level

3   we can hope to effect policy and behavioural change more readily at the municipal level

4   our work with the City of Richmond, British Columbia, may have generalizability to other communities.

In this part of the chapter, we explore three widely held positions about the best way to handle this reciprocal determinism. One calls for decentralized decision making about most social and health policies, while recognizing that the remaining national and corporate policies must be more supportive of, and sensitive to, local variations in needs. A second calls for maximum participation of individuals in community decision making. A third calls for coalitions of local organizations to mobilize and coordinate community resources more effectively and efficiently.

On the premise that the public perceives trade-offs between environmental reform and their own short-term quality-of-life considerations, we assume these decisions require local debate and decision. We seek ways of supporting and understanding the dynamics and resolution of the debate that must occur at the community level. The challenge is to find ways of facilitating local participation in planning and policy making for sustainable environmental reform and population health. This should be done while recognizing the inherent limitations in capacity currently existing at the local level for implementing healthful and sustainable policies and programs. In identifying the limitations, we hope to suggest ways in which centralized efforts can be directed toward the strengthening of local capacities.

Definitions

We narrow the scope of our discussion of health and social policies to population health and environmental protection. We are concerned here not with the major preoccupation of the American health-care reform debate or the Canadian debate on health-care renewal. These debates have been mostly about medical care and have paid little attention to the issues of population health. Even when they have employed population health analyses, they have tended to concentrate on the distribution of medical services rather than on the issues of social determinants of health, environmental protection, and sustainable development. The public debates around community and regional development have centred largely on issues of economic growth rather than on sustainable development. Even where sustainability or environmental impact have been debated, they have been divorced from issues of population health and other social qualities of life. It is as though the preservation of the environment and natural resources were ends in themselves rather than means to ensure other qualities of life.

We define "population health" as the epidemiological, social, and environmental condition of a community that minimizes morbidity and mortality, enables adaptation to changing environmental circumstances, ensures equitable opportunity to contribute productively to the community, and allows an optimal and sustainable quality of life. "Community" may be defined by geography, demography, common interests, or some combination of the three. Our focus here is on geographical communities bounded by sociopolitical lines, but also by their demography, resources, environment, and common interests. These delimiting conditions and their uneven distributions within communities make the sustainable and equitable development of health and the other qualities of life dependent on strategic and value-laden trade-off decisions. Whether some of these decisions must be made at higher levels of organization because of the ecology of regions or because of the inequitable lock on decisions by local power structures is a major question for this chapter.

Population health and sustainable development call for strategies that go beyond the provision of medical services, investments in economic growth, and preservation of physical environments. The additional strategies are associated with public health and community or regional planning, but more specifically with health promotion and environmental protection. "Health promotion" we define as "any combination of educational, organizational, economic and environmental supports for actions conducive to health" (Green and Kreuter 1999). This raises the question of what is health. We define "health" as the ability of an organism to adapt to environmental challenges (Green and Ottoson 1999). The organism may be a human individual or any other living thing, including a community or population. "Environmental protection" we define as actions designed either to protect the environment or to structure the environment in order to protect the health of a community. The actions in both health promotion and environmental protection may be those of individuals, families, corporations, communities, and policy makers at any level of government or organization. Some of the actions may be directed at purposes other than health but may have health consequences, such as social and economic policies, agricultural and industrial policies, and educational and transportation programs.

Theories, Policies, and Programs
Behind every policy is a theory or at least a presumption of cause-and-effect relationships. Senge (1992) refers to these loosely defined theories as "mental models." More formalized logic models for the planning, implementation, and evaluation of programs give more concrete expression to the presumed theories underlying policy. A theory explicit in some planning models (e.g., Kaiser Family Foundation 1987; Bracht and Tsouros

1990; Green and Kreuter 1999) is that people's participation in setting goals will enhance their commitment and response to the planned programs and the recommended behaviour. Implicit in most social marketing models of planning (e.g., Kotler and Zaltman 1971; Manoff 1985) is the theory that investigative methods using small numbers of people representing segments of a population can reveal a population's needs and substitute for widespread active participation in setting goals. These two competing but complementary theories have provided the justification for differing policies that support health-promotion programs (Green 1986a). We will examine these and related theories in various models of planning for health promotion, asking specifically which elements of these models account for the effective implementation of policies.

Implicit economic theories such as capitalism or socialism, and notions of centralized versus decentralized planning, also drive government actions and health promoting policies (Green 1988). Those policies that endure express widely accepted theories and are consistent with prevailing social norms and cultural ideologies. Broad acceptance of theory, however, does not make it valid or scientifically grounded. Principles link theory and policy. Those who frame policy often differ in their values, assumptions, and principles from those who formulate and test theories, and from those who implement programs, including the people who must implement them in their personal lives.

Policies arise from and influence governmental action, professional practice, and the health-related and environment-related behaviour of organizations, families, and individuals. Policy changes are often assumed to exert the most powerful influence in this chain of causation. However, practical and social realities have great influence over policy implementation. Professional and community discretion in adapting policies in the planning or implementation process can influence the application of government policies (Ottoson and Green 1987). Growing public awareness of technologies such as CAT scanners and silicon gel implants can drive the demand for high cost and even inappropriate medical procedures beyond the levels supportable by medical theories of need, political principles of universal and comprehensive access, and health policies of supply to meet demand. The public's appetite for the comforts and convenience of air conditioning and automobiles creates a demand for the excessive production and consumption of energy and secondary production of pollutants that compromise both environment and health.

Federal and Provincial Initiatives
Canadian health policy first gave prominence to the environment in the Lalonde report in 1974, which drew on the theory of the "health field" (Laframboise 1973). The Lalonde report shifted the health-policy debate

from nearly total preoccupation with the medical care system to at least some attention to lifestyle determinants and the environment. At the first international conference on health promotion, both the Ottawa Charter (1986) and the Epp Report (1986) on *Achieving Health for All: A Framework for Health Promotion* emphasized the environment as part of the equation for health promotion (Pinder 1988). The Ottawa Charter in 1986 gave fuller expression to the lifestyle construct in the context of social and economic determinants of health (Canadian Institute for Advanced Research 1991). Its major conceptual contribution, however, was its positioning of health not as an end in itself but as a resource for living a fuller, more socially productive life. The charter also redefined health promotion as a means of helping people gain control over the social and environmental determinants of their health. The second and third international conferences on health promotion in Australia and Sweden emphasized social policy and the environment, respectively.

Borrowing from the Lalonde report (Health and Welfare Canada 1974), the United States followed a similar pattern with its first *Surgeon General's Report on Health Promotion and Disease Prevention* (United States Department of Health, Education and Welfare 1979). This and the subsequent reports in the American *Healthy People* initiative gave equal weight to lifestyle, both narrowly and broadly defined, preventive health services, and environmental protection of health. The Americans, however, added a much stronger emphasis on specificity and concreteness with their *National Objectives* for health promotion and disease prevention (United States Department of Health and Human Services 1981, 1990). These documents set a framework for national and state policies in health promotion and disease prevention similar to the *Health Field* concept of Laframboise with its emphasis on determinants of health. The American national objectives also set a template for state policies. Many states followed the federal example with their own parallel state objectives in disease prevention and health promotion (Green 1980, 1990, 1996; McGinnis 1990). Subsequent implementation of these national and state policies and objectives for health promotion and environmental protection emphasized community participation in setting priorities and developing local resources to implement programs in support of them (Kaiser Family Foundation 1987).

The World Health Organization (WHO) and UNICEF jointly issued the Alma Ata Declaration (WHO 1978) and a global strategy of *Health for all by the year 2000* (WHO 1981), challenging member states to give greater attention to the primary health-care needs of their poorest and most remote populations. Primary health-care concepts, as articulated by WHO, placed the emphasis on highly decentralized planning and implementation. The most widespread Canadian implementation of this belief in local involvement was the Canadian Healthy Communities Project (Canada 1989;

Wharf and Wharf Higgins 1992; Hancock 1994). This project emphasized the participatory nature of health and social planning at the local level and the importance of intersectoral collaboration. A Healthy Community project needs support from local governments but is intended to be something other than an operational arm of government. The emphasis on intersectoral and public-private partnerships make the Healthy Community concept a special case of the marriage of health, social, and environmental interests at the local level. The withdrawal of federal support has slowed the development and evaluation of Healthy Communities projects, but federal initiative helped start it and provincial government support continues in those provinces developing new Healthy Communities projects (Berlin, Hoffman, and Sherwood 1991). These efforts have only begun to produce evaluations that might guide future sustainable community and environmental initiatives (Hayes and Manson-Willms 1990; Wharf Higgins and Green 1993).

We conclude from these experiences that federal or other centralized initiatives in setting broad goals, supporting demonstration projects at the local level, and funding research efforts can be crucial to the successful development of model community health and environmental programs. In Chapter 7, McIntosh and Woollard describe how one model of policy development and implementation regarding sustainable development functions at a municipal level in British Columbia. This research project explored the intersection of theoretical concepts associated with sustainability and real-world municipal politics, economy, and geography. The study period coincided with a general trend in Canada to deconcentrate and decentralize governance structures and facilitate citizen participation in policy-level decision making.

Deconcentration of Centralized Governments

The theory of deconcentrating refers to the spatial redistribution of administrative authority to local offices of the central government and has been discussed and promoted in Canada and the United States for more than two decades. Deconcentration places centralized governments in the faces of local communities. Within deconcentrated operating systems, public officials inform communities of problems and proposed solutions, while seeking inputs into a centrally controlled planning system. This style of participation, coined "participation as cooperation" (Green 1986a), depends on the individual's compliance with the centrally prescribed approaches to promoting health and sustainability. Deconcentration of centralized government services, for the most part, in Canada, has subsided for two reasons: (1) severe downsizing within the civil service over the past fifteen years has resulted in a reduced federal government presence in local communities, and (2) calls by the provinces for increased decision-making powers over their own affairs have resulted in more decentralized, rather than deconcentrated, operating contexts.

In addition to citizens' participation in local healthy community projects, other government initiatives such as the Planned Approach to Community Health (PATCH) and foundation grant programs[2] have offered innovative models of local initiative for health promotion and environmental protection. Meaningful lessons emerged from the PATCH programs and the foundation-supported community projects. These included the importance of technical assistance from central sources to apply state-of-the-art strategies in accomplishing local goals, and the need for patience and extensive time commitments when planning and developing local programs (Kaiser Family Foundation 1987; Green and Kreuter 1999). Also emerging from these projects was the recognition that one-time grants could not guarantee implementation of effective local programs, much less the institutionalization or sustainability of programs implemented (Steckler and Goodman 1989; Altman et al. 1991; Goodman and Steckler 1991; Altman 1995).

The strength of communities without centralized direction or support may lie largely in their private sector and educational sector resources and organizations. Most of these are highly decentralized in North America. Some 90 percent of businesses and industries are classified as small business, and most schools have local autonomy. The advantages of their flexibility and responsiveness to the people they serve are offset in part by their lack of resources and influence on decisions at other levels. This is the ultimate dilemma of all successful local initiatives; their success leads them to become models for central agencies that then refer other local groups to them for technical assistance or inspiration, but they seldom receive support for these added responsibilities.

Decentralization and Participation

"Decentralization" refers here to the transfer of some decision making to local authorities, and centrally determined guidelines. Decentralization brings the appearance of power closer to local communities, but it also places greater fiscal responsibility for health on local governments, as demonstrated by the shift toward decentralization in Australia, Canada, New Zealand, and the United States. In Canada and the United States, this has been done while leaving most of the highly centralized national, provincial, state, and corporate-financing mechanisms intact. Decentralization of responsibility in Canada and the United States has been accompanied by federal control of revenue-sharing with the provinces and states. However, the amount of money transferred from federal to provincial or state coffers in both countries has diminished. In Canada, where implementation of health care is under provincial jurisdiction, federal redistribution of tax points has reduced the provinces' ability to afford existing health-care systems. Thus, the positive potential for developing significantly increased social capital through self-determination does not seem to have been realized via decentralization in its current form. In Chapter 3, Carr provides a more detailed and complete discussion of social capital. Readers are encouraged to revisit the issues raised there and consider the following examples and discussion regarding planning for community health.

Local initiatives include public, professional, and political goals that often find themselves in conflict with each other and with the rights of individuals pursuing their own well-being and happiness. This has become a central problem of democracy today and could increase in the newly emerging democracies with fewer resources available to satisfy both social and individual needs.

Poverty, on the other hand, might seem to pull people together to attain mutual support. Long-standing economic hardship in the Atlantic provinces presents an example of the development of social capital as a necessary means of survival. In the United States, people living in urban neighbourhoods facing severe economic and social problems are also beginning to take up the challenge of civic responsibility, as this report from the *New York Times* (26 February 1996) indicates:

> Neighborhood groups are growing in number and in strength, taking on responsibilities that were once the province of government agencies and getting more attention from government officials. Fueled by shrinking local, state and Federal budgets and armed with fax machines, newsletters, a mastery of legal nuances, and enthusiastic members willing to give their money and time, they are moving beyond their traditional role of pestering officials to get potholes filled and streetlights fixed ... A survey by the Citizens Committee for New York City ... found that their number has gone from 3,500 in 1977 to 8,000 last year.

The question remains: Will our society pursue democratic decision making in the name of health and sustainability, or will we continue to focus on parochial self-interests?

How Health Promotion Has Pursued Decentralization
Among the assumptions derived from the theoretical underpinnings of health promotion, three have particular significance in the movement toward decentralization of planning and policy decisions: (1) the principle of participation; (2) the principle of local (decentralized) and personal control over the determinants of health; and (3) the principle of intersectoral action involving coalitions.

All three of these core themes have been interpreted to imply a preference for local rather than national control over the priorities assigned to various health concerns. The principles of participation and intersectoral action do not necessarily connote local rather than broad-scale approaches. It is not surprising, however, that such interpretations come at a time when economic imperatives serve to justify the retreat of central governments from their previous financial support to, and regulatory control over, programs that impact significantly on local environmental and health issues. This retreat also relates in many people's minds to a reactionary phenomenon manifest as antigovernment attitudes and demand for local autonomy. Added to this grim economic and political climate is the decline of neighbourhood communities, a result of a variety of social changes such as suburbanization. The resulting milieu has led to alienation, dehumanization of centralized services, and the disempowerment of local groups and individuals to cope with the problems of their communities (Green 1989).

These three themes seek to mobilize community resources against these sources of alienation, dehumanization, and disempowerment. Whether communities can regain sufficient capacity to take control over the determinants of their own health remains to be seen. However, The *New York Times'* report quoted above holds promise, as does work in Italy described in Chapter 2 by Hertzman and Kelly and in Chapter 3 by Carr, at least for those communities with civic traditions (Putnam 1993; Putnam, Leonardi, and Nanetti 1993). Commentaries in the health-promotion literature (Green and Raeburn 1988; Bracht and Tsouros 1990; Tsouros 1990) have tended to favour the community, rather than the health-care system or central government, as the centre of gravity for health promotion. Participatory approaches to assessing needs, planning, and evaluating programs continue to be favoured in health promotion (Green et al. 1995; Fetterman, Kafterian, and Wandersman 1996) and have begun to appear in environmental studies (Robottom and Colquhoun 1992). So far, the evidence has been inconsistent regarding the effectiveness of community health-promotion programs and Healthy Community policy initiatives in achieving their more modest behavioural and health objectives.

Paradoxes and Contradictions in the Three Principles
Can community participation be anything more than a superficial or so-called "spray-on solution" (Bryson and Mowbray 1981) to the needs for complex change in health policy and environmental protection? Perceptions of the social benefit of community participation generally range from benign to positive (Bracht and Tsouros 1990). Such initiatives are almost certain to find favour with current legislative bodies facing budget-balancing crises and with antigovernment factions, because they place responsibility for health and environmental programs and policies at the

local level. Will lay people in communities, workplaces, and corporations be willing and able to undertake the onerous task of confronting problems that grow out of alleged government and corporate mismanagement, or callousness (Hunt 1990)? Early studies of community development programs (Moynihan 1969; Gittel and Hoffacker 1980; Kweit and Kweit 1980; Farquhar et al. 1983) showed, at best, a mixed record of local successes. They were sufficient, however, to spawn a decade of more systematic quasi-experimental studies of larger magnitude and more generous funding, the results of which also have been mixed.[3]

The following section reviews the issues between the development of policies, whether centrally or locally, and their subsequent impact on health and environmental activities in local populations. These issues include clarification of goals of health-promotion contracts between organizations; clarification of who is responsible for accountability and to whom; finding ways to increase citizen participation without burdening the planning and implementation process with unmanageable structures; and issues of constitutionally limited powers and discretion for local decision making.

Issues of Who Controls the Goals and Programs

In considering the potential roles of various stakeholders in health and environmental decisions, we note a fundamental dilemma in the roles of the different levels of government. Many communities today lack the resources to resolve some of the complex problems they face, as well as control over outside influences. They have become increasingly beholden to external sources of support from their own headquarters or from other sources. As described in Carr's chapter of this volume, their social capital has been depleted. It has even been argued that the notion of community with a communality of interests is less tenable today than in earlier times in industrialized nations because communities are more interdependent (Hunt 1990).

Governments and other central funding sources, in turn, require a measure of focus, control, and accountability which community stakeholders may be reluctant to provide. The issue of ownership and goals becomes problematic when the central funding source requires a health-specific commitment but the local population wishes to focus on a different problem not defined as a priority by the central funding bodies. Indeed, when communities are invited to assess their own priorities, they commonly place on their list of concerns issues that lie outside the mandate of the funding agency. For example, a community group may receive funding from a research-oriented agency to examine health issues related to cardiovascular disease; however, the priorities within the community of interest are focused on creating jobs and stimulating the local economy. When local organizations contort their own priorities to fit a distant funding organization's priorities, they may find themselves out of step with the local base of support. When funding agencies attempt to contort their priorities to accommodate local demands, they face the question, Is everything health and is health everything?

Similarly, the need for accountability imposed by most central funding mechanisms encounters problems of locally funded organizations not having enough control or expertise to provide the monitoring required for accountability. These circumstances typically produce a rush of technical assistance from central to local organizations, welcomed or not. The outside experts often do not know enough about local circumstances to be as helpful as their substantive expertise might make them in more familiar territory, or they are held at arm's length from intruding on local prerogatives.

Moreover, frustration associated with this perceived lack of accountability is enhanced by the methodological difficulties of demonstrating "hard" outcome evidence over short periods of funding. The best-laid evaluation research plans are frequently undone by the realities of rigour, time, and funding. In addition, the "real world" in which policy decisions are being made dictates the practical context within which this type of academic question can be posed. As described by McIntosh and Woollard in Chapter 7, the Richmond, British Columbia, experience illustrated the importance of clear communication with community partners and the need to develop practical language to express more esoteric, theoretical concepts related to developing a model of sustainability.

Issues of Expecting Too Much of Public Participation
The demands for public participation in planning and the necessity of organizational partnerships in implementing programs have outgrown their practical feasibility within our current system. For example, the requirement by funding agencies for participation and for coalitions as conditions for grants has sometimes produced perfunctory participation, overworked volunteers upholding the appearance of participation, and staff devoting so much time to the care and feeding of coalitions that they have little left for program implementation. The participation issues, in particular, have plagued local planners for decades, with national programs calling for maximum feasible participation in policy and planning at the local level to qualify for central grant funds. The difficulties of finding volunteers for the labour-intensive work of serving on local policy-making or planning bodies has typically led to an overrepresentation of more affluent and retired people and professionals, which distorts the socioeconomic, educational, and age representation on such boards (Lomas and Veenstra 1995). Much work remains to be done to facilitate representation from other groups.

Community residents invited to participate in policy making for local organizations often find themselves pressed increasingly into voluntary duties to supplement the understaffed agency's paid workforce. Reducing some of the requirements and standards for public participation would solve some of these problems but would abrogate the central government's most troublesome issue with local planning – the monopoly of local power haves over local power have-nots. Central planning has been justified in large part on the grounds that it was needed to correct some of the local injustices perpetrated by those who control local power. Requirements for public participation in local decisions must stay, but new ways to reach out, support, and reward the participation of those that are typically underrepresented and overworked must be found.

Issues of Local Accountability

In a cost-conscious environment, is the purpose of community evaluation to reduce resources required, or to decrease funding allocations (Hayes and Manson-Willms 1990)? A genuine concern of some community centres is that accountability to higher levels of government will lead to loss of control over programs and resources. Health professionals and government officials may display a greater rigidity of attitudes toward acceptable interventions than is found among community members. The most promising alternative to the either-or standoff between funders and community grantees on issues of accountability may be the application of participatory research methods involving stakeholders actively in both the formulation and interpretation of program evaluations (Park et al. 1993; Green et al. 1995; Fetterman et al. 1996).

Possible Solutions

Coalitions as an Answer to the Resource Problem

Many federal, provincial, and foundation grants for community health promotion have attempted to address the dilemmas concerning local authority versus local resource deficits by requiring the local grantee to have a coalition. Some community health grant programs, for example, have required a coalition as a condition of application from the communities (e.g., Kaiser Family Foundation 1987; Feighery and Rogers 1990; Butterfoos, Goodman, and Wandersman 1996). Yet, there is little or no evidence that coalitions are necessary in all situations, and there is growing anecdotal evidence that they are dysfunctional in some situations. We can name five caveats for coalitions when imposed and poorly used at the local level:

1   Most organizations will resist giving up resources, credit, visibility, or autonomy.

2　Not everyone insists on being the coordinator, but nobody wants to be the one being coordinated.

3　So much goes into maintaining the coalition that little time, money, or energy is left for the program.

4　Those who come to regular coalition meetings often have little authority to make decisions on behalf of their organizations.

5　If the parent organizations at provincial or national levels have not formed a parallel coalition, the local organization may not be allowed to participate in the local coalition.

We believe that coalitions have served an important initial purpose in many community health and environmental programs, notably in establishing a community consensus on priorities, setting goals, and outlining a division of responsibility. Where they become increasingly dysfunctional is in a community's attempt to use them as a management tool for the implementation of programs. At the point of implementing specific strategies, coalitions should allow their members to pair off or proceed independently with strategy. The individual should be accountable to the coalition for outcomes, not for activities.

Another useful role that organizations can play is as advocators for legislation. Altman et al. (1991) identified obstacles to implementation of community priorities as perceived by community health professionals leading local coalitions, including those in the Kaiser Family Foundation Community Health Promotion Grant Program in the western United States. Although funding was rated as both a major obstacle and a high-priority objective, few communities listed seeking changes in legislation to secure such funding as a pressing priority for their coalitions. This inconsistency raises questions that have a strong bearing on practice. Do coalitions believe in their own potential to change funding formulas at any level of government? And if so, how can such action be facilitated and supported?

Victim-Blaming versus System-Blaming
Self-responsibility has been one of the philosophies guiding health education and health promotion in North America (United States Department of Health, Education and Welfare 1979; Green 1980). Its intent, usually, is positive in that it implies increased individual and community capacity to understand and change those factors affecting health. The application of the self-responsibility concept, however, has sometimes reassigned responsibilities to individuals that were previously assumed to be parental, governmental, corporate, or organizational. More insidiously, a blaming-the-victim policy sometimes emerges to replace regulations restraining industry and to substitute for social or health services or environmental control. Victims of genetic diseases, job exploitation, racial discrimination, or

commercial manipulation cannot be held solely responsible for their failure to control or cope with the genetic, environmental, and behavioural determinants of their health. The system-blaming counterpart of the victim-blaming argument also gets abused when its proponents use it as an attack on interventions directed toward individuals rather than systems, or those that seek behavioural change, or those that use educational methods.

A focus on individual responsibility diverts attention away from more distal but more important health determinants (Crawford 1977). The ideology of wise living promotes a false view that all individuals are equally independent of their surroundings and unconstrained by social and environmental conditions. Governments have appeared to endorse this ideology when they have argued that most of the remaining serious health problems are related to individual choice and self-imposed risks. This analysis is statistically correct but unfairly applied to those whose behaviour is conditioned by a lifetime of poverty, child neglect, poor education, unemployment, disability, and other conditions of living beyond their control. The health system's inability to improve efficiency, lower costs, and improve health status cannot be attributed simply to a general lifestyle failure on the part of individuals.

Responsibility implies a capability to control one's own actions. It also implies issues of accountability and liability. Capacity suggests the potential for positive, preventive action. Liability suggests the potential for being the primary agent of one's own destruction. Under the liability perspective, individuals are legitimate targets for professional- or government-driven interventions. The rationale for supporting individual approaches to minimizing liability rest on (1) social benefit, (2) equity, and (3) paternalism. Social benefit recognizes individual health as a social good, while equity presumes unequal distribution of costs among individuals is unfair. A more paternalistic rationale presumes that the government knows better or that the individual or community does not know enough.

Within the academic and research communities, these concepts become rhetorical whips to flog those who hold ideologically opposite viewpoints, in particular those concepts underlying the public health and health psychology disciplines (Roberts 1987). For example, the considerations of active versus passive and individual versus population approaches to prevention currently divide the two disciplines. Advocates for the public-health model vigorously argue the passive, structural intervention as the most important strategy while deprecating the fundamental tenets of health psychology and behavioural health that produces little in the way of productive action. Economists, medical faculties, social workers, nurses, and other disciplines all define health-promotion issues differently, and each frames the action arena differently, each lays the emphasis on government versus individual responsibility differently. Regardless of the ideological implications of where they lay the emphasis of their analysis within ecological systems, each has an essential contribution to make to the planning, implementing, and evaluating of health-promotion programs. This is where the concentric circles portrayed by ecological analysis come to the rescue of interventions at each of the levels.

Participation in Community versus Community Participation

The near consensus that community participation is a laudable goal has not produced unanimity of definition. Participation is often misunderstood and poorly applied. Professionals at the community level may lack the necessary skills to develop a plan of action that takes adequate account of complex political and social dimensions (Tsouros 1990). Academic and governmental experts on the other hand, are often characterized by local participants as skeptical, uncooperative, and fearful of losing control (Siler-Wells 1988; Green et al. 1995).

One of the problems in fostering community participation in formal decision-making processes is the paucity of resources at the community level, where direct participation of citizens can occur (Piette 1990). The "actionalist sociology" of Touraine (1978) describes different levels of society. The level of social organization involves concrete groups or existing entities in society. They have norms and means of fulfilling their objectives. The objectives of an organization or group are adapted to the limitations of its resources. Community participation usually means people participating in the allocation and use of the scarce resources of these organizations. Organizations, groups, or communities are both direct and indirect results of the second level of society: the institutional or corporate and local governmental level. The third level (state, provincial, or national) is where power to determine knowledge requirements, to allocate resources, and to manage resources resides. It falls to the most centralized third level to assure some degree of equity in the distribution of resources across other levels (Whitehead 1990). Concerns at central levels regarding equity in health depend on the ability of local organizations to make their voices heard and to communicate the realities of the inequitable distribution of health resources to these higher levels of organization. Good data systems for surveillance are helpful, but data require interpretation. Our use of the term "community participation," therefore, means more than just participation *in* community organizations; it means participation *of* communities and their constituent organizations in decision making at more centralized levels.

The Role of Governments in Citizen Participation

The theory of participation and its expression in national and international health policies has its foundation in generations of community development research (Green 1986a). Two patterns of participation are discernible in international health. The first is an historical pattern within countries that mirrors the changes in WHO policies over several decades. The second reflects the differences among nations in levels of development of democratic institutions and the corresponding distribution of national policies on health education and promotion explicitly calling for greater citizen participation in planning.

Official international endorsement of the theory of participation can be traced to a statement in the original WHO constitution (1946) that "informed consent and active cooperation are of utmost importance in the improvement of the health of the people." Later documents (WHO 1978, 1981) continued this theme, but its operation continued to emphasize cooperation of local people with centrally planned programs. The World Health Assembly of 1978 adopted a view to "fostering community participation in health development," which shifted the emphasis from central planning to local initiative and central government responsiveness to locally defined priorities.

Second, historical patterns across countries reflect a full range of participation, ranging from limited participation *within* organizations and communities to participation *of* organizations and communities in the affairs of higher levels of governments. Advocacy for local concerns has become increasingly refined as a professionally crafted art. Media advocacy, in particular, has emerged as a powerful tool for both professionals and lay people committed to initiating social and policy change at all levels (Wallack 1994).

Achieving Effective Participation

Citizen participation within the local community often requires the acquisition of new skills and new roles (Hunt 1990). The skills may be acquired only through trial-and-error experience. Early on in any health-promotion project, the political ramifications must be addressed. If the aim is to achieve real changes in policies and practices, existing structures must be challenged, and this is unlikely to happen effectively if participants in community decision making are the same people who hold positions of authority. Incumbent leaders and agencies may pay only lip service to meaningful change, as it involves lay or community participation. For example, citizens are invited routinely to comment on government proposals to revamp or alter transportation infrastructure (e.g., new highways and bridges). This type of citizen consultation, however, focuses traditionally on the technical aspects on the proposal. As would be expected, very few citizens have the expertise required to make informed comments on the technical aspects of such plans. Such approaches to participatory decision making result in untenable relationships between citizens and the paid experts. Situations like this retard the ability of citizens to have useful involvement in decision making because they are less able to obtain a valid and meaningful place at decision-making tables. Giving an effective voice to citizens within a milieu dominated traditionally by professional experts may be viewed as presumptuous or confrontational, and may fail to gain the support necessary to recruit participants effectively or to translate participation into policy changes. What is needed is a decision-making process that accounts for and respects the valuable input of the technologic professional and the well-informed citizen.

The Complementarity of Percolating Up and Filtering Down
Whether the changes in public sentiment regarding health and the environment stimulated government policy through a process of percolating up, or whether public sentiment was influenced by a trickling down, remains to be documented. Evidence of both processes at work in some of the national and local policies can be found (Green 1986a). Indeed, the top-down and bottom-up demands appear to be complementary in some ways. In interactions between governments and communities, two areas of conflict typically emerge: immediate versus postponed action, and mass campaigns versus local activities (Kok and Green 1990). Central governments want direct, mass action and visible campaigns. Communities want local organization and interpersonal health promotion. Agents of the health organizations that stand between the government and the communities also may have conflicting agendas and sensitivities to the needs of other stakeholders. If the preferences of all these stakeholders could be met, a better program would likely result, but resource constraints force choices to be made.

Efforts must be made to find the most comprehensive and effective strategy to achieve health benefits through a multifaceted approach. The approach should be targeted at numerous levels of intervention, involving active and passive as well as individual and population approaches. As Downie, Tannahill, and Tannahill (1996) conclude, "a top-down governmental intervention cannot bring about health for all in the WHO sense of health. What is needed is a new sense of community responsibility or citizenship." Community members and government representatives must negotiate the trade-offs with sensitivity and flexibility. Neither side has a monopoly on truth; both sides have access to knowledge the other lacks.

Participatory Research and Evaluation
A critical element in community organization work involves what Freire (1973) terms a "critical consciousness." Critical consciousness invokes a level of collective reflection and action. It suggests that individuals and

communities not only have a capacity for individual and collective choice, but that they can develop the ability to assess their own health needs and to take action. Taken together, the concepts of self-reliance and critical consciousness avoid the "psychology of dependence." Freire (1972) also suggests a "cultural synthesis" in which the government and the community work together to define needs and implement solutions.

Too often, government and other technical assistance agencies hold an unassailable conviction about the worth of their intervention and the benefits it would confer (Hunt 1990). This philosophy engenders a scenario in which would-be helpers, for example, governments, seek out those whom they feel are in need of being helped. Freire (1972) characterizes any intervention that begins from the *weltanschauung* or worldview of the helpers to be one of "cultural invasion." Although Freire's position involves a consideration of cross-cultural issues, it also has significant relevance to the question of allocation of health resources in general, and the inherent companion questions of accountability between local and central stakeholders.

A cross-cutting principle found equally in learning theory and in community studies is that people learn and act more reliably if they have concrete feedback on their actions. Methods for self-assessment have been increasingly advocated in preference over external research (Freire 1972, 1973; WHO 1981; Green 1986a, 1986b). Methods, manuals, and software have been developed to support communities in self-study for needs assessment, priority setting, monitoring, and evaluation of programs (Green et al. 1994; Pelletier, Kraak, and Ferris-Morris 1994; Pelletier and Wolfe 1994; British Columbia 1995a, 1995b; Green and Kreuter 1999). The potential for these tools to be communicated across geographic boundaries, updated, and made increasingly accessible to diverse communities increases with the availability of new information technology.

Pressures for universities to demonstrate their relevance to communities and for science in general to demonstrate its utility in a period of budget reductions have converged with the growing sophistication of communities concerning research methods, a demystifying of scientific methods, and an increasing access to all sources of information. These colliding trends have revived an interest in participatory research in which the subjects of research become co-researchers in learning about their own needs, resources, and solutions (Green et al. 1995). Health-promotion practice has led the way toward fostering participatory research. This seems to be a natural step considering its interdisciplinary nature, long-standing ethos of participation and relevance, and its broad view of the key concept – health. It is no longer necessary for communities to call in outside experts to research their issues, and when they do use outsiders, they can negotiate a more favourable arrangement to meet their own needs from the research.

The big box retail study in Richmond provides a good case example of the challenges faced by both academics and communities when conducting participatory research. The study was undertaken as a result of an expressed need in Richmond to develop a better understanding of the impact of big box retail stores on the appropriate carrying capacity and social caring capacity of Richmond. However, some task force members expressed their discomfort with taking on the additional work required to complete this study. The resulting tensions around the roles of task force members, community leaders, and municipal staff members were not able to be resolved through a process of consensus-building, while the work in Richmond continued. Our inability to resolve this issue is cited by McIntosh and Woollard as one of the factors that led to a general decline in the interest and involvement by the task force as whole with the community.

Devolution of Centralized Governments

"Devolution" refers here to the transfer of significant decision-making power to local authorities, with only broad principles determined by central governments. Devolution brings the mechanisms of power closer to communities. The successful development of a devolved system for decision making to support healthful and sustainable living relies on (1) citizens demanding action along with the rhetoric regarding participatory approaches and (2) processes for decision making that facilitate and support creative, problem-solving efforts regarding the inevitable trade-offs that accompany a healthful and sustainable way of living.

For a moment, we will assume that the former condition may be fulfilled easily, although this is a point that will be revisited later in the chapter. As demands for citizen participation in decision making grow, and our system of governance continues to decentralize, federal, provincial, and local governments may increasingly seek to establish specific mandates between elections. During past times of great political and bureaucratic turmoil, governments have held direct votes or referendums on controversial issues to legitimize specific mandates (Boyer 1992). The political value in heeding the opinions of the people, as expressed during referendums, is perhaps most apparent when the direct vote centres on an issue with controversial overtones. This is often the case with health and environmental matters such as transportation, fluoridation, land use, alcohol control, or tobacco reduction.

The referendum is the most familiar tool of direct voting to Canadians and has been used frequently over the years to obtain opinions on a wide variety of issues relating to healthful and sustainable communities. Referendums have been held on issues such as alcohol control (nearly every year since the 1898 vote on Prohibition), on fluoridation issues within municipal governments, and on transportation (e.g., the referendum held in Prince Edward Island regarding the proposal to build the

Fixed-Link Crossing). People living in Canada have considerable experience with referendums on policies; yet, we do not fully understand the capacity of the referendum process.

The referendum process presents a double-edged sword to the public, elected representatives, and public servants. One edge of this sword seems to cut a new path for potential increases in the quantity, and possibly quality, of citizen participation in decision making at the local, provincial, and federal levels. The other edge cuts a swath through many of the time-honoured principles of both parliamentary (i.e., representational) systems of government and community-development approaches to consensus-building for healthy and sustainable communities. A closer examination of both the positive and negative capacity of the referendum process is warranted before making further comment about the role of referendums in a devolved operating context.

Positive Capacity of Referendums

Arguments to support increased use of referendums in Canada as beneficial supplements to our parliamentary system rest on the premise that they increase citizen participation in decision making. This, in turn, is vital to a healthy democratic society and results in decisions perceived to have a special level of legitimacy. Decisions reached during referendums guarantee the satisfaction of at least those citizens who cast votes on the winning side. Given that the winner has received the most citizen support, referendums are often characterized as democratic means of making decisions on policy issues.

Negative Capacity of Referendums

A careful distinction exists between legitimacy and wisdom. Referendums may increase the former but do not necessarily guarantee the latter. The case against holding increased numbers of referendums is predicated on arguments relating to competencies of the electorate and responsibilities of elected officials.

As a supplement to our traditional democratic methods of representation, the referendum presents a conundrum for those who believe in community-development approaches to healthy and sustainable communities. For example, the finite period for the debate preceding a referendum can result in a process that more closely resembles a pressure cooker than a forum for reasoned discussion. This observation concurs with the popular idea that our current system of governance places disproportionately high value on speed, at the expense of effective program and policy development (Saul 1995). Thoughtful, broad-based discussion is essential in the implementation of policies that promote healthy and sustainable communities. Such discussions take time – time to argue about trade-offs between competing values, to reflect on the factors that contribute to the general health of the public, and to build consensus around the breadth and depth of policies. Forcing emotional and intellectual energies into a thirty- or sixty-day campaign runs counter to this end. Participatory approaches are based on democratic processes and depend on building trust between interest groups, rather than administrative efficiency. Time frames that are too short can inflict volunteer burnout from the intensity of the citizen participation required during a referendum (Bochel, Denver, and Mcartney 1981; McGuigan 1985; Butler and Ranney 1994).

Democracy guarantees all citizens the right to express freely their position on an issue. An uneven playing field, however, can result in an imbalance between the spoken word of the average citizen and a flood of expensive campaign materials and other means of exerting influence. Power imbalances, including financial expertise and political influence, often exist between opponents during a referendum campaign. Referendums too often have become more about public relations than about broad-based discussion and participatory decision making. Special-interest groups have the ability to finance their way into the "hearts and minds" of the citizenry, and members of the government, by generating factual information, purchasing television time, making campaign contributions, lobbying, and intimidating, to promote a particular viewpoint (Zimmerman 1986). Recent experiences with referendums in Canada illustrate that special-interest groups seem adept at garnering media time and tend to portray their interests as representative of the people, regardless of the amount or quality of consultation with the average citizen. In contrast, citizens, unlike consultants, bureaucrats, and politicians, are usually not paid for their involvement, that is, their work, in decision making. This presents a considerable imbalance in the time, effort, and expertise that citizens are able to dedicate to discussions about public policy. Individuals are greatly challenged to find a forum for, or the resources with which to share, their opinions.

Most importantly, in its current form, the referendum process precludes stakeholders from searching for common ground; the referendum demands that one side wins and the other loses. There can be no negotiated settlement within the confines of the rules and regulations of most referendums. The referendum process pits one side of an issue in diametrical opposition to the other, as required by a process that relies on either-or decision options. Most health and environmental issues related to sustainability, however, are not so easily dichotomized. Thus, the referendum question and the public debate process divides at least two stakeholder groups, usually leading to confrontational rancour rather than reasoned discussions. The emotion necessary to generate citizen interest in public-policy issues often serves as fuel for confrontation and drives out open-minded exploration and resolution. It is little wonder that many citizens have become disenchanted with participation in decision making about public policy.

Can Communities Make Decisions that Support Health and Sustainability?

The short reply to the question of whether communities can make decisions that support health and sustainability is: It depends. However, the bases for this retort are worth noting. The reply depends on citizens demanding that creative, problem-solving action accompany the existing rhetoric regarding participatory approaches. To successfully develop a devolved system that supports healthful and sustainable living, the role of the citizen in decision making will need to change radically, as will the processes involved. Perhaps the greatest challenges are the philosophical and practical tasks of working with communities to develop civic-mindedness. Changes required to sustain citizens' healthful civic-mindedness depend on the organizational skills of existing professional and lay leaders working currently within communities. Communities need to learn ways to effectively harness emotional energy, which is generated frequently during public discussions of health and environmental issues, in creative, problem-solving ways, rather than in divisive winner-take-all disputes. To support this community organizing work, all science-based disciplines must apply existing technologies in more creative, healthful, and sustainable ways and develop new technologies that support citizen participation. Auto-diallers, a technology used to automatically speed-dial and leave public information messages with large volumes of households, have been demonstrated to increase community capacity by "spreading the word" effectively.

Based on experiences in developing local community service centres (referred to as CLSCs in Quebec), O'Neill (1998) cautions those planning citizen-based movements for promoting health through social change. It is imperative to recognize the possibilities and limits of participation within the existing political structure. Restructuring existing decision-making structures and institutions according to participatory models must dovetail with efforts to increase civic-mindedness. As has been described in this and other chapters, citizens, bureaucrats, and politicians face a number of institutional barriers to broad-based participation. The way public business gets done in our society must evolve in concert with changes in civic attitudes if long-term and meaningful advances toward healthful and sustainable living are to be made. In this light, we recommend that governments abandon the referendum as an antiquated and ineffective tool for decision making. The work of making healthful social change is simply too colourful to rely on an instrument that views issues in black and white. In making the first steps toward changing our institutions for decision making, we should look to the potential presented by participatory democracy, such as Fishkin's (1991) ideas of deliberative opinion polls and rolling community conventions. What our society needs are citizens "capable of common purpose and mutual action by virtue of their civic attitudes and participatory institutions" Barber (1984, 117).

Challenges for Healthy and Sustainable Communities

Significant challenges face governments, health professionals, and the public in their efforts to improve health and to increase community involvement in sustainability, including:

1 placing environmental sustainability on public, professional, and political agendas
2 achieving equity in the determinants of health
3 restructuring existing systems for decision making about policy to enable community participation
4 allocating resources to the organizations bringing about community change
5 increasing intersectoral collaboration.

Governments may play a leading role in meeting these challenges. The federal government can offer technical assistance and funding to existing organizations that support community efforts. Governments and the private sector must reallocate resources and funds within the health sector and target additional funds toward health promotion. Money must be provided to improve evaluation techniques and to fund health-promotion initiatives. Piecemeal solutions, however, are unlikely to generate enduring change in health behaviours or institutions. A specific dollar allotment must be targeted for environmental health promotion. In a recent example of such a move, the government of the Northwest Territories of Canada earmarked 1 percent of its annual health budget for dedicated health-promotion activities to rise to 6 percent. In that region, local versus centralized distribution of the percent set aside is not so problematic, but in the United States, or in large provinces in Canada, this would be a critical consideration.

Health and environmental impact assessment statements should be included on all legislative, treasury board, and cabinet submissions. The availability of health impact analysis and other means of planning policy first need to be enhanced through the development of health goals; the provision of technology and training, including the use of planning software, communications systems, and data record linkages; and the development of monitoring systems. The rate of continued development and nurturing of communities depends on the ability of governments and communities to pursue the positive effects to be gained by adapting technology for use in planning, implementation, and evaluation of policies. British Columbia's Ministry of Health, for example, developed guidelines for health impact assessment but found that they could not be implemented effectively without first developing health goals and targets for the province.

Community initiatives depend for their success on the adaptation of theory, policy, and technology to produce services at regional and local levels. Policy can improve the quality of health and environmental programs only if those who implement the policies know how to transform them into effective programs. In addition, communities must be prepared to successfully construct a health or environmental problem and be able to present the issues to the media, elected representatives, and potential allies within a sea of concerns and competing agendas (Hannigan 1995). With an active and politically savvy community, public and governmental agencies tend to be more responsive and officials tend to be more sensitive to publicly expressed needs. Community organizations also tend to work more cooperatively than in those communities where the public waits for government and other organizations to provide leadership in health matters. If the public seeks more information, participates more actively in debating priorities, and watches more vigilantly the process of policy development, the problems are more likely to be dealt with in ways that assure public acceptance. Researchers and communities need to work closely to examine alternative strategies for making decisions about policy. It is unlikely that strategies reflecting only the extremes of direct democracy or of closed-door decisions by an accountable elite will suffice. It is predictable that some strategies will work better for some communities than for others. Developing a better understanding of the process of finding that best mix of participationist and representationist theory and practice will prove to be one of the most interesting questions to be pursued during the next decade of community research.

Conclusions

Government has at least three roles in the development of healthy and sustainable communities: (1) listening to the people and their concerns, (2) sharing leadership and resources across disciplines to enhance environmental protection and population health efforts, and (3) providing the infrastructure to maintain momentum to produce sustainable improvements in health and environment. The question remains as to the extent to which an essentially locally derived process can affect conditions that become regional, national, and global in scope (Hayes and Manson-Willms 1990). Can a cross-country network of projects demand changes in the priorities of senior levels of government and act as a stimulus for an integrated social movement toward sustainable development and health for all? Our conclusion is that such a cross-country network represents a good beginning. In doing so, we recognize that prescribing a single, best formula for all communities is precluded by the need to take into account the particular issues in environmental and population health planning that might pertain to any given planning effort. That said, we conclude this chapter with some suggestions for action at individual, community, and societal levels.

Challenges: Individual, Community, Societal

As individuals, we often become overwhelmed by negativity. We need to begin to talk with our neighbours, coworkers, and other associates as a way to reaffirm the existence of a problem-solving capacity which provides a balance for the self-destructive side of humanity. In doing so, individuals need to cultivate the power that exists across personal, professional, cultural, geographical, and ideological linkages to achieve healthful and sustainable living. As we talk about the issues, we need to move beyond the media-speak that dominates our daily dialogues. This demands a lengthy education process that may take generations to realize its full impact. Rather than become overwhelmed, individuals need to view these changes in dialogue as the first step toward creating critical consciousness and, ultimately, a healthful and sustainable legacy.

Communities must learn to negotiate effectively with governments and industries for health and sustainability. Communities need to develop strong power bases by organizing critical masses of the electorate, workforce, and consumer market. Although the power imbalance that exists currently between citizens, government, and industry reflects a "David versus Goliath" struggle, there are success stories from which we can learn. One example is the movement toward self-determination within Aboriginal communities that have successfully negotiated land claims.

Cost-effectiveness, efficiency, and sustainability issues will dominate our society during the twenty-first century, as growing populations face shrinking resources. Ecological perspectives will strengthen regional planning in some spheres. In others, growing distrust of centralized planning and government control will hasten the proliferation of highly fragmented groups seeking control over their own health. This will be the largest challenge to the global perspective that ecological approaches to planning must embrace. Within our society, information systems will reign as the technology that will enable a reconciliation of regionalized or more centralized planning. This reconciliation will ensure more equitable distribution of resources within increasingly decentralized systems of decision making, planning, and implementation intended to better address the concerns of particular populations.

For example, a user-friendly software, entitled EMPOWER, is being developed for use by citizens and street-level bureaucrats. The acronym

EMPOWER stands for "expert methods of planning and organizing within everyone's reach." Citizens' abilities to influence decision making, planning, and implementation may be further enhanced by their use or access to other technological tools, including access to auto-diallers, communication and information collection via the Internet and the World Wide Web, expanded use of linked databases, and widespread access to producing and manipulating video and other image-making media. As technological resources expand, more remote communities, such as the BC sawmill towns described by Ostry in Chapter 8, may be able to access and disseminate information in a fashion and with speed unheard of before the development of the World Wide Web. By creatively integrating enabling technologies with individual and community efforts, our society may achieve a new sense of civic-mindedness that will result in decision making to support healthful and sustainable communities.

Acknowledgments
We are indebted to Lynne Blair, Leland Brown, James Frankish, Joy Johnson, Chris Lovato, Meredith Minkler, David Pelletier, Freya Peters, and Abraham Wandersman for comments on earlier drafts. This work has benefited from the support and debates of the University of British Columbia Task Force on Healthy and Sustainable Communities. In particular, we thank Peter Boothroyd, Robert Woollard, Aleck Ostry, and Clyde Hertzman for their helpful comments. We have drawn also on work conducted under grants from the British Columbia Ministry of Health and Health Canada, for the evaluation of Heart Health Programs, the British Columbia Consortium for Health Promotion Research, and for Dr. Shoveller's doctoral dissertation research at the University of British Columbia.

Notes
1 Parts of this paper were presented by L. Green with C.J. Frankish at the Fourteenth Annual Bristol-Myers Squibb/Mead Johnson Nutrition Research Symposium, "Beyond Nutritional Recommendations: Implementing Science for Healthier Populations," Cornell University and National Academy of Science, Washington, DC, 5-7 June 1995, and at the Group Health Cooperative and University of Washington School of Public Health and Community Medicine conference on community approaches to health promotion, sponsored by the Henry J. Kaiser Family Foundation, 10-11 October 1995. Other parts of this paper were presented by J. Shoveller at the Fourth National Conference on Health Promotion, 9-12 June 1996, and the Ninth Annual Meeting of the International Association on Health Policy in Montreal, 13-16 June 1996.
2 Notably the Carnegie, Ford, Kaiser, Kellogg, Rockefeller, and Kansas Health Foundations, and now the California Wellness Foundation, have demonstrated leadership in this arena.
3 Mixed results might mean that much knowledge remains to be developed or put into practical designs for planning or program content. It could also indicate that the quasi-experimental research approach to large-scale community programs of this type is inappropriate, or perhaps good program concepts were not well executed. Anecdotal evidence is mounting regarding what can happen when the locus of attention shifts to local decision making, leaving states with regulatory powers. For detailed reports on the results of this research, refer to the following, as well as the editorials that accompany each of these articles: Holder and Giesbrecht 1989; Farquhar et al. 1990; Shea and Basch 1990; Altman et al. 1991; Holder and Howard 1991; Gerstein and Green 1993; Leujoker et al. 1994.

References
Altman, D.G. 1995. "Sustaining Interventions in Community Systems: On the Relationship between Researchers and Communities." *Health Psychology* 14: 526-36.
Altman, D., J. Endres, J. Linzer, K. Lorig, B. Pitney, and T. Rogers. 1991. "Obstacles to and Future Goals of Ten Comprehensive Community Health Promotion Projects." *Journal of Community Health* 16: 299-314.
Barber, B.R. 1984. *Strong Democracy: Participatory Politics for a New Age.* Berkeley: University of California Press.
Berlin, S., K. Hoffman, and D. Sherwood. 1991. "National Project Funding Canceled. Challenge: The Multiplier." *Canadian Public Health Association Newsletter,* May (special edition).
Bochel, J., D. Denver, and A. Mcartney, eds. 1981. *The Referendum Experience: Scotland 1979.* Aberdeen, Scotland: Aberdeen University Press.
Boyer, P. 1992. *The People's Mandate: Referendum and a More Democratic Canada.* Toronto: Dundurn Press.
Bracht, N., and A. Tsouros. 1990. "Principles and Strategies of Effective Community Participation." *Health Promotion International* 5: 199-208.
British Columbia. Ministry of Health and Ministry Responsible for Seniors. 1995a. *Health Impact Assessment: Guidelines.* Victoria: Population Health Resource Branch, BC Ministry of Health and Ministry Responsible for Seniors.
–. 1995b. Ministry of Health and Ministry Responsible for Seniors. *Health Indicator Workbook: A Tool for Healthy Communities.* 2nd ed. Victoria: Population Health Resource Branch, BC Ministry of Health and Ministry Responsible for Seniors.
Bryson, L., and M. Mowbray. 1981. "Community: The Spray-On Solution." *Australian Journal of Social Issues,* November: 265-7.
Butler, D., and A. Ranney. 1994. *Referendums Around the World: The Growing Use of Direct Democracy.* Washington, DC: American Enterprise Institute Press.
Butterfoos, F.D., R.M. Goodman, and A. Wandersman. 1996. "Community Coalitions for Prevention and Health Promotion: Factors Predicting Satisfaction, Participation and Planning." *Health Education Quarterly* 23: 65-79.
Canada. 1989. *Canadian Healthy Communities Project.* Ottawa: Canadian Healthy Communities Project.
Canadian Institute for Advanced Research. 1991. *The Determinants of Health.* (Research CIAR Publication no. 5.) Toronto: Canadian Institute for Advanced Research.
Canadian Unity Information Office. 1978. *Understanding Referenda: Six Histories: Australia, Newfoundland, Ireland, Norway, Denmark, United Kingdom.* Ottawa: Ministry of Supply and Services Canada.
Crawford, R. 1977. "You Are Dangerous to Your Health: The Ideology and Politics of Victim-Blaming." *International Journal of Health Services* 7: 663-80.
Downie, R.S., C. Tannahill, and A. Tannahill. 1996. "Justice, Health and Society." In R.S. Downie, C. Tannahill, and A. Tannahill, eds., *Health Promotion: Models and Values.* 2nd Ed. (184-98). Toronto: Oxford University Press.
Epp, J. 1986. *Achieving Health for All: A Framework for Health Promotion.* Ottawa: Health and Welfare Canada.
Farquhar, J.W., S.P. Fortmann, J.P. Flora, C.B. Taylor, W.L. Haskell, P.T. Williams, N. Maccoby, and P.D. Wood. 1990. "Effects of Community-Wide Education on Cardiovascular Disease Risk Factors – The Stanford 5-city Project." *Journal of the American Medical Association* 264: 359-65.
Farquhar, J.W., S.P. Fortmann, P.D. Wood, and W.L. Haskell. 1983. "Community Studies of Cardiovascular Disease Prevention." In N. M. Kaplan and J. Stamler, eds., *Prevention of Coronary Heart Disease: Practical Management of Risk Factors,* 170-82. Philadelphia: W.B. Saunders.
Feighery, E., and T. Rogers. 1990. *Building and Maintaining Effective Coalitions: How-To Guides on Community Health Promotion.* Palo Alto: Health Promotion Resource Center, Stanford Center for Research on Disease Prevention.

Fetterman, D.M., S.J. Kafterian, and A. Wandersman, eds. 1996. *Empowerment Evaluation: Knowledge and Tools for Self-Assessment and Accountability.* Thousand Oaks: Sage Publications.

Fishkin, J.S. 1991. *Democracy and Deliberation: New Directions for Democratic Reform.* New Haven, CT: Yale University Press.

Freire, P. 1972. *Pedagogy of the Oppressed.* New York: Seabury Press.

–. 1973. *Education for Critical Consciousness.* New York: Seabury Press.

Gerstein, D., and L.W. Green, eds. 1993. *Preventing Drug Abuse: What Do We Know?* Washington, DC: National Academy Press.

Gittel, M., and B. Hoffacker. 1980. *Limits to Citizen Participation.* Beverly Hills, CA: Sage Publications.

Goodman, R.M., and A. Steckler. 1991. "Integrating Qualitative and Quantitative Evaluation Methods." *Hygie* 10: 16-20.

Green, L.W. 1980. "Healthy People: The Surgeon General's Report and the Prospects." In W. McNemey, ed., *Working for a Healthier America.* Cambridge, MA: Ballinger.

–. 1986a. "The Theory of Participation: A Qualitative Analysis of Its Expression in National and International Health Policies." *Advances in Health Education and Promotion* 1, Pt. A: 211-36.

–. 1986b. "Individuals vs. Systems: An Artificial Classification that Divides and Distorts." *Health Link* 2: 29-30.

–. 1988. "Policies for Decentralization and Development of Health Education." *Rev. Saúde Públ. San Paulo* 22: 217-20.

–. 1989. "The Revival of Community And Public Obligation of Academic Health Centers." In R. Bulger and S. Reiser, eds., *Integrity in Health Care Institutions: Humane Environments for Teaching, Inquiry and Healing.* Ames: University of Iowa Press.

–. 1990. *Preface of Healthy People 2000: Objectives for the Nation in Health Promotion and Disease Prevention.* Boston: Jones and Bartlett.

–. 1996. *Commentary in Healthy People 2000 Midcourse Review and Revised Objectives.* Boston: Jones and Bartlett.

Green, L.W., A. George, M. Daniel, J. Frankish, C. Herbert, and W. Bowie. 1995. *Participatory Research in Health Promotion.* Ottawa: The Royal Society of Canada.

Green, L.W., R. Gold, J. Tanm, and M.K. Kreuter. 1994. "EMPOWER/Canadian Health Expert System: The Application of Artificial Intelligence and Expert System Technology to Community Health Program Planning and Evaluation." *Canadian Medical Informatics,* November-December: 20-3.

Green, L.W., and M.K. Kreuter. 1999. *Health Promotion Planning: An Educational and Ecological Approach.* 3rd ed. Mountain View, CA: Mayfield.

Green, L.W., and J. Raeburn. 1988. "Health Promotion. What Is It? What Will It Become?" *Health Promotion International* 3: 151-9.

Green, L.W., and J.M. Ottoson. 1999. *Community and Population Health* (8th edition). Toronto: McGraw-Hill.

Hancock, T. 1994. "Health Promotion: Did We Win The Battle, But Lose the War?" In A. Pedersen, M. O'Neill, and I. Rootman, eds., *Health Promotion in Canada: Provincial, National and International Perspectives,* 350-73. Toronto: W.B. Saunders.

Hannigan, J.A. 1995. "Social Construction of Environmental Problems." In J.A. Hannigan, ed., *Environmental Sociology: A Social Constructionist Perspective,* 32-57. London: Routledge.

Hayes, M., and S. Manson-Willms. 1990. "Healthy Community Indicators: the Perils of the Search and the Paucity of the Find." *Health Promotion International* 5: 161-6.

Health and Welfare Canada. 1974. *A New Perspective on the Health of Canadians.* Ottawa: Ministry of Supplies and Services.

Holder, H., and N. Giesbrecht. 1989. "Conceptual Issues: Perspectives on the Community in Action Research." In N. Giesbrecht et al., eds., *Research, Action, and the Community: Experiences in the Prevention of Alcohol and Other Drug Problems,* 27-40. Rockville, MD: Office for Substance Abuse Prevention, Alcohol, Drug Abuse, and Mental Health Administration, OSAP Prevention Monograph-4, DHHS Pub. no. (ADM) 89-1651.

Holder, H.D., and J. Howard, eds. 1991. *Community Prevention Trials for Alcohol Problems: Methodological Issues*. New York: Praeger.

Hunt, S. 1990. "Building Alliances: Professional and Political Issues in Community Participation." *Health Promotion International* 5: 179-85.

Kaiser Family Foundation. 1987. *The Community Health Promotion Grant Program*. Menlo Park: The Henry J. Kaiser Family Foundation.

Kok, G., and L.W. Green. 1990. "Research to Support Health Promotion in Practice: A Plea for Increased Co-Operation." *Health Promotion International* 5: 303-8.

Kotler, P., and G. Zaltman. 1971. "Social Marketing: An Approach to Planned Social Change." *Journal of Marketing* 35,3: 3-12.

Kweit, R., and M. Kweit. 1980. *Improving Citizen Participation in a Democratic Society*. New York: Praeger.

Laframboise, H. 1973. "Conceptual Approach to the Analysis and Evaluation of the Health Field." *Union Médicale du Canada* 102: 1128-33.

Leujoker, R.V., D.M. Murray, D.R. Jacobs, M.B. Mittleark, N. Bracht, R. Carlaw, R. Crow, and P. Elmer. 1994. "Community Education for Cardiovascular Disease Prevention: Risk Changes in the Minnesota Heart Health Program." *American Journal of Public Health* 84: 1383-93.

Lomas, J., and G. Veenstra. 1995. "If You Build It, Who Will Come?" *Policy Options* 16: 37-40.

Manoff, R.K. 1985. *Social Marketing: New Imperative for Public Health*. New York: Praeger.

McGinnis, J.M. 1990. "Setting Objectives for Public Health in the 1990s: Experience and Prospects." *Annual Review of Public Health* 11: 231-49.

McGuigan, P.B. 1985. *The Politics of Direct Democracy in the 1980s: Case Studies in Popular Decision-Making*. Washington: Free Congress Research and Education Foundation.

Moynihan, D. 1969. *Maximum Feasible Misunderstanding*. New York: Free Press.

O'Neill, M. 1998. "Community Participation in Quebec's Health System: A Strategy to Curtail Community Empowerment?" In D. Coburn, C. D'Arcy, and G.M. Torrance, eds., *Health and Canadian Society: Sociological Perspectives,* 3rd ed., 517-30. Toronto: University of Toronto Press.

Ottawa Charter for Health Promotion. 1986. *Health Promotion* 1: 3-5.

Ottoson, J.M., and L.W. Green. 1987. "Reconciling Concept and Context: Theory of Implementation." In W.B. Ward and M.H. Becker, eds., *Advances in Health Education and Promotion,* vol. 2., 353-82. Greenwich, CT: JAI Press.

Park, P., M. Brydon-Miller, B. Hall, and T. Jackson. 1993. *Voices of Change: Participatory Research in Canada and the United States*. Toronto: Ontario Institute for Studies in Education.

Pelletier, D., V. Kraak, and M. Ferris-Morris. 1994. *The CBNM Problem Solving Model: An Approach for Improving Nutrition-Relevant Decision-Making in the Community*. Ithaca: Division of Nutritional Sciences, Cornell University.

Pelletier, D., and W. Wolfe. 1994. Nutrition Monitoring and Action: Convergent Lessons from the U.S. and Developing Countries. Paper presented at the 122nd annual meeting of the American Public Health Association, Washington, DC, 30 October.

Piette, D. 1990. "Community Participation in Formal Decision-Making." *Health Promotion International* 5: 187-97.

Pinder, L. 1988. "From 'A New Perspective' to the 'Framework.'" *Health Promotion International* 3: 205-12.

Putnam, R.D. 1993. "The Prosperous Community: Social Capital and Public Life." *The American Prospect* 13: 35-42.

Putnam, R.D., R. Leonardi, and R.Y. Nanetti. 1993. *Making Democracy Work: Civic Traditions in Modern Italy*. Princeton: Princeton University Press.

Roberts, M. 1987. "Public Health and Health Psychology: Two Cats of Kilkenny?" *Professional Psychology: Research and Practice* 8: 145-9.

Robottom, I., and D. Colquhoun. 1992. "Participatory Research, Environmental Health Education and the Politics of Method." *Health Education Research* 7: 457-69.

Saul, J.R. 1995. *The Unconscious Civilization*. Toronto: House of Anansi Press.

Senge, P.M. 1992. *The Fifth Discipline: The Art and Practice of the Learning Organization.* New York: Doubleday.

Shea, S., and C.E. Basch. 1990. "A Review of Five Major Community-Based Cardiovascular Disease Prevention Programs: Part 1. Rationale, Design, and Theoretical Framework." *American Journal of Health Promotion* 4: 203-13.

Siler-Wells, G. 1988. *Directing Change and Changing Direction: A New Health Policy Agenda for Canada.* Ottawa: Canadian Public Health Association.

Steckler, A., and R.M. Goodman. 1989. "How to Institutionalize Health Promotion Programs." *American Journal of Health Promotion* 3: 34-44.

Touraine, A. 1978. *La Voix et la Regard.* Paris: Editions du Seuil.

Tsouros, A. 1990. "Healthy Communities Means Community Action." *Health Promotion International* 5: 177.

United States. Department of Health, Education and Welfare. 1979. *Healthy People: Surgeons General's Report on Health Promotion and Disease Prevention.* Washington, DC: Public Health Service, Pub. no. DHEW-PHS-79-55071.

United States. Department of Health and Human Services. 1981. *Promoting Health/Preventing Disease: 1990 Objectives for the Nation.* Washington, DC: Public Health Service.

–. 1990. *Healthy People 2000: National health promotion and disease prevention objectives.* Washington, DC: Public Health Service, Pub. no. DHHS-PHS-91-50212.

Wallack, L.M. 1994. *Media Advocacy and Public Health: Power for Prevention.* Newbury Park, CA: Sage Publications.

Wharf, B., and J. Wharf Higgins. 1992. "Healthy Communities." In B. Wharf, ed., *Communities and Social Policies in Canada.* Toronto: McClelland and Stewart.

Wharf Higgins, J., and L.W. Green. 1993. "The APHA Criteria for Development of Health Promotion Programs Applied to Four Healthy Community Projects in British Columbia." *Health Promotion International* 9: 311-20.

Whitehead, M. 1990. "The Concepts and Principles of Equity and Health." *Health Promotion International* 5: 217-28.

WHO (World Health Organization). 1978. *Alma Ata, 1978: Primary Health Care.* Geneva: WHO, Health for All Series, no. 1.

–. 1981. *Global Strategy for Health for All by the Year 2000.* Geneva: WHO, Health for All Series, no. 3.

Zimmerman, J.F. 1986. *Participatory Democracy: Populism Revived.* New York: Praeger.

Part 3:
Case Examples and the Reason for Hope

This final section of the volume ends with two case examples. The first study describes an attempt to put sustainability in action in the municipality of Richmond. The study documents the political difficulties that new sustainability policies face at the level of municipal government, which is probably the level of governance where these kinds of initiatives must be seen and made to work. The second case study is based on a cohort of sawmill workers employed in fourteen BC sawmills, three of which are located within a stone's throw of Richmond on the Fraser River, and six of the remaining eleven mills located along the Strait of Georgia within sixty kilometres of the Fraser River Delta. Both case studies speak, directly in the case of Richmond, and less directly in the case of the sawmill study, to issues of Fraser River Basin sustainability.

Besides the geographic fit, these illustrations are complementary in their focus. In the Richmond study, the success and failure in attempting to put sustainability in practice at the municipal level are outlined in detail so that readers come away with a sense of the "real politik" facing sustainability activists. In the sawmill study, the focus is technical rather than political as the author attempts to show how the ecological footprint tool described in Chapter 1 might be adapted to assess the changing ecological impact of an industry on a forest ecosystem. Together the case studies illustrate a range of political and technical sustainability concerns that face the Fraser River ecosystems.

The complementarity of these case studies, focused as they are on very different outcomes, arises because the issue of consumption is at the core of both studies. For example, the Richmond study describes in some detail how the municipality deals with a looming big box retail development project.

Big box retailing, as well as many of the retail, real estate, and industrial developments that take place within municipalities, involves the same kind of rationalization of production that has occurred with increasing rapidity in the BC sawmill industry and other industries worldwide. Increased efficiency and production leads to higher sales at the big box retail outlet. In the sawmills, gains in industrial efficiency lead directly to a faster pace of tree extraction from the forest ecosystems that supply its logs. The economic rationale for both types of development, the one within a municipality and the other as part of an industrial strategy, is based on unsustainable consumption.

As outlined in the Richmond example, the "issues must contain 'business case' contexts and terminology" in order to succeed. It is often difficult to cast the benefits of community sustainability in direct economic terms. This same problem occurs in the forest-products industry within and near the Fraser River Basin. However, in this case, concerns about the sustainability of the forests increasingly have an economic rationale as nontraditional forest uses, particularly from tourism, are providing an increasingly strong economic counterweight to the clear-cutting mentality which has dominated British Columbia's forest industry for so long.

Thus, as outlined in the Conclusion of this volume, there is prospect for hope. In the case of the forest industry, alternative users of the forests are increasingly bringing their concerns to the negotiating table at the grassroots, community, and municipal- and provincial-government level. The ability of forest companies to clear cut with impunity has been restricted as these alternative users of the forests gain economic and political clout.

These local signs of success are useful in countering what Robert Woollard, in the Conclusion of this volume, calls the "twin traps of denial and learned helplessness" which can paralyze sustainability activists. Also, as Woollard points out, "We did not slide unwillingly and inevitably into our current pattern of gross overconsumption. There are trends in the economy, and in our political and social relationships, that have served to simultaneously reinforce our consumption and insulate us from the realization of the ecological consequences of that consumption. These forces are subject to change."

7

The City of Richmond: Reflections on Sustainability in Action

Janette McIntosh and Robert F. Woollard

We believe that an understanding of sustainability can best be achieved through its practical application. This chapter outlines the processes involved in the joint initiative between the University of British Columbia Task Force on Healthy and Sustainable Communities and the City of Richmond, in British Columbia, Canada. Much has been written about the general framework and models for sustainability; however, the literature is inadequate in terms of the realistic applications of these models. This is due, in part, to methodological concerns on the part of academics and the difficulty in maintaining a long-term relationship between academia and municipal decision makers. This chapter describes the iterative process of our work together, including the successes, frustrations, and pitfalls of this process. Our description attempts to achieve a practical level of detail, while not overwhelming readers with nongeneralizable observations.

The Task Force on Healthy and Sustainable Communities came together from a range of disciplines, with the assumption that no single perspective or area of expertise was sufficient to address the mass of issues subsumed under the rubric of sustainability. Indeed, the task force was the beneficiary of an evolving consensus among policy makers that the increasing specialization of an academic culture, based on reductionism and quantitative analysis, had reached the point of diminishing returns as far as complex policy issues, such as sustainability, were concerned.

Why Community-Based Research?

As we turn to the discussion of our specific working relationship with the City of Richmond, it is important to consider two further aspects of our work: the importance of community interaction in refining the theoretical framework being developed, and the choice of the municipality as the appropriate level for such interaction. The specific criteria used to select the City of Richmond will be discussed later in this chapter.

The overarching question that was of interest to members of the task force was, Why do urban communities in North America act in a fashion that is, by any reasonable definition of the term, unsustainable? From our various disciplines we brought our individual concerns about ecological sustainability, health status, social equity, and resource consumption. These concerns reflected that the collective actions of society are resulting in the deterioration of conditions that are essential to our long-term survival. These conditions are at various stages of urgency and tractability but are generally moving in the wrong direction. Insofar as there was no shortage of either models or data to document these trends, we focused on why they were not being used to redress the drift away from sustainability. The agencies that supported our research shared this interest.

It was evident that no further speculation or model-building would be beneficial unless it was subjected to the "real world" in which sustainability-related policy decisions are being made. The disjunction between our society's stated support for sustainability and the contrary results of our collective actions could be addressed only by exploring the realm in which this disjunction takes place. Review of the literature on sustainability demonstrates that little has been published in this area. While some disciplines represented on the task force have histories and methods that address community interaction, the scope of "sustainability" left us apprehensive about our ability to identify and honour the conventional fine line between research and community development. Was the task force, for example, to do participatory research (Green et al. 1995)?

After significant discussion, the task force concurred that only through community-based research could we move beyond dry theorizing into the practical realm of testing the validity and utility of our ideas. Our chosen approach did bring a certain momentum to this task. The structure of the task force reflected our view that any attempt to approach a concept as broad and pervasive as community sustainability required a variety of perspectives and methods.

We also believed that if we could communicate with a nonacademic partner, we could overcome some of the communication problems inherent in working across our own academic boundaries. This would be particularly true if the communication was with a partner that was keen to develop the practical expression of our concepts and findings. If our concepts and models made sense in the context of day-to-day decision making for sustainability, it was very likely we were moving toward a deeper understanding of the area. On the other hand, if we were incapable of articulating an understandable and useful model for sustainability, it would mean that we were not developing a cohesive interdisciplinary understanding of the issues. We thus moved into the iterative process described below – one whereby concepts were developed and data collected by the task force, issues were presented by the community, and exchanges took place to refine our respective approaches.

Why a Municipality?

Once we decided to move in the direction of community interaction, we had to deal with the question of scale. What level of action or governance would be most usefully explored: national, provincial, municipal, or organizational? Task force members William Rees and Robert Woollard had worked previously on a report for the City of Vancouver entitled *Clouds of Change* (City of Vancouver 1990). This report recommended that policy actions be implemented at the municipal or regional level in order to have a practical impact on greenhouse-gas production. Therefore, issues such as urban form, zoning, and transportation policies, while influenced by higher levels of governance, find their ultimate practical expression through myriad daily decisions made by municipal and regional councils. Our experience with the City of Vancouver led us to believe that this would be the most fruitful level to explore the disjunction. (See Chapter 4 for an analysis of *Clouds of Change*.) Study at the municipal level promised to be not only manageable but also most likely to bear fruit in increasing our understanding of why we behave unsustainably.

A municipal community is not homogeneous. While a city represents a geopolitical entity, it is invariably composed of many smaller communities – communities based on common interests, ethnicity, socioeconomic status, and neighbourhoods. This complex interwoven skein can be intimidating as a whole, so we chose to address it at four levels: elected officials, senior municipal staff, formal community consultative committees, and informally engaged citizens.

What follows is a description of our work with the City of Richmond. We hope that the lessons learned from our research are sufficiently generalizable to facilitate others in undertaking similar projects elsewhere.

Why Richmond?

As a first step in selecting a community, a list of fourteen communities in British Columbia was developed based on population trends, economic activities, geographic regions, and communities' expressed interest. This was scaled down to six communities, based on cost of research, accessibility, and generalizability factors. The following selection criteria were used to further refine the choices: census data on population, immigration, density, percentage increases, age groups, education levels, employment, and income. Jurisdictional overlaps between health units, local health areas, school districts, and regional districts were also considered, as were urban form issues, Healthy Communities initiatives (see Chapter 6 for a discussion of the Canadian Healthy Communities Project), economic activity, and development trends. Each community was then rated by population size, geographic area, and distance from the University of British Columbia. Signs of intersectoral and innovative planning efforts, evidence of leadership, and willingness to participate in a joint research initiative were significant factors considered in our decision making.

For research cost and accessibility reasons, the list was reduced to three communities: Maple Ridge, Richmond, and Delta. The anticipated population growth and development trends, the jurisdictional boundary overlaps, and the Healthy Communities initiatives that were being funded in two of these communities were also factors of great interest to the task force. A presentation was made to all three municipalities by the task force chair and coordinator. Our contacts with the City of Richmond demonstrated it to be the most responsive and ready to participate in this joint initiative with the task force (Betz 1991).

The City of Richmond is an island city in the Fraser River Delta floodplain immediately south of Vancouver. (See Figure 7.1.) Richmond has undergone dramatic growth; its population grew from 108,492 in 1986 to 126,625 in 1991 (Canada, Census Canada 1987, 1992), and, further, from 145,000 people in 1996 to 154,700 in 1998 (City of Richmond 1996, 1999). The population mix is changing rapidly because of immigration from Asian countries such as Hong Kong, the Philippines, India, Taiwan, and mainland China (Canada, Employment and Immigration 1994). While English remains the dominant language, 31 percent of the student population speak Chinese at home (City of Richmond 1996). There is a mix of agricultural, aquatic, residential, industrial, commercial, recreational, and natural land uses. The city has a diversified economy, which has expanded rapidly beyond its original base in agriculture and fisheries. Thus, contrary to popular perception, Richmond is not solely a "bedroom community" in which most residents commute to Vancouver. Because Richmond is an island community, measurement of traffic and functional flows was possible. These factors, together with a commitment on the part of Richmond City staff, led the task force members to select it as the first case study community for our research on planning healthy and sustainable communities.

Research Process
On 23 January 1992, the task force began working with members of Richmond's senior administration and representatives from the departments of Planning, Health, and Parks and Leisure. What became a four-year working relationship began with meetings to clarify objectives and direction. The work evolved through an iterative process facilitated by open communication, graduate student research projects, and an overall sense of commitment by both groups. A number of "integrative techniques" (Klein 1990) were

Figure 7.1

City of Richmond, British Columbia

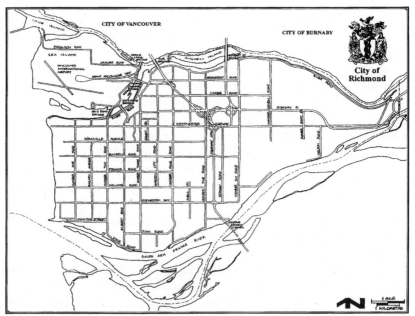

Source: City of Richmond (1993).

used. These included regular meetings, periodic reports and reviews, joint presentations and papers, and joint organizing and planning. Detailed information was gathered for this volume using notes from various meetings held in Richmond during the life of this project.

A number of key themes and facilitative factors for effective partnerships had been identified by the fall of 1993 and were refined with input from the workshop participants at the provincial "Making It Work! New Directions in Health" conference, held in late October 1993.

The four themes that emerged from this iterative process were vision, communication, action, and reflection. As Figure 7.2 indicates, these connect in a cyclical fashion, with each facilitating the others.

- *Vision*, or shared commitment to purpose, can be facilitated by a variety of factors. It requires ideas and knowledge, imagination, respect, commitment, and opportunities to revisit the vision, as well as having the means for taking action.
- *Communication* requires development of a common language and working relationship based on mutual trust and respect. It can be further facilitated by communication skills, open-mindedness, flexibility, adaptability, and humility.

• *Action* can be facilitated by factors such as specific goals and products, means to accomplish set goals (e.g., resources, manageable timelines, and regular contact), and effective translation of theory to practice. Patience is a key factor, as people have different needs and priorities.
• *Reflection* involves evaluation and feedback. Some of the facilitative factors are confidence, honesty, constructive criticism, and specific resources.

As shown in Figure 7.2, the key themes and facilitative factors were useful for reflecting upon the first two years of the project and guiding our work during the remaining two years.

The task force and our Richmond counterparts had the same goals in mind: first, to develop concepts related to sustainability; and second, to apply these concepts within a real community through policy and decision making. New ideas emerged and gave direction, language, and focus to the research. The theories and concepts have been explored through graduate student research projects and case studies as described below.

Research Outcome I: Conceptual Development
The concepts related to healthy and sustainable communities presented in this chapter were developed primarily from existing theory and related literature. For example, the ecological footprint analysis is an extension of Carrying Capacity Theory applied to humans (see Chapter 1). Some concepts were subsequently refined and revised through the exchange of ideas between partners in the course of the work. Others, such as social caring capacity, evolved by identifying additional, equally important social dimensions of the research. (See Introduction and Chapter 3.) As other chapters describe the appropriated carrying capacity/ecological footprint and social caring capacity concepts in detail, we focus here on the development of the conceptual framework and a brief summary of the appropriated carrying capacity and social caring capacity linkages.

The task force initially adopted a model for sustainability based on the work of Hancock et al. (Canadian Medical Association 1991) (see Figure 7.3). This conceptual model defines sustainability in terms of a balance among economic, environmental, and social health objectives, such that all can be sustained over the long term. A community, policy, or project must consider all three realms to ensure both their separate and collective long-term viability. This approach served a useful integrative function in a variety of presentation and workshop settings. It has heuristic value in shifting individuals and departments from a narrow focus on their primary realm of interest to an acknowledgement of the relevance and significance of the other two realms. It was, therefore, seen as a useful tool for broader thinking and a descriptor of a desirable state.

However, it did not translate into an effective tool for achieving

Figure 7.2

An interdisciplinary model: themes for realizing vision and action

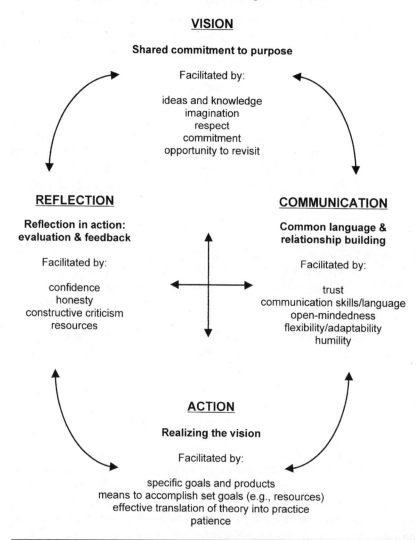

VISION

Shared commitment to purpose

Facilitated by:

ideas and knowledge
imagination
respect
commitment
opportunity to revisit

REFLECTION

**Reflection in action:
evaluation & feedback**

Facilitated by:

confidence
honesty
constructive criticism
resources

COMMUNICATION

**Common language &
relationship building**

Facilitated by:

trust
communication skills/language
open-mindedness
flexibility/adaptability
humility

ACTION

Realizing the vision

Facilitated by:

specific goals and products
means to accomplish set goals (e.g., resources)
effective translation of theory into practice
patience

sustainability. While it implied that there are inherent trade-offs between realms to achieve the desired state, it did not provide for a mechanism to make such trade-offs explicit. While it was extremely valuable in communicating the necessity of linking the various realms in policy development, it failed the test of utility for decision makers – if it could not make the trade-offs explicit, how could it provide an opportunity for the community to

Figure 7.3

Three key ingredients of community sustainability

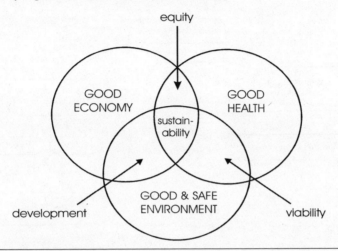

Source: Boothroyd et al. (1994).

choose? We, therefore, had to place this model within a broader context, where it became a focusing device in a cycle of change toward sustainability. A number of iterations led to the following expanded version of the social learning process (Figure 7.4).[1]

Previous chapters have outlined the power of the ecological footprint tool and the concept of social caring capacity as key factors in long-term social viability. If properly applied in the manner represented by the expanded model, we have found that these tools and concepts help to stimulate a desire for change toward sustainability. They provide a means to assess which policies are likely to be most effective in moving society in the desired direction, and they create the possibility of measuring the effectiveness of the chosen policies. While there are issues of scale when we apply the model to various policies and projects, this broad conceptualization has been helpful in advancing our collective understanding, and potential operationalization, of a sustainable community.

Health concerns are prime factors in a community's interest and ability to move toward sustainability. Most non-Aboriginal Canadians have a health status that is enviable by global standards. However, it is arguable that this is being purchased, in part, at the expense of the health of our global and local ecosystems and community well-being. To better represent the reality that human systems are, in fact, subsystems embedded in natural systems, we developed the following conceptualization of the relationships among the health of individuals, their community, and their ecosystem.

Figure 7.4

Community change towards sustainability

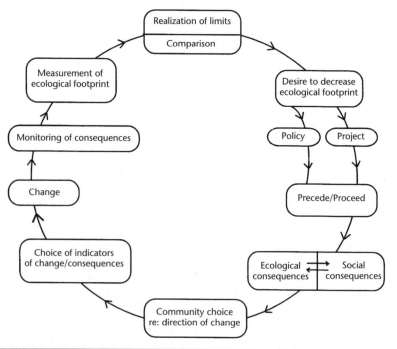

Source: Woollard et al. (1999).

Figure 7.5 shows a nested hierarchy in which an individual existing within a community derives his or her health from that community, and in turn contributes to its health (see Chapter 6). The community is in a similar state of obligate dependence on the health of its sustaining ecosystem while contributing (for good or ill) to the health of that ecosystem. As we moved into a greater understanding of the theory of complex adaptive systems (Boothroyd et al. 1994), this hierarchical conceptualization became even more useful in understanding the dependency relationships among these three levels in the system (see Introduction).

Our work with the City of Richmond also underscored the importance of arriving at an understanding of the relationship between the concepts of appropriated carrying capacity (later rephrased as "ecological footprint") and social caring capacity. It became obvious that any planned major reductions in the ecological footprint would have to be achieved in a way that did not seriously disturb the social health of the community. Conversely, it raised the possibility that various ways of improving the social caring capacity of a community might actually *offset* some of the

Figure 7.5

Order of health: ecosystem, community, and personal health

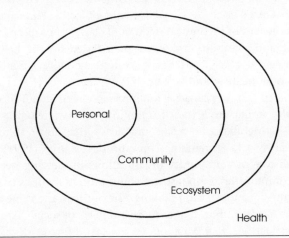

Personal

Community

Ecosystem

Health

Source: Boothroyd et al. (1994).

demands that community was placing on the ecosystem. (See Chapter 3 for detailed discussion on this dilemma.)

Research Outcome II: Concepts – Theory to Application

As for the conceptual frameworks described above, the application of theory to practice involved several iterations as new issues and interests emerged. These issues and interests generally relate to product, process, and policies (and politics) involving people and their interactions (for instance, working relationships) that led to shaping the interdisciplinary model (Figure 7.2). The key themes of the model, vision, communication, action, and reflection will be examined more closely below through the examples of our own research with the City of Richmond.

Vision: Defining the Research Agenda through a Shared Commitment to Purpose

Vision, for the purposes of this research, is defined as a related collection of shared concerns, goals, or interests. A common vision can be developed through sharing ideas and knowledge, developing a mutually respectful relationship, sharing a joint commitment to the realization of the vision, creating opportunities to revisit the vision, and having a plan as well as the means to act. A number of student research projects were conducted during the summer of 1991, and these proved to be valuable in shaping our ideas and research agenda.

Five graduate students explored various topics and issues relevant to healthy and sustainable communities. Konkin (1991) examined the nature of traditional health indicators in British Columbia and called for more socially relevant and useful indicators. Lawson (1991) emphasized the need for a balanced look at subjective and objective indicators, while pointing out the lack of theoretical rigour and clarity of purpose in existing quality-of-life and liveability-index research. Based on the belief that a community needs to consider at least its current ecological situation before acting to become healthy and sustainable, Wackernagel (1991) suggested that appropriated carrying capacity might be an effective indicator for policy makers to understand their community's relationship to nature. Perkins (1991) highlighted several practical urban-form solutions for achieving healthy and sustainable communities. Nairne (1991) carefully examined the role of community organizations in creating healthy and sustainable communities, emphasizing communities' abilities to carry out their own planning and decision making. She outlined the value of indicators as change agents rather than as mere monitors of social change.

These investigations were valuable to the task force in developing an understanding of the connections between local communities and their larger spatial and political context, whether it was provincial, national, or global. They also served to focus the thinking of our Richmond counterparts as they came to grips with the practical expression of sustainability.

Several meetings and workshops took place in 1992 to clarify goals and determine a specific research focus. Among the issues identified by the City of Richmond staff were social and community needs associated with densification (the redevelopment of the downtown core area), changing population and neighbourhoods, preservation of the Agricultural Land Reserve, and waste management. All these issues relate to the larger policy area of land use. Richmond was facing the prospect of adding 40,000 more people to the city centre area by the year 2010. Meetings were held with citizens who were members of the City Centre Steering Committee and Richmond Community Services Advisory Council's Social Issues Task Force to explore specific design issues related to shared public spaces, safety, and accessibility. At the same time, the appropriated carrying capacity concept and the calculations were also being refined and applied to the City of Richmond. Thus, we jointly identified the need to explore ways to apply the concept of sustainability as it relates to land use, our natural resources, and social networks.

Communication: Developing a Common Language and Working Relationship

The various opportunities for dialogue and exchange that we had while working together allowed the researchers and staff to develop a sense of trust and respect. Two-way communication skills are essential in building trust and respect within a group as ideas are exchanged and modified. Tied to a person's ability to listen is the capacity to maintain an open mind so that flexibility and adaptation can mark the development of ideas. Thus, humility becomes a key facilitative factor in communicating thoughts and ideas within a group with diverse backgrounds and professional interests.

Formal and informal communication was established between the groups, primarily through the task force coordinator and selected staff members in the Planning Department. As noted earlier, the integrative techniques (Klein 1990) used in the research process primarily centre around effective communication. The methods used are described below as a general overview of the project.

During the first year of the joint initiative, 1992, there were three large group meetings, four subgroup meetings, and six workshops or consultations for the purposes of clarifying our goals and determining our research focus. The workshops and consultation meetings were designed to get input from citizen advisory groups on social and environmental issues. We began 1993 with a joint strategic planning workshop, followed by two workshops exploring the concept of social caring capacity. A joint presentation between the City of Richmond and the task force followed in the spring of 1993 at an international health-promotion conference in Vancouver. Efforts were made during the summer to bring practical relevance to the work by involving six research students in projects directly related to, or specified by, the City of Richmond. In the fall of 1993, as a final acknowledgement of the two-year Sustainable Communities Initiative funded by the Science Council of British Columbia, the task force and the City of Richmond coorganized and cohosted a symposium in Richmond entitled "Sustainability in Action: How do we make it happen?" This featured our joint efforts on theory and practice (Task Force on Healthy and Sustainable Communities 1994).

A transition was marked in 1993 and 1994, as the task force joined a new research initiative, the Lower Fraser Basin Ecosystem Study, funded by the Federal Tri-Council Secretariat. At the same time, the City of Richmond held municipal elections that resulted in changes to council leadership and its agenda. Following a symposium debriefing meeting in October 1993, a "working group" meeting was held in November with people who remained interested and able to continue working together. Goals and objectives were reviewed and refined, and a general outline of steps to be taken was discussed. An agreement was reached regarding the role and function of the smaller working group, rather than for the larger, corporate groups in Richmond and the task force as a whole. A letter of endorsement for our joint initiative was received from the City of Richmond's director of planning in early December (Mann 1993). This gave us added confidence to pursue further research interests, including the social caring capacity concept, the linkages between the ecological footprint or appropriated carrying capacity and social caring capacity concepts, and their policy relevance and applications.

Another joint presentation related to our work was made between one of the Richmond planners and the task force coordinator at a Design Week '94 sustainability conference in early March. Also, following the City of Richmond's stated interest in examining the impacts of big box retail[2] complexes on sustainability, a case study approach was taken to explore various criteria for evaluating the impacts. A small working group consisting of five to seven members met regularly throughout the year. The Big Box Retail Case Study resulted in setting the groundwork for a sustainability checklist, which was developed with the City of Richmond planning staff later in 1994 and 1995.

Our working relationship changed over time. Critical to this evolution was the enthusiastic involvement of Richmond's senior officials. It was essential, as it is in any participatory model of research, to have the staff and members of the task force involved in the discussions and design of the research throughout the process (Green et al. 1995). We came to realize the importance of having the councillors onboard, since they directly affect the corporate agenda and the various roles and mandates of their staff. Council members, in this case, were key enablers for taking action.

Action: Realizing the Vision
Once there was philosophical agreement on the concept of sustainability, we could set the agenda in motion. However, patience and flexibility were required throughout this time. Some of the issues that arose during our research will help explain the actions that followed.

Background
Some unanticipated issues affected our research, including staff changes within the City of Richmond in late 1992 and early 1993; the postponement of Richmond's City Centre Plan; adjustments within the Advisory Committee on Environment, a citizen advisory group; municipal elections in November 1993, resulting in organizational restructuring in late 1994 and early 1995; and changes in focus and dynamics within the task force during 1994 and part of 1995.

One of the pivotal events in our work was the change in Richmond staff leadership. The manager of Policy Planning, one of the key initiators of this project, left the City of Richmond in the fall of 1993. Shortly after that, a senior staff member from the Health Department, who was involved in our research, changed departments. This affected the project in several ways: loss of key leadership and continuity slowed the conceptual development and focus; the level of interest and commitment changed to a more product/output-based approach; some staff members were lost to other projects and mandates; and the issues became more focused within the Planning Department, with less involvement from other departments.

In early 1993, Richmond staff members were notified of council's decision to postpone the public consultation phase for the city centre plan (Mann 1993). A joint strategic planning workshop, held late in January 1993, helped recapture some of the staff and task force members' interest and enthusiasm for a continued working relationship aimed at applying the concept of sustainability in their planning efforts.

The involvement of Richmond's citizens through various advisory groups, such as the aforementioned Social Issues Task Force, was helpful in our research. Unfortunately, the environmental groups in Richmond, while present, were not particularly focused at that time. We received limited input and participation from one of Richmond's formal consultative committees, the Advisory Committee on the Environment, because of structural and administrative issues of their own. Some of these stemmed from political decisions and actions related to a particular development site in Richmond.

There is value in having a ripe political climate and the right timing for this kind of initiative. The project began with positive support from all sides. Our work climaxed in the fall of 1993 when it involved many staff members, managers, and councillors at the symposium "Sustainability in Action." The symposium provided each of us with the opportunity to not only introduce the concepts described above to a general audience but to also explore ways to make them more real and useful to community members and decision makers. In November 1993, a municipal election resulted in fewer "green" and more "prodevelopment" members of council. Furthermore, it was felt by staff and council that the late 1994 to early 1995 organizational restructuring created a "leaner and keener" approach to projects with greater emphasis on output and cost-effectiveness. The task force was dealing with its own issues during this time, such as differences in approach to research, presentation, authorship, and leadership styles. This precluded it from the development of an effective working relationship with the new city council, something that would have made ongoing work more effective. As we demonstrate later in this chapter, the City of Richmond has undergone a further transformation that has reversed some of the areas of concern evident in 1995.

Examples of Action
In taking action, we recognized the importance of having (1) specific goals and anticipated products; (2) the means to accomplish set goals, such as resources, manageable timelines, and regular contact, both within and between groups; and (3) an effective translation of theory to practice.

These three points will be further explored through the examination of some projects that we undertook with the City of Richmond.

Specific Goals and Products   Cooperative interagency work becomes more rewarding the more directly relevant and tangible the products. In the case of Richmond, this success took three different forms: the 1993 summer student research projects; the Big Box Retail Case Study; and the development of a sustainability checklist.

Summer Student Research Projects: During the spring of 1993, we defined research topics that were relevant and useful to both parties. The City of Richmond's expressed interest and concern was related to urban form, transportation, and community economic-development issues. The task force remained interested in the ecological footprint/appropriated carrying capacity and social caring capacity as decision-making tools for sustainability. Thus, topics were chosen and researched by graduate students, resulting in the following papers:

- "The Social Caring Capacity of a Community: A Literature Review," by Lesley Aronson and Melanie Charles.
- "The Freedom to Stay: Transportation and Appropriated Carrying Capacity in the Context of Richmond's City Centre," by Graham Beck.
- "Urban Form and Appropriated Carrying Capacity: An Examination of the 'City Centre' of Richmond, BC," by Anthony Parker.
- "Community Based Economies Planning for Healthy and Sustainable Communities: The Case of Richmond, BC," by Molly Harrington.
- "Environmental Awareness and Sustainability Efforts in the City of Richmond: A Case Study," by Joanna Sale.

Much of the research took place in Richmond or used information provided to the student researchers by Richmond staff and residents. Each paper was presented as a report to the City of Richmond and findings were presented in workshops at the fall symposium, "Sustainability in Action." Some of the research was also incorporated into Richmond's City Centre Area Plan and its Implementation Strategy (City of Richmond 1995).

Big Box Retail Case Study: In late fall of 1993, the task force was invited by the City of Richmond staff to participate in an application of the sustainability principles and framework. The priority issue selected by Richmond was big box retail, as some decisions had to be made on a large, multinational home-improvement chain that had submitted a development application to council. As a result, some members of the task force got involved in the discussion and planning efforts with the City of

Richmond. The first meeting with members of the Advisory Council on the Environment was held in January 1994 to discuss the sustainability concepts and how the framework might apply to the big box retail issue. Since council had already requested an economic impact assessment from its staff on the large-scale home-improvement proposal for early May, the group decided to focus on identifying related ecological and social concerns and developing a logical decision-making framework that would include all three key ingredients of sustainability (Figure 7.3).

A working group was set up to develop a draft sustainability decision-making framework for big box retail and to refine and categorize relevant questions. By mid-March 1994, the group was discussing a skeleton sustainability impact report for the purposes of reviewing the questions under these headings: public health, social equity, community character, transportation, land-use, civic design, and economic impacts. Discussion also began on the measurement of some of these effects. The economic issues were designated to two City of Richmond staff members, and the ecological and social-related issues were referred to two task force members. This led to discussions of the format of a sustainability report to council. The working group sought input from various staff of Policy and Planning for the next draft prepared by Richmond. The economic impact study was presented to council before bringing all of the broader concepts together. The comments received at that presentation were to be incorporated into the next presentation scheduled for August, at which time the ecological and social dimensions would be included.

In early July, for reasons unknown to the group, the development application was withdrawn. Despite the sudden loss of immediacy, some Richmond staff members felt the need to set some policies related to the big box retail issue and other developments, and expressed their desire to continue working with us on a sustainability framework.

Sustainability Checklist: The same working group that examined the big box retail issue met, at Richmond's request, in August 1994 to discuss the necessary refinements of a draft sustainability report and the details of the next steps. Richmond staff hoped that this effort might lead to council's endorsement of an overall strategy toward sustainability. There were four outstanding issues related to the draft:

1   the inclusion of off-site considerations in order to have people think about broader impacts
2   the clarification of where ecological footprint and social caring capacity fit in
3   the degree of specificity required for the form's questions and responses

4   the appropriate scale of application (e.g., residential or large developments only).

A detailed work plan was developed with a goal to present the material
to council in December 1994. However, because of competing priorities
resulting from Richmond's organizational restructuring and the lack of formal communication and focus given by the task force to this project during this time, the working pace slowed significantly.

In early July 1995, the task force received a copy of the newly revised sustainability checklist prepared by one of Richmond's Planning staff members. Planners with the Environment and Land Use Section of Urban
Development intended that the checklist be filled out by developers in
conjunction with applications for development permits or major subdivi-
sions. It was designed to meet a number of objectives:

1   to raise consciousness about the relationship of development to
impacts in the community
2   to provide a tool for developers to present information and for planners to assess developments
3   to standardize the information exchange between staff in Urban
Development and the developers
4   to provide a yardstick to measure if, and how, developers are making
projects more sustainable (Beran 1995).

Following revisions based on input from staff and task force members, a
report to council was submitted by the manager of Environment and Land
Use with two staff recommendations:

1   Council authorize a six-month test of the sustainability checklist, on a
voluntary basis, with rezoning and development permit applications.
(This would exclude rezoning permits for single-family or duplex units.)
2   Before the end of the six-month trial period, staff be directed to report
back to council on a more permanent policy and procedure for the sustainability checklist (Atienza 1995).

One of the task force cochairs, Robert Woollard, together with Eleanor
Atienza, Richmond's manager of Environment and Land Use Section, were
invited to make a joint presentation to council on 2 October 1995. The
presentation was in two parts: a conceptual introduction to sustainability
and an explanation of the checklist. Following a discussion, one of the
councillors, who was an enthusiastic supporter of the checklist, moved
that the recommendation be amended so that the sustainability checklist

would become mandatory for all rezoning and permit applications, except for rezoning to single-family and duplex dwellings. This recommendation was defeated by a vote of six to two. One week later, one of the councillors reintroduced the original staff recommendation for consideration. Following statements from each elected official, a vote was taken, and the recommendation was defeated by a tie vote of four to four. Those in favour, including the mayor, felt that active planning for sustainability was necessary and wished to begin addressing it at the level through such efforts as the sustainability checklist. It was seen to provide some guidance toward more ecological and socially conscious design and development. Those opposed expressed concerns about costs and resources, demands on staff time, duplication of existing efforts, more bureaucracy and red tape, and the belief that bylaw changes would be more appropriate. Despite some enthusiasm, it appeared that cynicism and lack of enthusiasm toward sustainability issues remained.

Means to Accomplish Set Goals   Actions, such as the projects and initiatives described above, are best facilitated by having strategies for achieving the set goals. These include manageable timelines, regular contacts, and resources, primarily in the form of financial and personnel commitments. Money was required to develop and refine the ecological footprint concept through investment in a PhD student, summer student research projects, and conference attendance. A full-time research coordinator, acting as a key liaison between the two organizations, was essential for the maintenance of research focus and progress. The various summer projects had defined timelines with a particular focus. This made the research efforts more productive and useful to both groups involved. The Big Box Retail Case Study and sustainability checklist were spread out over time, and thus more susceptible to the changes and demands within the structures and organizations involved. The summer research projects engaged all researchers and staff members in the project since they communicated with one another frequently through formal and informal meetings. Similarly, the Big Box Retail Case Study progressed with regular contacts in focused, task-oriented meetings. These experiences underlined the importance of clear goals and timelines, a problem orientation, and effective resources to respond to the problems.

Effective Translation of Theory to Practice   A key factor in translating theory into practice is the ability to share relevant concepts that are mutually developed and explored. In this case, the task force was interested in applying the conceptual tools that were being developed and refined in a "real world" context; the City of Richmond was interested in some practical ways to take action toward sustainability. The challenge of translating theory into a usable language, and applying it in a policy and decision-making framework, remained throughout the project.

The ecological footprint concept was perceived by Richmond officials as academic and not translatable into policy because of the language, calculation details, and the seemingly less relevant global scale of the concept. The concept was powerful in the broader context of shifting consciousness about the problem of overconsumption. However, questions remained regarding the utility of the tool during the efforts made to apply the ecological footprint concept to the Big Box Retail Case Study and the sustainability checklist. It proved cumbersome when attempts were made to apply it at the practical decision-making level. Applications such as the approach to big box retailing and the development of a sustainability checklist were attempted, but neither project received enough resources nor data to allow for adequate refinement, calculations, and comparisons.

Similar observations could be made about the social caring capacity development and application. It was expected that this would be developed further and applied jointly with appropriated carrying capacity within the municipal context. However, a number of factors contributed to delays in linking the two concepts and applying them within the City of Richmond. These were mainly a later start in conceptualization for social caring capacity (in 1993 as opposed to 1991 for appropriated carrying capacity), a lack of resources, lack of a "champion" to devote time to researching the concept, and the differing expectations regarding the conceptual development and its use.

While resource constraints and external factors limited the full deployment of some of the tools at the various scales of application within the City of Richmond, their heuristic value was apparent to both researchers and City staff (City of Richmond 1995; Westland Resource Group 1998). The work was responsive to Richmond's needs at the time, even though it did present some challenges for researchers working within resource and disciplinary constraints. There is a role for researchers in the continuation and expansion of this work with Richmond, and possibly in exploring similar work with other communities within the Lower Fraser Basin.

Reflection: Reflection in Action
Reflection requires time for evaluation and feedback. To effectively reflect within a group, the people involved should have trust and confidence in one another, give constructive criticism, and be able to make resources, such as time and money, available for this purpose.

What became most evident through this research process is the need to assess what is being done while continuing to act, a phrase Donald Schön (1987) has termed "reflection in action." This differs from the more traditional research method of observing, analyzing, and, sometimes, observing again. The research with Richmond was dependent on our ability to reflect, take stock, and revise our own actions based on the environment in which action is taking place. For example, the Big Box Retail Case Study was derived from a real need expressed by Richmond. Similarly, the shift from the conceptualization of the appropriated carrying capacity/social caring capacity cycle of change model to a simplified sustainability checklist was a reflection of Richmond's need for a simplified, product-oriented approach appropriate for council. This change in approach required a rethinking by the task force of its role in relation to the City.

During the Big Box Retail Case Study, questions were raised within the task force about the nature of our involvement with Richmond and the research direction. Members endorsed the sustainability framework of decreasing appropriated carrying capacity and increasing social caring capacity. However, some members expressed their discomfort with the apparent consultative role that was being taken on, and the expectations we might be building at the community level. They felt that the task force should conduct research and not participate in community development. An argument was made for continuing the discussions with Richmond on the big box retail issue as one concrete example of the application of the appropriated carrying capacity and social caring capacity concepts. Proponents of this argument felt that we should take the opportunity to gather data and explore the utility of the concepts, and prepare for later integration of the social caring capacity tool as it develops. These proponents claimed that this exercise would be useful for maintaining the relationship we had built with Richmond. Although it was a practical link to the social caring capacity research, the concept was still being tested and redefined through community focus groups. Work with Richmond continued without a consensus being reached by the task force as to how to proceed. This may have been one of the main reasons for the decreased interest and involvement by the group as a whole with Richmond.

Upon reflection, a number of observations can be made related to the inner workings of the task force and the nature of interdisciplinarity. First and foremost, the task force is an interdisciplinary group, which began "a process for achieving an integrative synthesis" (Klein 1990) with the issue of sustainability and a commitment to make a difference. With time and opportunities for dialogue, a shift occurred from a multidisciplinary group to an interdisciplinary group. Second, time was required (approximately two years) to produce comfortable relationships within this group; there were fundamental value shifts. For example, the concept of the ecological footprint expanding beyond ecological principles to health (Figure 7.5), the notion of health promotion exploring some ecological foundations (Green, Potvin, and Richard 1996), and the newly explored connections between health, wealth, and consumption (see Chapter 2). Third, attempts were made to resolve the differences in disciplinary language, approach, and worldviews. Overall, despite some failures, those attempts have been successful. Fourth, resources were allocated for a full-time coordinator to manage the task force activities. This helped maintain focus, direction, and action. Last, the task force has been involved in ongoing reflection in action. We have shifted thinking and direction throughout this research and continue to reflect on our actions in order to explore future opportunities to work together.

The four years of joint work by the task force and the City of Richmond have taught us several important lessons. The positive experience included the opportunity to work together within changing times, ideas, and mandates; the ability to jointly plan and organize the "Sustainability in Action" symposium in September 1993; and the process of shared decision making used in defining our research. The more challenging lessons related to communication between, and within, the two groups. These included the translation of academic language into something meaningful to communities, the nature of leadership and representation, the limitations of organizational structure, and the issue of timing as it relates to the changing political climate and community needs.

Specifically, the structural and organizational issues that have been identified relate to the scope and length of the project, the size of bureaucracies involved, and the degree of buy-in by the City's senior officials and management. The scope was thought to have been too big and the time period too long. This affected staff involvement and the overall level of commitment. Designing projects with immediate and manageable timelines was perceived to be more effective. Long-term projects risk losing their sense of urgency and passion unless the specific goals are revisited regularly. The difficulty of working within large bureaucracies was compounded by changes in management, council, and organizational structure, all of which took place in Richmond within one-and-a-half years. Staffing, mandates, demands, and expectations needed to be adjusted accordingly. Lastly, it was noted that the City administrator and departmental heads were not included early enough in the process. Having their support was strongly recommended to gain the necessary backing and interest from council, management, and staff.

A number of Richmond officials expressed their hopes for continuation of the project, either by implementing the concepts or forming a renewed partnership. There is also an overall sense of disappointment as goals were only partially realized. Most agreed, however, that the foundations have been laid for various initiatives already started within Richmond City. Should such a renewed phase two come about, it has been suggested that the task force seek the senior-level decision makers' buy-in early on in the project. An appropriate timing for approaching council might be after an election, when new players are introduced. In one Richmond official's view, the timing might be right now as the Greater Vancouver Regional District and the City of Richmond are both presently "requiring a true response to environmental and economic concerns" in this region.

The interactive nature of community-based research initiatives, such as this one with the City of Richmond, takes time to nurture and develop. Throughout the relationship it is necessary to maintain open communication, both within and between the organizations involved, to ensure support by all members. Having a designated contact person in each group can facilitate this process, especially in the exchange between the groups involved. Also, at the beginning, and during the project as deemed necessary, efforts must be made to:

1   begin with clearly stated objectives, timelines, and resource expectations and revisit them frequently throughout the project
2   learn the City's bureaucratic structures and establish contact with the appropriate persons in order to win their support
3   introduce the project and concepts being explored by the group to council and have periodic updates
4   maintain a broad representational base and level of involvement.

These will not only help clarify roles in the process of working together but will also secure a well-accepted, stable, and long-term relationship.

Conclusions and Future Considerations

From summative interviews conducted with Richmond officials, a picture emerged of a level of government severely constrained in its scope of action and consideration. The importance of this level of government was referred to earlier in this chapter, as it has the *potential* to control major inputs into the ecological and social health of the community – and by aggregate action, the major global ecological issues. The admonition from another generation to "think globally, act locally" was seen to have great potential at this level.

However, it is also at this level that the major portion of the disjunction between global words and local actions takes place. It is important to understand why this is the case. While the forces unleashed at the local level (such as greenhouse gases) have tremendous cumulative impact on the global commons, there are global and national forces that act in the opposite direction. For example, two of the major international and national political forces impacting on Richmond are cutbacks as a method of deficit reduction and the downloading of increased responsibilities and decreased resources to carry them out to lower levels of government. These two trends meet at the municipal level, where responsibilities for service are shifted to a level of government that cannot, by law, run a deficit. One staff member stated that "downloading is killing community council." In the initial debilitating period of response, before more effective patterns were re-established, there was a tendency to refer matters back to staff as a method of deferring spending. Proposals that had a clear product, with a clear end point and cost, are more likely to get a favourable response.

Issues must contain "business case" contexts and terminology so they can be handled as discrete entities. While general concepts such as "built form" are of interest, they too must be crafted in very local terms in order to be processed. Direct benefits, such as reduction of energy consumption or accessibility for the disabled, are manageable; more general issues of community sustainability are not. The Richmond City Council, in common with many other local governments, is often more sensitive to various interest groups (including community groups and developers) than to its staff. On many issues, for example, people with disabilities, there are specific lobby and advocacy groups. However, in the City of Richmond, environmental organizations and advocacy groups did not have a very strong voice. Because of the lack of a sense of immediacy surrounding environmental issues, the voice of concern for longer-term ecological health tended to be overpowered by a number of other issues. This is another general trend noted in our society (Saul 1995) wherein advocacy has shifted away from broad social concerns to specific competing groups. Outsiders tend not to be accepted if they are representing a specific interest within the community.

The abiding conundrum is that municipal polities tend to be parochial, while the issues are much larger. It would appear that individuals are waiting for some as yet undefined larger force to change the workings of council so that new policies can be developed to support sustainability. Thus, waiting has replaced direct lobbying in support of the environment. This sense of waiting for someone or something else to force change toward sustainability is not unique to Richmond. It derives, in part, from the inherent difficulty of understanding the full ecological and social ramifications of *any* decision. In the absence of such understanding, there is a natural tendency to focus on very immediate issues, whose direct consequences are obvious and of importance to the individual or group making the decision. If the larger ecological and social forces seem inexplicable and immutable, there is even more reason to wait and see what happens. Particular and immediate environmental concerns – such as development of agricultural land – might find some advocates and opponents, but the larger context of sustainability is less amenable to thoughtful discussion by a municipal council. Given that the agenda is crowded by numerous issues competing for limited attention and resources, it is understandable that council members might be disinclined to add further complexity to their lives. It is equally predictable that the community at large might adopt a posture of "wait and see" in the face of potential threats to its future health.

The cross-linking of issues on the agenda – a necessary prerequisite for meaningful action toward sustainability – presents further difficulties. For example, while rapid transit had an intuitive appeal for linking Richmond with the Vancouver region, its desirability was compromised by the realization that densification of the city centre would be a required condition. Since disaggregating this package would be counterproductive as far as automobile use is concerned, this is an example of how the separation of issues into discrete "manageable" portions contributes to the disjunction between an expressed desire to act sustainably and support for initiatives that would allow it. One of the Richmond officials comments that "we are building into a higher density mentality in our kids and they will not be interested in commuting." A generational change may be required. The question abides: Do we have the time?

The working relationship with Richmond has proven to be invaluable at many levels. By refining and honing our information, knowledge, and management tools, we can affirm the *possibility* that a pattern of isolated, parochial decision making might move into a more inclusive and balanced era. In this way, when decisions are made, their social and ecological consequences will have equal place with their economic consequences. We have had more than a glimpse into the workings of a city wrestling with the problem of sustainability. We have also had an opportunity to compare it with at least one other municipal government (see Chapter 4), and received reassurance that some of our findings have a degree of generalizability. Some of the successes that Richmond has enjoyed give us hope that, while the notion of sustainability may be complex and difficult, it will *not be impossible* to achieve.

The bulk of this chapter represents descriptions of and reflections on a four-year intense relationship with the City of Richmond. Subsequent to 1996 and the previous defeat of the proposal for a trial of the sustainability checklist, interaction between the task force and the staff of the City of Richmond diminished. At that point, it was clear that *formal* consideration of the integrated concept of sustainability was unlikely to proceed in any meaningful way. Follow-up discussions in 1999 indicated that this was an accurate prediction. Equally accurate were the predictions about downloading of responsibilities from provincial to municipal jurisdictions without attendant resources. The provincial granting program has seen significant reductions. The cumulative impact of these and other related concerns might have been expected to lead to a demoralized, less responsive and less adaptable (hence less sustainable) municipal governing structure. Certainly this appears to have been the case in many jurisdictions in Canada.

In fact, the opposite appears to have obtained in Richmond. When members of the task force reinterviewed three senior staff with whom we had worked before and one new manager at Richmond City Hall, it was apparent that the accomplishments of the intervening three years were considerable and were at variance from what might have been predicted. These interviews did not provide a deep or broad enough examination to constitute a meaningful assessment of the interdisciplinary model outlined in Figure 7.2. However, certain elements taken together with the consistently upbeat nature of the conversations are relevant to the considerations of this volume.

While we must be circumspect in extrapolating too much from limited data, it is apparent that in a substantial way, there has been a transformation of the way business is conducted at City Hall. This was apparent from the time of initial contact with custodial staff as task force members approached City Hall through the very welcoming and efficient reception staff, passing staff members who spontaneously stopped to offer direction, up to the clear and enthusiastic descriptions of the new state of affairs by the four management staff. It was interesting to note that while the formal construct of a "policy on sustainability" had no obvious presence, there were strong elements of sustainable decision making in the re-envisioned City of Richmond. A detailed strategic planning exercise had resulted in a new vision statement that appeared to have remarkable acceptance at all levels. Their vision "for the City of Richmond to be the most appealing, liveable, and well-managed community in Canada" (City of Richmond 1998) has apparently found significant resonance in a modified policy-development and decision-making structure. This seems to have effectively broken down a number of the barriers that previously compromised integrated decision making around such things as transportation policy. A specific anecdote worth mentioning is a recent exercise wherein all the senior managers went on a community bus tour together to share observations about the active projects and policies that were animating their current work plans. It appears that in addition to this, many of the formal and semiformal community consultation processes have evolved in a way that has re-engaged the environmental and other areas of citizen concern that were outlined as "waiting" in earlier sections of this chapter. Many elements of this transformation are consistent with those outlined earlier in this volume, most particularly in Chapters 3, 5, and 6, and the Conclusion. Further, more detailed research will be required to see how closely this new way of doing business approaches the "model for change" outlined in the Conclusion of this volume. The iterative nature of our community interactions will need to be extended to see how a modified model of change might better reflect the lived experience of the City of Richmond.

In conclusion, the use of a particular geopolitical example, in this case the City of Richmond, in the interdisciplinary, community-interactive exploration of the concepts of health and sustainability has been extraordinarily useful in refining and validating our work. This has developed more robust models and greater insight into the difficulties of translating high-sounding ideals into the practical expression of lived lives in democratic communities. Clinicians in the field of chronic stress disorders have defined a concept of "learned helplessness" whereby people (and animals) confronted with unresolvable sources of stress enter a stage where even obvious solutions to problems are not taken because of an inability to respond. We apply this concept to populations and link it to the concept of "social denial" in the conclusion of this volume. These concepts have been nested in the broad theory of complex adaptive systems. Our practical relationship with the City of Richmond has provided an extraordinary opportunity to validate their relevance. What is striking about our more recent experience with the City is how rapidly a transformation in attitude appears to have taken place. This would certainly be consistent with the process of change envisioned under adaptive systems theory. Should an opportunity arise, we would like to explore in some detail this transformation to see if some of the concepts and models outlined herein have some explanatory value. If this is the case, and if the transformation is what it appears to be, that is, a move in the direction of sustainability, the experience may be used to rekindle hope in other communities.

Acknowledgments

We are grateful for the contributions made by the initial contacts in each of the municipalities in the early stages of this research: Mr. John Bastaja, planner, District of Maple Ridge; Ms. Marga Betz, manager, Policy and Planning, City of Richmond; and Mr. Wayne Dickinson, director of the Planning Department, Corporation of Delta. We would like to thank the ongoing involvement and support of staff and management at the City of Richmond, including Ron Mann, Eleanor Atienza, David Brownlee, Kari Huhtala, Suzanne Carter, Carolyn Morrison, Hilda Ward, Brent Zaharia, and Jenny Beran. Also, we would like to thank the City of Richmond mayor, Greg Halsey-Brandt; Councillors Evelina Vaupotic and Corisande Percival-Smith; and administrator, Johnny Carline.

Notes

1 A detailed explanation of this model can be found in the Conclusion of this volume.
2 "Big box retail" refers to very large warehouse-style retail outlets usually developed on industrial land to reduce land and tax costs.

References

Atienza, E. 1995. *Report to Committee of the Whole*. Prepared for Richmond City Council for consideration by manager, Environment and Land Use, Urban Development Division, City of Richmond, BC, 12 September.

Beran, J. 1995. Memorandum. Circulated by Planner, Urban Development Division, City of Richmond, BC, 7 July.

Betz, M. 1991. Letter written by acting director, Planning Department, the Corporation of the Township of Richmond, BC, 30 July.

Boothroyd, P., L. Green, C. Hertzman, J. Lynam, S. Manson-Singer, J. McIntosh, W.E. Rees, M. Wackernagal, and R. Woollard. 1994. "Tools for Sustainability: Iteration and Implementation." In C.M. Chu and R. Simpson, eds., *Ecological Public Health From Vision to Practice*, Chapter 10. Nathan, Queensland: Institute of Applied Environmental Research, Griffith University (Australian edition); Toronto: Centre for Health Promotion, University of Toronto (Canadian edition).

Canada. Employment and Immigration Canada. 1994. *Canadian Immigration: Immigration Figures from 1991 Census*. Ottawa: Employment and Immigration Canada.

Canada. Census Canada. 1987. *Population Figures for 1986*. Ottawa: Government of Canada.

–. 1992. *Population Figures for 1991*. Ottawa: Government of Canada.

Canadian Medical Association. 1991. *Health, the Environment and Sustainable Development – The Role of the Medical Profession*. Ottawa: Council on Health Care and Department of Health Services.

City of Richmond. 1995. *City Centre Area Plan and Implementation Strategy*. Richmond: City of Richmond.

–. 1996. "The Population Figures for 1995." *Hot Facts* 3, 15.

–. 1998. *Strategic Management Plan Executive Summary*. Richmond: City of Richmond.

City of Richmond. 1999. "The Population Figures for 1998." Richmond.

Green, L.W., M.A. George, M. Daniel, C.J. Frankish, C.P. Herbert, W. Bowie, and M. O'Neill. 1995. *Study of Participatory Research in Health Promotion: Review and Recommendations for the Development of Participatory Research in Health Promotion in Canada*. Ottawa: Royal Society of Canada.

Green, L.W., L. Potvin, and L. Richard. 1996. "Ecological Foundations of Health Promotion." *American Journal of Health Promotion* 10,4: 270-81.

Klein, J.T. 1990. *Interdisciplinarity: History, Theory and Practice*. Detroit: Wayne State University Press.

Konkin, B. 1991. "Health Indicators/Regions and Overlapping Jurisdictional Boundaries in British Columbia." A background paper for the Task Force on Healthy and Sustainable Communities, University of British Columbia, Vancouver.

Lawson, J. 1991. "The Use of Livability Indexes in Achieving Healthy and Sustainable Communities." A background paper for the Task Force on Healthy and Sustainable Communities, University of British Columbia, Vancouver.

Mann, R. 1993. Letter from director, Planning Department, City of Richmond, BC, 7 December.

Nairne, K. 1991. "Governance and Community Organizations: Structural Barriers and Opportunities to Healthy and Sustainable Communities." A background paper for the Task Force on Healthy and Sustainable Communities, University of British Columbia, Vancouver.

Perkins, R. 1991. "Modifying Urban Form to Attain Healthy and Sustainable Goals." A background paper for the Task Force on Healthy and Sustainable Communities, University of British Columbia, Vancouver.

Saul, J.R. 1995. *The Unconscious Civilization*. Concord, ON: House of Anansi Press, University of Concord.

Schön, D.A. 1987. *Educating the Reflective Practitioners: Toward a New Design for Teaching and Learning in the Professions*. San Francisco: Jossey-Bass.

Task Force on Atmospheric Change. 1990. *Clouds of Change*. Vancouver: City of Vancouver.

Task Force on Healthy and Sustainable Communities. 1994. *Sustainability in Action: How Do We Make It Happen?* Conference Proceedings, University of British Columbia, Vancouver.

Wackernagel, M. 1991. "Land Use: Measuring a Community's Appropriated Carrying

Capacity as an Indicator for Sustainability." A background paper for the Task Force on Healthy and Sustainable Communities, University of British Columbia, Vancouver.

Westland Resource Group and City of Richmond staff. 1998. *State of the Environment Report.* Richmond: Westland Resource Group.

Woollard, R., M. Wackernagel, W.E. Rees, A. Ostry, J. McIntosh, S. Manson-Singer, J. Lynam, C. Hertzman, L. Green, M. Carr, and P. Boothroyd. 1999. "The Community as a Crucible: Blending Health and Sustainability." In M. Healey, ed., *Seeking Sustainability in the Lower Fraser Basin: Issues and Choices.* Vancouver: Institute for Resources and the Environment / Westwater Research.

8
The BC Sawmill Industry:
A Case Study of Community and
Ecological Sustainability
Aleck S. Ostry

The fishing to extinction of Canada's East Coast cod and the attendant collapse of outport communities is a graphic illustration of the dependence of human communities on the integrity of natural ecosystems. Such a link is most visible and immediate in communities directly dependent on the extraction and primary processing of the natural products of local ecosystems. Canada is unique among Western industrialized countries in having large numbers of communities involved in direct exploitation of nature. This is part of Canada's historical and economic legacy.

According to Harold Innis, much of Canada's economic history has been based on the discovery of natural resources, consequent community formation to facilitate their extraction, resource depletion, and finally, community disappearance (Hayter and Barnes 1990). This Innisian "cycle of destruction" which began with Canada's fur trade economy is less publicly acceptable today because natural resource depletion is increasingly equated with ecosystem compromise and ultimately with reduced liveability for human beings.

In Chapter 1 of this volume, William Rees asked the general question, Are humans living within nature's means? He also asked the more specific question, Just how healthy or sustainable is the ecological niche that industrial society has carved out for itself? The purpose of this case study is to use the ecological footprint, also described in detail in Chapter 1, to answer this second question, posed in the context of BC's sawmill industry.

The forest ecosystems that sustain BC's forest-products industry and communities, while not as compromised as the fish stocks and fishing communities of Newfoundland, are under increasing pressure. In British Columbia, for example, "50 percent of all the public timber cut has been felled in the last 13 years. The most rapid acceleration has primarily been in the BC interior, with 50 percent of the total cut being done since 1977 – the northern regions of Prince George and Prince Rupert have an even faster acceleration rate" (Travers 1993, 189). In addition, "much of this acceleration has been above the Ministry of Forests' own estimates of the sustainable yield" (Travers 1993, 190).

At the same time, employment in forest-based manufacturing in most industrial centres of the province has shrunk to record postwar lows. The increased rate of natural capital depletion using a smaller industrial workforce has been made possible because of the dramatic technological changes that began in the forest-products manufacturing sector in the late 1970s and early 1980s. Large segments of the industry had, by the early 1980s, moved from "Fordist" assembly line mass production methods to "flexible" methods of production and work organization. This was made possible largely by a combination of new markets and new computerized production technology (Barnes and Hayter 1995).

The increasing rate of tree consumption combined with a diminishing labour force poses a twin sustainability challenge. On the one hand, forestry-based communities receive less revenue in the form of direct wages and municipal taxes from local mills (Regional Data Corporation 1994). If there is no diversification within the affected community, or if the public sector does not step in to create forestry-related jobs in areas such as silviculture and forest-roads maintenance, the economic base is reduced and the structure of the local labour market altered. At the same time, the ecosystems from which logs are extracted to feed the mill are placed under greater pressure. There is some similarity to the Newfoundland cod fishery, in that the dynamic of increased rates of natural capital consumption with seemingly less community benefit than in the past is a feature common to both and which may be unstable over the long term.

From a traditional economic perspective, such a scenario may be acceptable and even desirable because greater throughput of raw logs and more efficient technology in mills means greater productivity and short-term wealth generation. Viewed through a sustainability lens, however, increased productivity associated with large-scale, permanent job loss and increased rates of forest destruction could have negative consequences. From the ecosystem and community health perspective, enhanced industrial productivity is desirable if it leads to lower resource throughput, perhaps by increasing the value-added component of the resource in the manufacturing process and creating job opportunities in local communities.

To better understand the impact of the recent industrial revolution in BC forests on both communities and ecosystems, and to reformat the discussion in terms of ecosystem and community health, we will examine the changing ecological footprint of several of the major sawmills in the province between 1950 and 1985. This is done using a database of information on approximately 26,000 BC sawmill workers, gathered to investigate the occupational effects of antisapstain chemicals, in combination with sawmill production data gathered during this time (Hertzman et al.

1997). The job-history information in the database is used to determine changing employment patterns in these mills. For mills located in forestry-dependent communities, changing employment opportunities will have direct effects on the economic sustainability of the community. Thus, employment change can be linked with community sustainability. In addition, using a survey of employed and laid-off forest-industry workers during the period 1978 to 1985, an estimate of the economic impact within the community of technological restructuring in sawmills is obtained (Cohen, Couture, and Allen 1988). By linking these studies, a discussion of recent changes in BC's sawmill industry in terms of both community and ecosystem sustainability is undertaken.

The period for this study focuses on the years between 1978 and 1985. It should be noted that the technological revolution in the industry has continued and the results shown for the period under investigation may underestimate current effects. For example, according to Marchak, "in gross terms 966 cubic metres of timber supported a job in 1980, but 1,300 cubic metres was required in 1993. In the major employment area, sawmilling and plywood production, 48 percent more timber is required to support a job in 1993 than in 1980, including jobs in management, plants, production, transportation, and infrastructure" (Marchak 1995, 95).

The Empirical Base

Sawmill Workers' Cohort
The cohort was gathered between 1987 and 1992 in order to investigate the effects of an antisapstain chemical, chlorophenol, on worker health. It consists of 26,487 men who worked for at least one year between 1950 and 1985, in at least one of fourteen large sawmills located in four regions of the province: the Lower Mainland, the Interior, Vancouver Island, and the Southern BC Mainland Coast (see Table 8.1). Because complete information on job history is available in eleven of the study mills for the period 1950 to 1985, temporal and regional changes in employment can be tracked. Because three of the mills were not built until the 1960s, data for early periods are missing.

Forestry Sector Labour Adjustment Study
Produced in 1988 for Employment and Immigration Canada, this longitudinal study linked Statistics Canada and Revenue Canada files for the years 1978 and 1985 in order to study income changes among Canadian forestry workers (Cohen, Couture, and Allen 1988). Data were individually linked but are presented in grouped form for confidentiality reasons. Income data for workers and their spouses and unemployment data for workers in the BC sawmill workforce are available for the period 1978 to 1985. This is con-

Table 8.1

Sawmill locations

Location	Number of workers	Start-up year
Vancouver	2,232	<1950
Vancouver	2,467	<1950
Vancouver	2,705	<1950
Vancouver Island	2,681	<1950
Vancouver Island	2,126	<1950
Vancouver Island	2,402	<1950
Vancouver Island	1,991	<1950
Vancouver Island	1,507	<1950
Vancouver Island	2,247	<1950
Coast Garibaldi	2,797	<1950
Coast Garibaldi	674	1963
BC Interior	766	1966
BC Interior	1,402	1966
BC Interior	490	<1950

venient, as this time frame straddles the major restructuring period in the industry and overlaps with the last few years of the sawmill workers' cohort study. By linking the cohort study data with the economic study, demographic changes occurring between 1978 and 1985 can be translated into likely economic impacts for sawmill workers and their families at the community level.

Labour Demography for the Cohort
For the initial analysis, three mills built in the 1960s were excluded from the analysis; the remaining eleven study mills reflect the demographic reality of the larger, established sawmills for the entire period of 1950 to 1985. It should also be noted that because the minimum eligibility for entrance into the cohort was one year of employment between 1951 and 1985, this study does not capture the experience of the most transient segment of the workforce.

Figure 8.1 shows that in all eleven mills, employment grew by approximately 30 percent during the boom in the 1960s, peaking in 1973. From 1973 to 1979, employment remained high and fairly stable, but from 1979 to 1985, employment dropped by about 40 percent. In exact terms, employment in the eleven mills dropped from 8,457 to 4,896 workers, a total of 3,561. One thousand and seventy-eight workers lost their jobs in 1982 alone. Based on patterns of employment loss, the post-1979 period appears unique.

Of the 3,561 workers who lost their jobs between 1979 and 1985, 2,232

Figure 8.1

Total number of workers in eleven study mills, by year

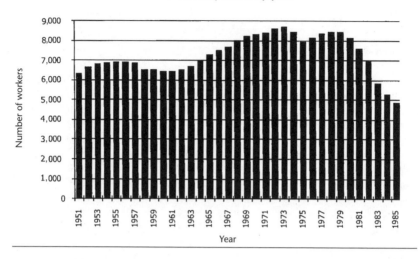

were actively terminated and 1,329 retired or were retired. In a labour market where layoffs usually proceed in terms of strict seniority, one would expect younger workers to bear the brunt of employment layoffs. The extent to which older workers were affected by employment downturns depended on the degree to which mills adopted policies of encouraged or forced early retirement. These data indicate that, during the recession of the early 1980s, about one-third of workers were let go through both normal and possibly early retirements.

Most job losses, however, were active terminations, meaning that the downturn affected mainly the younger segment of the workforce. Because community viability is directly related to the ability of young workers to obtain local employment, the age-specific changes in termination profile across periods and regions are informative. Figure 8.2 shows the change in the rate of active terminations for the sawmill cohort from 1955 to 1985. Layoffs are considered active terminations, while terminations due to illness, disability, or retirement are not. Active terminations are emphasized because these are more likely to reflect the size of the real "bite" of economic change in the workforce.

Using a life-table approach, age-specific person-years of employment were constructed with active termination rates for four periods between 1950 and 1985. These were standardized for mortality using 1981-5 cohort mortality rates. The standardization was performed because the number of deaths in the cohort in the 1980s was much higher than in the 1950s. By standardizing for mortality across periods in this way, comparison of active termination rates across time is more accurate.

Figure 8.2

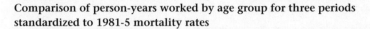

Comparison of person-years worked by age group for three periods standardized to 1981-5 mortality rates

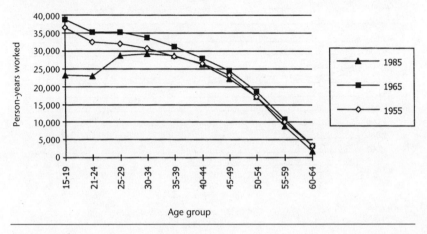

Age group

In Figure 8.2, active termination rates are modelled over time by showing the decline in the number of person-years worked for ten age groups in three different periods. Active terminations reduced the person-years worked in 1981 to 1985 by 20 percent compared to 1961 to 1965. Seventy-eight percent of these lost person-years were within the age groups fifteen to thirty-five, with particularly hard losses for those under the age of twenty-five. Again, this is not surprising given that the order of layoffs is strictly seniority-based and the absolute number of jobs lost was very high.

It is interesting to look at the regional differences in these age-specific termination patterns, both because labour markets tend to be regionally organized and because different regions often depend on different forest ecosystems for their log supply. To accomplish this task, we need to move to an analysis of all fourteen study mills so that the BC Interior can be included in the regional comparison. By using data from all mills, we can compare and contrast the periods 1966 to 1970, the earliest period for which we have data from the cohort encompassing the widest possible regional variation, with 1981 to 1985.

Figures 8.3 and 8.4 show standardized person years of employment for four regions during 1966 to 1970 and 1981 to 1985, respectively. (As in Figure 8.2, these have been standardized to 1981-5 cohort mortality rates.) The person-years of employment for those under thirty-five years of age are dramatically different in the two periods. Also, in both eras, those under thirty-five bear the largest employment loss, particularly in the Vancouver and Vancouver Island regions, and particularly during the recession of the early 1980s.

Figure 8.3

Person-years worked by age group in four regions during 1966-70

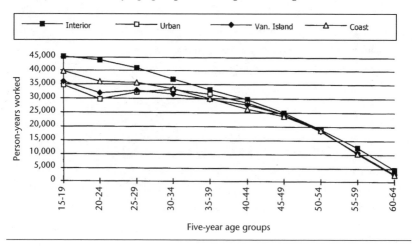

Figure 8.4

Person-years worked by age group in four regions during 1981-5

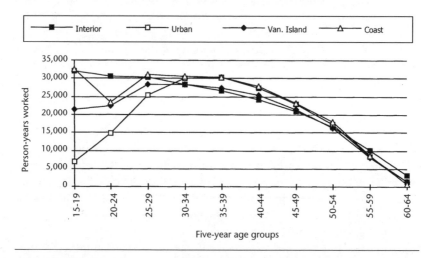

Figure 8.5 shows the net hiring rates (number hired : number actively terminated) for four regions in BC from 1951 to 1985. Vancouver Island mills appear to have gone through a dramatic reversal in hiring practices after the recession of the early 1980s, given the steady rates of hiring over the decades leading up to the recession.

The Interior shows a different pattern from the other regions. The

Figure 8.5

Five years' net hiring rates for four regions

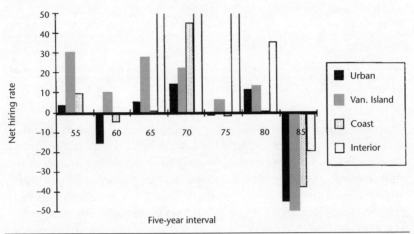

Interior was opened up for lumber manufacturing in the mid-1960s as the government granted companies access to previously unexploited interior forests. New plants were built with the latest technology. The high-net hiring rates for the fifteen-year period 1965 to 1980 reflect the synergy between new technology and new access to untapped forest ecosystems. Although, like the other regions, net hiring in the Interior became negative during the 1981-5 period, the recession's impact on these rates was approximately half that of the other regions.

Another way to compare the impact of the latest recession on the different regions is to compare annual net hiring rates for the pre- and post-1980 periods. (See Table 8.2.) Before 1980, the pattern of net hiring was variable, with the Interior showing explosive expansion. Vancouver Island mills had moderate growth in their hiring rates, at 3 percent per year, followed by coastal mills with hiring rates about half this figure. Finally, mills in the Lower Mainland had growth of about half a percent per year. However, as the preceding figures show, the older, established, forest-based communities on Vancouver Island have faced the greatest change in hiring patterns since the recession of the early 1980s.

The impact on Vancouver Island can be seen more clearly by looking at the pattern of job migration between the fourteen mills in the cohort. Between 1951 and 1985, 499 workers moved from one study mill to another. The workforce at these mills appears to have increased its mobility rate over time, since approximately two-thirds of these migrations occurred after 1973. The number of migrations during the height of the boom, 1973 to 1979, was the same as for the recessionary period of 1979 to 1985.

Table 8.2

Annual net hiring rates[1] per year before 1980 and after 1985

Net hiring rates per year	Interior	Urban	Vancouver Island	Coast
Pre-1980	16.4	0.6	3.0	1.4
Post-1980	–3.0	–6.7	–7.3	–6.3

1 Net hiring rate = (New Hires - Active Terminations)/Number of workers expressed as a percentage.

These migrations do not completely capture actual regional migration patterns of workers in the industry because movement to nonstudy mills is not recorded, and because migrations may be distorted by patterns of corporate ownership which might have facilitated migrations as intracompany mill transfers. However, even with these limitations, gross migration patterns are discernible. Of the 499 migrations between mills, 208 were within-region migrations. Of these, 87 percent represented movements among the six Vancouver Island mills. Figure 8.6 shows the pattern of the remaining 291 between-region migrations. These are gross between-region migration figures that do not take into account denominator factors such as size or number of mills within a region. However, the data are useful because they show no migrations from the Interior to the other three regions.

Because cohort migration between the regions will largely be a function

Figure 8.6

Interregional migration of workers in the sawmill cohort, 1973-85

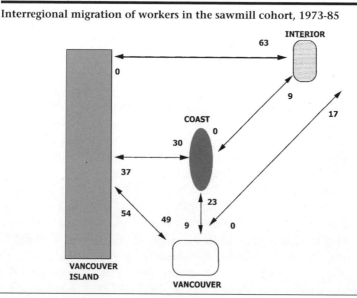

Table 8.3

Regional emigration and immigration[1] and rates per mill[2]

	Interior	Coast	Vancouver	Vancouver Island
Emigrants	0	55	94	142
Immigrants	89	53	58	91
Emigration rate	0	28	31	24
Immigration rate	30	25	19	15
Net emigration rate/mill	–30	+3	+11	+9

1 Expressed as total number of workers.
2 Expressed as total number of workers/number of mills.

of the number of mills in each region, emigration rates can be expressed as the number of workers per mill leaving the region of origin. Likewise, regional immigration rates can be expressed as the number of workers entering the region divided by the number of mills in that region. These rough denominators mould the data so that the relative contribution of each region can be ascertained.

Using this rough denominator, Table 8.3 indicates that Vancouver and Vancouver Island have the highest net emigration rates per mill, and the Interior region the lowest.

Summary
These data indicate that employment losses following the recession of 1981 were more drastic than for any other recessionary era after 1950. Workers under the age of thirty-five appear to have been most affected. Across regions, it appears that the younger workers in Vancouver Island and Vancouver mills suffered the greatest job losses. Migration data confirms these trends by showing that cohort workers who moved to another cohort mill tended to move away from the Vancouver and Vancouver Island mills and toward the newer Interior mills and the historically less exploited forest ecosystems.

Community Sustainability
The impact of labour structure change and mobility will be most noticeable in mill towns, that is, towns in which the sawmill is the only large employer. Towns such as Tahsis, Chemainus, and Youbou on Vancouver Island are mill towns that historically have depended primarily on their sawmills. Port Alberni, Harmac, and Powell River are larger mill towns in which the sawmill has historically been a less important part of an integrated forest-products manufacturing complex. Finally, the mills in Vancouver are a small part of a complex urban labour market.

Table 8.4

1985 status of 100 sawmill workers employed in BC sawmills in 1978

Number of workers in 1978	Number of workers in 1985	Income of workers in 1985 (in 1985$)
100	56 still in mills	35,906
	6 in other forestry industry job	33,761
	21 in jobs outside forestry industry	21,147
	2 UIC	6,306
	15 no job/no UIC	0

Notes: Core workforce in 1985 is 56 percent of its size in 1978 and in 1985 had an average income of $35,906. Only 6 percent of workers in sawmills in 1978 were able to move "sideways" into another high-income sector of the forestry industry. If we assume the people receiving unemployment benefits or with jobs outside the forestry industry are available potentially as a "peripheral" workforce for the sawmills, this peripheral labour market operates at an average wage level 45 percent less than the core ($19,850 versus $35,906).

Table 8.5

Estimated income in 1978 and 1985 for sawmill workers in the cohort, assuming rates of layoff and subsequent income levels from the forestry sector labour adjustment study (1985 dollars)

	1978	1985
Estimated wages from twelve mills	332,238,218	186,053,042
Income from workers who obtained other forestry industry jobs		19,934,293
Income from workers who obtained nonforestry industry jobs		41,091,370
UIC income		1,166,988
Totals	332,238,218	248,245,693
Net loss		83,992,525

According to this hierarchy of communities in our database, sustainability in small mill towns may be more directly assessed by examining the fate of their sawmills. It is more difficult to make the connection between the fate of labour forces and the fate of a community in complex labour markets. However, insofar as changes in sawmill labour demography reflect broader shifts in the forest-products manufacturing labour force, they provide indicator data on the potential community impact of these changes. Such data are strongest for the most mill-dependent towns.

Most of the sawmills in this study initiated major capital investments in technology in the late 1970s and early 1980s. The dramatic shift in employment after the recession of the early 1980s represents a combination of cutbacks in production and replacement of labour by capital-intensive equipment. Absolute, regional, and age-specific employment after years of fairly stable employment patterns show a dramatic shift by 1985.

The cohort survey indicates that about 60 percent of the sawmill workforce employed during the peak years in the 1970s remained employed in the mills after the recession of the early 1980s. These results are similar to those found in the Forestry Sector Labour Adjustment Study, which indicates that 56 percent of BC sawmill workers employed in 1978 were still employed in a sawmill in 1985 (Cohen, Couture, and Allen 1988, 19). The latter study found that, of the 100 workers who had a sawmill job in 1978, 44 had lost their sawmill jobs by 1985. (See Table 8.4.) They found that 62 percent of these workers managed to find another job by 1985. However, of these, only 16 percent found employment somewhere in the forestry industry other than a sawmill. Eighty-four percent of those who managed to find another job found one outside the industry. By linking this information to income tax files, they were able to ascertain that workers who found jobs elsewhere within the forestry industry kept their incomes stable. However, those who obtained jobs outside the industry were earning 33 percent less in 1985 than their sawmill jobs had paid in 1978: $31,435 compared to $21,147. In addition, a total of 17 percent of the workers employed in a sawmill in 1978 were unemployed by 1985.

When we combine the information from both the cohort study and the labour adjustment study, it is clear that there has been a large loss of jobs from the sawmill and forestry sector, and that this job loss has the most severe impact on young workers and those near retirement. It is also clear that even for those who obtained reemployment, income levels earned in 1985 were drastically reduced from 1978 levels. (See Table 8.5.)

If one assumes that no migration took place in the affected communities between 1978 and 1985, there is a net income loss of $83,992,525 just in terms of personal income. This does not include lost municipal tax revenue and any associated downturn in local economic activity.

Summary

Labour demographic changes for small sawmill towns are more directly translatable to community sustainability than for urban regions and more diversified midsize towns such as Port Alberni.

Given this fact, and combining the cohort study with the Forestry Sector Labour Force Adjustment Study, it is clear that the approximately 40 percent employment losses in the sawmill cohort probably translated to a minimum 25 percent income loss for the community, assuming that the unemployed workers did not out-migrate. If one assumes out-migration took place, and this is a much more likely scenario in single-mill towns, then overall economic loss to the community was greater than 25 percent. In addition, as the termination-by-age-group data indicates, the brunt of employment loss has been borne by the younger workers, who in turn were more likely to choose out-migration. Future community growth may therefore be compromised, as young workers leave these largely hinterland communities and such communities' demographic patterns are skewed toward an older age group, leading to their premature senescence.

Besides these direct losses, there are a number of less direct fiscal and health-related losses. There are costs to the municipality in lost forest-company taxes, as well as losses to municipal, provincial, and federal governments in other tax shortfalls resulting from the employment downturn. For example, according to a recent survey by the Regional Data Corporation, municipal tax revenue in Powell River dropped by 15 percent between 1990 and 1993. The same study indicates an increase in the economic dependency ratio, which is a measure of the extent to which transfer income from other levels of government enters the community to replace the income lost from industry layoffs (Regional Data Corporation 1994).

Unemployment creates indirect costs for all levels of government. Both the anticipation of unemployment in employed groups of workers and unemployment itself have been linked to a range of disease outcomes, including heart disease and psychiatric disorders (D'Arcy and Siddique 1985; Westin, Schlesselman, and Korper 1989; Mattiasson et al. 1990; Jin, Shah, and Svoboda 1995). In 1995, the suicide rate among the unemployed in BC was eleven times that of the total labour force (British Columbia 1995, 24). The suicide rate for young males is usually high, but the impact of unemployment may render this group even more vulnerable. The health consequences of unemployment are enormous. They are paid for by tax dollars, but the cost is not usually included in the accounting process when the cost of technological change in industry is measured.

Direct and indirect health and other welfare-related costs of labour force reduction can be viewed as a public subsidy to labour force structural change carried out within the private sector. If total company income remains stable or even increases after these structural changes in the labour force, and if taxpayers cover the health and welfare costs incurred by these changes, then a massive public subsidy of the private sector will have occurred. Furthermore, it will have occurred within an ideological and political atmosphere in which the federal government has been withdrawing massive funds from health, welfare, unemployment insurance, and labour force retraining, placing the burden of this hidden public subsidy increasingly on the provincial government. In addition, the subsidy will have occurred in the political environment of the 1980s and 1990s, when private enterprise unfettered by government is the supposed panacea for modern economic woes.

Clearly, changes in mill technology affect labour force demography and community sustainability. Because long-term sustainability of the forest-based community ultimately depends on the long-term sustainability of the forest ecosystems that supply its mills with logs, it is important to ground changes in technology, labour demography, and community sustainability within a construct of ecosystem health. The first step is to attempt to gauge the changing ecological footprint of these mills over time.

Ecosystem Sustainability

In British Columbia, the pressure on forest ecosystems has increased dramatically. The annual allowable cut (AAC), the volume of trees the ministry allows to be cut on forest tenures in the province, amounted to 60.8 million cubic metres in 1975. By 1980, this had increased to 66.7 million cubic metres. By the middle of the decade, it was up to 67.3 million cubic metres, and by the end of the decade, it was 74.3 million cubic metres. This amounts to an increase of volume allocated in forest tenures of about 1 million cubic metres per year since 1976. By the 1980s, "the capacity of current operating mills exceeded the AAC by about a third" (Travers 1993, 18).

It is clear, therefore, that after the mid-1970s, the rate at which the carrying capacity of the BC forests has been appropriated increased significantly. This increase has, for the entire decade, hovered above the ministries' own estimates of ecosystem sustainability. In effect, ecological appropriations above an ecologically sustainable limit have helped fuel the shift toward a more technology-intensive industrial system.

One way of measuring the impact of such a change is to determine the ecological footprint of each mill, or the quantity of logs each mill consumes over time. Ideally, one would want to know the exact quantity of logs consumed per unit time. This information is not available, but estimates of annual mill production are available for eight of the fourteen study mills for selected years from 1949 to 1985 (Miller Freeman Directory 1986). These data can be used to examine the mills' changing impact on the ecosystems that supply them with logs.

The ecological footprint is therefore proportional to the volume of lumber produced per mill during each of the five periods for which data are available (see Figure 8.7). The eight large coastal mills show a greater than 60 percent increase in their production volume from 1949 to 1965 and, therefore, a 60 percent increase in ecological footprint. Thereafter the rate of increase slows, but the footprint per mill in 1985 is still nearly twice its 1949 size. As an aside, it should be emphasized that an increased rate of production of wood means increased logging, which, in turn, means more road-building and encroachment into wilderness areas, with consequent impacts on forest sustainability.

During this period, 1949 to 1985, the number of workers in these mills

Figure 8.7

Lumber production per mill in eight large coastal sawmills, 1949-85

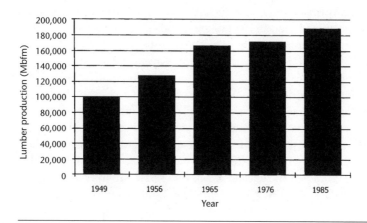

Figure 8.8

Lumber production per worker in eight large coastal sawmills, 1949-85

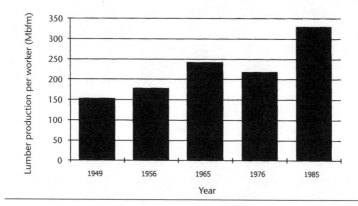

first increased, reaching a peak in the late 1970s, and then decreased drastically in the early 1980s. It is therefore instructive to consider the changing ecological footprint of a sawmill worker, expressed as millions of board feet (Mbfm) per worker, for this period. (See Figure 8.8.) Clearly, by 1985, technology had increased the ecological footprint of each sawmill worker from 154 Mbfm to 330 Mbfm.

Summary
The rate of increase in lumber production per mill accelerated fastest between 1956 and 1965 as the industry moved away from recession and

entered the boom period of the 1960s and 1970s. Over the twenty-year period 1965 to 1985, lumber production at the eight coastal mills increased by only 10 percent. Lumber production increased more rapidly than this in the industry as a whole, probably because rates of increase were faster in the Interior, which was the first region to move to new sawmill technology. Thus, our sample of eight large coastal mills is really a snapshot of production in a less technologically advanced sector of the sawmill industry.

The eight mills do not show a startling increase in the rate of draw-down of natural capital in an era when the rest of the industry consumed more of British Columbia's forests than ever before. In fact, these data show that the large increases in production occurred in the late 1950s and early 1960s. However, Figure 8.8 illustrates that on a per worker, rather than a per mill, basis, the increase in productivity, or the individual workers' ecological footprint, between 1976 and 1985 is the largest in the history of these mills.

Conclusion

The ecological footprint is an estimate of a specific populations' consumption of major resources measured in terms of the amount of land *in continuous* production necessary to sustain the group's rate of consumption. In this study, an attempt has been made to adapt the concept to a resource-extracting industry. Accordingly, the sawmill, rather than a population group, is the unit of consumption and, because turning trees into lumber is a relatively crude primary manufacturing process, most of the footprint can be assessed fairly directly by measuring lumber production.

It should be emphasized that this approach results in a considerable underestimation of the ecological footprint because per annum sawmill lumber production is a crude proxy for the number of trees consumed each year. Also, the size of the land base required for a constant flow of trees to a sawmill depends on logging intensity and general forestry and silvicultural policies and must always expand as accessible stands of this largely nonrenewable resource are logged off. An underestimation of the size of the footprint also results because not included are measures of wastage involved in milling trees to lumber, the energy required for logging the trees, building logging roads, and other extractive infrastructure, as well as the energy expenditure required to operate the sawmills.

In reality, the sawmill is a site where raw natural capital is transformed rather than consumed. Furthermore, the ecological footprint is usually assigned to the population that is the site of consumption of the mill's lumber. Assigning an ecological footprint to the site of transformation rather than consumption decouples the linkage between the consumption of specific population groups and its impact on the ecosystem.

The inherent danger in using the ecological footprint in this way is that its utility as an educational and analytical tool may be blunted. During the 1980s and 1990s, for example, Japan has become the final destination for an increasing number of trees processed in BC coastal mills. These changes in the BC lumber market result in an increased ecological footprint for Japan in general and for various Japanese cities and regions in particular. By focusing on transformation rather than final consumption, the specific links between consumption in Japan and ecosystem draw-down in British Columbia are not made explicit.

There are advantages, however, in assigning ecological footprints to the site of the extraction and transformation of natural capital. First, for a nation like Canada, which engages heavily in direct natural resource extraction with minimal value-added manufacturing and export, the trade-off between ecosystem depletion and community benefit needs to be explicit in order to determine the sustainability of the transformation process both for communities engaged in the process and ecosystems supplying the natural resource.

Second, the ecological footprint, as it is generally used, is calculated from a range of essential items and expressed in land area needed to produce them. The power of the concept lies in its ability to make explicit the impact on ecosystems of the general consumption patterns of a defined population. While the ecological footprint links consumption patterns to nature and expresses the impact of consumption in terms of land area needed to support it, there is no identification of the location or type of land-bases or ecosystems being exploited. Because it is primarily a planning and educational tool, the ecological footprint focuses on the final consuming population rather than on the specific ecosystem being consumed or the population groups engaged in transforming natural products on their way to the final site of consumption.

Canadian industries such as sawmilling, fishing, and mining, which are heavily reliant on the direct harvesting and minimal processing of products of natural ecosystems and which have communities that are highly dependent on these industries, lend themselves to a particular adaptation of the ecological footprint. The approach is centred on the specific ecosystems and associated communities engaged in their extraction and transformation, rather than on the population consuming the products. The focus on minimally transformed natural products, such as the number of fish caught or the quantity of lumber produced, produces a rough indication, albeit an underestimation, of the direct draw-down of natural capital, as well as locating the site of this draw-down. This approach links the costs and benefits of transformation with *site* or *region-specific* ecosystem exploitation.

The measure of community sustainability used in this study was also somewhat crude, being based on the number of hourly pay jobs in sawmills. The measure excluded salaried and contracted workers, and any mechanisms by which reductions in the number of hourly pay jobs within sawmills may have been offset or transferred by increases in related employment within the sawmill communities. In spite of the crudeness of the measure of community sustainability used in this investigation, it is clear from other studies of sawmills during the recession of the early 1980s that the loss of hourly pay jobs in mills were largely mirrored by reductions in salaried positions, contracted work, and office staff, indicating that fluctuations in hourly pay mill jobs are a fairly valid indicator of changes in community benefit from mill employment.

The discussion has until now focused on underlying methods and their limitations. But what are the main findings of this investigation? The case study, involving about 20 percent of workers in the coastal sawmill industry, showed that the downturn of the early 1980s was particularly hard on young workers. In part, this was because of the seniority-based system in the mills which ensured that those with less seniority, who are generally the younger workers, are most likely to be laid off. When this finding is analyzed in relation to between-mill migration patterns and the Forest Labour Adjustment Survey, it is clear that younger workers in older sawmill communities with increasingly less viable nearby forest ecosystems have either moved away from these communities and the entire industry, or, if they have remained in the industry, have tended to move to the interior of the province with its newer mills and, most importantly, its less exploited forest ecosystems.

The increased personal ecological footprint of those workers who remained in the industry is a function of a new industrial strategy that replaces labour investment with capital. New technologies enable workers to be more productive. While each worker can transform more trees into lumber than ever before, as a group there were about 40 percent fewer of them after the recession. Even with this drastically reduced and more aged workforce, the ecological footprint of the eight coastal mills for which we have data increased between 1976 and 1985 principally because of increased productivity per worker.

A classical or neoclassical economist might be pleased with such productivity increases, but an ecological economist might see these in a less positive light. The new technical infrastructure now in place in most sawmills is more capable than ever of accelerating the pace of forest ecosystem drawdown. This enhanced production capacity was established at a time when BC's coastal forest ecosystems, which have historically been overharvested, are under increasing pressure from other forest sector uses, such as tourism.

Interestingly, as illustrated in the previous chapter by McIntosh and Woollard, big box retail development in Richmond, BC, shows that this issue of enhancing capacity while at the same time reducing employment opportunity also occurs in urban centres and in sectors other than forestry.

The kinds of urban developments discussed in the Richmond case study, in contrast to the forestry situation described in this chapter, are harder to link to effects in specific ecosystems, which may make it more difficult to mobilize concern around environmental effects of such development.

Richmond and other urban centres in the Lower Fraser Valley basin were situated, during the late nineteenth and early twentieth century, virtually on the edge of wilderness areas. Most of the jobs in these urban centres were related to the direct extraction and primary manufacture of products of local ecosystems, mainly fish and wood. These kinds of jobs, in Richmond, have almost entirely disappeared now, as urban land prices have skyrocketed and both logs and fish have become less abundant.

In an historical sense, the rise in importance, particularly during the mid-twentieth century, of BC's mill towns, was partly due to the phenomenon of disappearing forestry resources. The shift of primary manufacturing to mill towns and away from urban centres such as Richmond was due to efficient consumption of the forests in the immediate periphery of urban areas. As has been shown in this chapter, resource depletion has progressed to a stage where the mill towns and mill-town jobs, particularly in BC's coastal communities, may also soon disappear.

In the latest phase of this process, as the coastal forest ecosystems are depleted, the mills and the jobs move to the BC interior. The infrastructure left in place in the coastal mills is the most efficient the industry has ever seen. The irony of this situation is that the coastal forest ecosystems are moving into their least productive phase at a time when a more efficient industry is creating intense production pressure. The efficiency of production methods ensures that more can now be taken from the forest ecosystems.

The changes are felt at the community level. The direct impact is job loss, reduced incomes, and a smaller tax base. The indirect losses range from increased migration of young workers, increased community instability and senescence, and increased health and welfare costs associated with community instability and employment losses. These losses are likely particularly strong in small, highly dependent mill communities. Indirect costs such as these are not usually part of the accounting procedure. The extent to which the government must step in to deal with health and social costs incurred in industrial restructuring amounts to a public subsidy usually unrecognized by the private sector.

Calculation of the ecological footprint used in conjunction with measures of community sustainability can usefully illuminate the linkages and trade-offs that occur in some industries at the level of ecosystem and community health. While the results of this particular case study may not be encouraging, the development and application of new planning and conceptual tools like these may at least begin the process of making these trade-offs explicit.

References

Barnes, T.J., and R. Hayter. 1995. The Restructuring of Forest Communities: Flexibility Perspectives. Paper presented at the Joint Simon Fraser-University of British Columbia Conference on Harold Innis and the BC Forest Industry, February.

British Columbia. Division of Vital Statistics. 1995. *Quarterly Digest* 5,2.

Cohen, K., L. Couture, and D.R. Allen. 1988. Forestry Sector Labour Adjustment Study. Paper prepared for Employment and Immigration Canada, Labour Canada, Industry, Science and Technology Canada.

D'Arcy, C., and C.M. Siddique. 1985. "Health and Unemployment: Findings from a National Survey." *International Journal of Health Services Research* 15,4: 609-35.

Hayter, R., and T.J. Barnes. 1990. "Innis's Staple Theory, Exports, and Recession: British Columbia, 1981-1986." *Economic Geography* 12,1: 156-73.

Hertzman, C., K. Teschke, A. Ostry, R. Hershler, H. Dimich-Ward, S. Kelly, J. Spinelli, R. Gallagher, M. McBride, and S. Marion. 1997. "Cancer Incidence and Mortality in a Cohort of Sawmill Workers Exposed to Chlorophenols." *American Journal of Public Health* 87,1: 71-9.

Jin R.L., P.C. Shah, and T.J. Svoboda. 1995. "The Impact of Unemployment on Health: A Review of the Evidence." *Canadian Medical Association Journal* 153,5: 529-40.

Marchak, P.M. 1995. *Logging the Globe.* Montreal: McGill-Queen's University Press.

Mattiasson, I., F. Lindgarde, J. Nilsson, and T. Theorell. 1990. "Threat of Unemployment and Cardiovascular Risk Factors: Longitudinal Study of Quality of Sleep and Serum Cholesterol Concentrations in Men Threatened with Redundancy." *British Medical Journal* 301: 461-6.

Miller Freeman Lumber Directory, 1950-85. 1986. Vancouver.

Regional Data Corporation. 1994. *Projected Impacts of Land-Use Changes on Vancouver Island upon forest Sector Work Force and Income Support Programs.* Vancouver: Union of BC Municipalities.

Travers, O.R. 1993. "Forest Policy: Rhetoric and Reality." In K. Drushka, ed., *Touch Wood: BC Forests at the Cross Roads.* Madeira Park, BC: Harbour Publishing.

Westin S., J.J. Schlesselman, and M. Korper. 1989. "Long-term Effects of a Factory Closure: Unemployment and Disability during Ten Years' Follow-up." *Journal of Clinical Epidemiology* 42,5: 435-41.

Conclusion: Working Together and the Prospect for Hope

Robert F. Woollard

[Hope] is a state of mind, not a state of the world. Either we have hope within us or we don't: it is the dimension of the soul, and it's not essentially dependent upon some particular observation of the world or estimate of the situation.
– Vâclav Havel (Heaney 1995, 4)

In light of the data and ideas contained in this volume, it is appropriate to pause and reflect on Vâclav Havel's statement. At the most basic level, we must confront the question: Is there any hope for a healthy and sustainable world? Is there any realistic prospect that a majority of the world's population, or even those in the Lower Fraser Basin, can change its present patterns of consumption? Can people learn and respond to the ecological consequences of their actions and build a society that is in harmony rather than at odds with its sustaining ecosystems?

If the answer to these questions is "no," then the entire work of the task force is at best an absurdist exercise. A detailed description of the inevitable demise of human society and many of its members is of little more utility than the prophet standing on the street corner waving a sign stating that "The End Is Nigh." Given what we have discovered about the power of human denial, such a book (no matter what the truth of its assertions) would presumably be treated like the prophet on the corner – with bemused pity and contempt.

We must, therefore, believe that our questions can be answered in the affirmative. Part of this can derive from what Havel refers to as a "dimension of the soul" independent of the reality in which we find ourselves embedded. Such a hope, while essential if we are to make any attempt to change from our present self-destructive course, is not sufficient in itself to point our feet in that new direction. Given the size of our ecological footprint, it matters that we take the right direction and that we do so urgently. To do so, our hope must be tempered with reality.

There are two levels at which we must address reality and hope. The first is at the social and political level. We can have a hopeful vision of a peaceful and sustainable world, but have no faith that the political process can get us there. As evidenced by the words of the current American Vice-President Al Gore, quoted in the introduction to this volume, lack of faith in the process can become an excuse for giving up hope. To temper the bleak hopelessness that could result, both society and individuals frequently undertake to discount the reality and urgency of the present ecological crises. This process is facilitated by what we have referred to as "social denial" in earlier chapters of this volume. This has led to a better understanding of the mechanisms of a dysfunctional political process. From this we derive some elements of an antidote to the despair so often associated with our political prospect. If political lethargy in the face of a pressing danger comes from an inability to accept the problematic rather than from ignorance, then our approach to change should be fundamentally different. Instead of waiting for a political messiah, we should develop calculated means to understand the roots of denial and provide feasible political alternatives and the mechanisms to implement them. We might consider the historical collapse of the seemingly invincible Aztec Empire (Fernandez-Armesto 1995). Professor Fernandez-Armesto points out that "the power of the Aztec state to levy tribute was both the source of its weakness and a daunting measure of its strength. Only the scale of consumption among the hegemonic communities in and around Lake Texcoco can show the degree of their dependence on the resources of the hinterland" (ibid., 197).

Through the use of surviving tribute-lists, the author outlines the scale of consumption enjoyed by the concentration of citizens in the capital city. He further points out that notwithstanding the technological advantages (and the help of apocalyptic mythology) the final defeat of the city at the hands of the Spaniards and their hinterland allies derived from excessive dependency on what amounts to ecological footprints displaced to a great distance. "Instead of being overwhelmed by superior morale or superior technology, Tenochtitlán was starved and plagued into surrender. An empire nourished by tribute could not survive the severance of supply. The densely populated community crowded onto a small island could not endure without the huge inputs of food the Empire supplied" (ibid., 197). This can be seen as an example of the vulnerability that accrues to a society overly dependent on an ecological footprint extended into the hinterland.

The parallels with the current state of the City of Richmond are sobering. While the relationships with its widely dispersed hinterland are not specifically hegemonic in the sixteenth-century sense of the concept, there is clearly a dependent relationship with production well away from the Lower Mainland of British Columbia. While we cannot measure this relationship through tribute-lists such as those used by Professor Fernandez-Armesto, our studies of the ecological footprint create a starkly similar picture of concentrated consumption in precontact Tenochtitlán and in Richmond at the close of the twentieth century. The hegemony that maintains this grossly inequitable level of consumption is now in the hands of international corporatism using the mantra of "globalization" rather than the imperial hegemony of European monarchies under the mantra of the expansion of Christendom. It is worth noting that both the regional hegemony of the Aztec Empire and the power of the royal houses of Europe to do anything other than entertain and amuse have slipped into the pages of history.

At a certain level, this could lead to a degree of nihilism about the prospects for a sustainable Richmond. On the other hand, since its current unsustainable state is heavily dependent on a seemingly invincible hegemony of consumer-oriented multinational corporatism, history may also provide a lesson in optimism insofar as this hegemony may be far more vulnerable to change than we can currently imagine.

The second level at which we can address reality and hope is the one we have sought to demonstrate in this volume. This rests in an attempt to understand the reality of how systems work, how change and adaptation occur, and where we might begin to induce a newer, healthier, and more sustainable society. In this respect, there are no simple answers. The absence of simple answers is frequently taken to assume there are no answers and, thereby, no cause for hope. Again, to come back to Havel's definition of hope, we should see this as a stimulant to the exploration for complex, difficult, but nonetheless real answers. Not only are the answers likely to be complex and difficult, but there is a profound urgency in finding them as we approach the end of the twentieth century. As we embark on our search for these solutions, we must keep in mind that we do not have to understand their final shape in order to be optimistic about finding them. In this regard, one other aspect of Havel's view of hope might give us some reassurance: "It is not the conviction that something will turn out well, but the certainty that something makes sense, regardless of how it turns out" (Heaney, op. cit., 5).

The eminent historian Eric Hobsbawm, in reflecting on the rate of economic growth in the second half of the twentieth century, observes that:

> if maintained indefinitely (assuming this to be possible), [such economic growth] must have irreversible and catastrophic consequences for the natural environment of this planet ... It will not destroy the planet or make it absolutely uninhabitable, but it ... may well make it uninhabitable for the human species as we know it in anything like its present numbers. Moreover, the rate at which modern technology has increased the capacity of our species to transform the environment is such that ... the time available to deal with the problem must be measured in decades rather than in centuries. (Hobsbawm 1994, 569)

This presents an excellent précis of the dilemma that this volume seeks to reflect. Hobsbawm goes on to suggest that "the objective of ecological policy must be both radical and realistic." This volume seeks to respond to that dual challenge using our second definition of "realistic."

We have looked at biophysical processes and their limits, social processes and their constraints, global trends and their influences, local activities and their effects, why things don't work and how they might be made to. The radicalism arises from the analysis. Evidently, things must be done differently, but it is not quite so evident precisely how they must be done. In this regard, we have made some specific suggestions. However, the underlying assumption is that people and their communities must explore the consequences of their actions and accept a different way of acting. In essence, we must substitute an ethic of concern and stewardship for the existing ethic of individualism and growth. This has an inherent radicalism in a society based on consumption. It nonetheless offers some resonance with much traditional religious and social thought – thoughts that have preceded by centuries our more recent short-lived fling with limitless technological enhancement.

The First Halting Steps

In the above discussion, we have invoked the thoughts of poets and historians because we believe that the basic concept of sustainability has a profoundly moral dimension. From the beginning of our work together, the members of the task force assumed that we would require a respectful attention to a broad range of intellectual disciplines in order to achieve any understanding of this complex concept. Indeed, as mentioned, the very genesis of our working relationship was a consensus among ourselves and our funding agencies that the traditional division of knowledge into various disciplines had reached the point of diminishing returns in addressing such fundamental societal issues. What was required was an opportunity to work together across disciplines and with the "real world" of policy makers and communities in order to arrive at a collective understanding that would transcend any particular view. The absence of a representative from the humanities on the task force has been a source of concern from very early in our deliberations. Nonetheless, we simultaneously realized that there was an issue of scale in interdisciplinary work. It appeared that beyond a particular workable size, an interdisciplinary group would fail to develop or maintain the robust intercollegiate relationship necessary to develop the synergy of the various perspectives. Instead, the perspectives appeared to function more in parallel. Despite this, and perhaps as a consequence of our practical working relationship with the City of Richmond, we have developed a broad picture of *sustainability* in action. We recognize, however, that many of the details and effective processes remain to be contributed by others. We do not believe that we in the Lower Fraser Basin have the luxury of time in coming to grips with these issues.

For that reason, we seek to present what Nobel Laureate Murray Gell-Mann called "a crude look at the whole" (Gell-Mann 1994, xiv). It may not totally satisfy those with particular disciplines and arcane methods, but readers are invited to see the broad conceptual basis for thinking about, addressing, and practising sustainability.

On the way to doing this, we will present some observations about the task itself so that others can build upon our successes, avoid our mistakes, and carry forward the search for solutions.

A Model for Change

We have earlier referred to "complex adaptive systems" or "self-organizing systems." These ideas are fundamental to our work, since the essence of sustainability over time is the ability to adapt effectively to changing circumstances. The general tenets of system theory have been around for a very long time (von Bertalanffy 1968). Much of the recent ecologic work and other research, such as that done by the Santa Fe Institute (Waldrop 1992, 32; Gell-Mann 1994; Kauffman 1995), has refined various concepts and enhanced our understanding. Such theories as have arisen have not given us a clear, replicable, and predictive model of sustainability. This should not disappoint us, since an expectation of such a model would signal a misunderstanding of the fundamental tenets of the theory.

It is essential to understand that, as we approach the idea of a healthy and sustainable system, we are not dealing with a simple, linear, explanatory model. We are not even seeking a complex and interwoven series of linear casual factors. In appealing for an integrated look at the whole, Gell-Mann explains:

> The reason is that no complex, non-linear system can be adequately described by dividing it up into sub-systems or into various aspects, defined beforehand. If those sub-systems or those aspects, all in strong interaction with one another, are studied separately, even with great care, the results, when put together, do not give a useful picture of the whole. In that sense, there is profound truth in the old adage "the whole is more than the sum of its parts." People must therefore get away from the idea that serious work is restricted to beating to death a well defined problem in a narrow discipline, while broadly integrated thinking is relegated to cocktail parties. (Gell-Mann 1994, 346)

Fundamental to the understanding of a complex adaptive system is the realization that it must be capable of sensing its internal and external environment, recognizing changes in those environments, and mounting an effective response that maintains or re-establishes an equilibrium that allows it to persist over time. The task force, in seeking to apply these general principles, has arrived at a model to describe a healthy and sustainable community (Figure 7.3; see p. 207). Like the theory that spawned it, the model is capable of being applied to a number of scales and in response to a number of circumstances. This particular model is based on the presumption that the communities in the Lower Fraser Basin are going to have to drastically curtail current levels of consumption as an absolute prerequisite for any possibility of being sustainable. That this must be accomplished in a way that allows our social systems to adapt is the second arm of the dilemma we face.

This model is also capable of leading the communities to adapt more effectively to required reductions in their ecological footprints. Part of the adaptation is an assessment of the social consequences and societal values related to a reduced ecological footprint. The development of tools and units of measurement is an integral part of the feedback loop. This results in an increased degree of acceptability, and presumably responsiveness, to the feedback loops created.

While this model has some descriptive utility at various community levels, its primary use will be found when it is applied to particular choices within particular communities. For example, if a city is confronting a decision about transportation policy, it can develop a series of accepted measurements that can be integrated into a cycle-of-change model. This can then serve two purposes. First, it may have some predictive value that will assist in the political decision-making process about the most sustainable of a series of choices. Second, if there is concern about the likely outcome of a particular policy or project choice, measurements can be built into the model so that the community can adapt to the reality of the outcome, even if it is different than that predicted. Consequently, it provides the community with the general opportunity to function as a complex adaptive system.

We have no illusions about the complexities of the task of putting such an overall model into operation on a consistent basis. Nonetheless, we have had numerous opportunities to present the model for the consideration of others, and it appears to have significant heuristic value. Recent (1999) meetings with senior managers at Richmond City Hall indicate that in many important ways, the general principles of assessing and measuring choices are being increasingly integrated into the planning and policy development process. In addition, we have had experience with operationalizing and assessing various segments of the model.

It is immediately obvious that this model of sustainability is a dynamic one. It is not a picture of some past Arcadia or a future Utopia. It will work only with the sustained commitment of all segments of society. Much of the content of this volume is aimed at gauging the elements that go into a functional model. Thus, we have looked at the role of social denial in rejecting the very idea of ecological footprints and the social imperative that it carries. We have refined the measurement of the ecological footprint so that it will withstand the scrutiny of those whose vested interests might enhance their level of denial. We have examined the intimate connection between consumption and health as measured both at the international and at the community levels. We have sought to understand the ways in which community cohesion could be developed so that at least the possibility of collective action is attained. We have reviewed decision-making systems, the development of health within communities, and the ways in which those decisions might be more closely linked to the broad aim of community health and sustainability. We have reflected upon the particular experience with the City of Richmond in hopes that this will be of value to future researchers who may seek to expand upon our first halting steps.

The work that has been done and the suggested steps that follow are capable of facilitating a fundamental shift toward sustainability. Readers should not be intimidated by either the enormity of the task or the absence of simple solutions already on the shelf. That each individual, each community, and each government must shape the particular tools and solutions to be used should not detract from the fundamentally simple concept: *We must, and can, dramatically reduce our consumption while enhancing our social well-being. These goals, far from being contradictory, are synergistic – progress toward one moves us closer to the other.* Both the sterility of automobile-dependent suburbs and the vibrancy of integrated working and living communities should reassure us in that regard. As for "getting there from here," there is increasing evidence that an approach tantamount to muddling through, with constant adaptation to changing circumstances, is more effective than an attempt at a grand design that may prove both unrealizable and wrong.

This should not detract from the importance or the urgency of the issues we face. However, because of this, we have fallen into the twin traps of denial and learned helplessness. Cooperation is replaced by conflict wherein the major forces advocating growth, and those opposing forces that support conservation, paint convincing pictures of Armageddon – on the one hand economic and on the other ecologic. Between lies a hopeful future – despite the soul-deafening cries of the current neoclassical economic orthodoxy. On the other hand, "even today, the most zealous friends of the earth become understandably impatient with the shuffles and scuffles, compromises and bargains of politics when the 'death of nature' is said to be imminent, and the alternatives presented as a bleak choice between redemption and extinction" (Schama 1995). Such a situation can be paralyzing. The way out of the box is through the individual and collective actions, which are called for later in this chapter.

What remains is to reflect on the general nature of interdisciplinary research and then to return to the issue of hope.

Reflections on Interdisciplinary Research

The real joy (and true effectiveness) of interdisciplinary work rests in that time between the breaking down of discipline-centred conventions and the onset of self-centred concern about ownership of specific parts of the enterprise. The process is somewhat like the exciting years in personal development when one is first exposed to an unbearable wealth of ideas to explore and paths to choose. This often occurs after completing high school, when conventional success in responding to well-defined norms suddenly seems to be thin wine indeed when compared to the challenges facing the society of which one is a fledgling member. The rich possibilities for doing things differently, coupled with a wonderful sense of not knowing that it cannot be done, result in an optimism rarely equalled later in life. There is a later period when the practical realities of family and financial responsibilities can reduce opportunities for idealism ... one by one until the dull hand of convention again reasserts itself.

So it can be with interdisciplinary research. The very success within one's own discipline that makes one attractive as an interdisciplinary collaborator is often the first barrier to effective collaboration. A determined and coordinated attempt needs to be made to overcome the idea of intellectual ownership that has been the hallmark of this success. Such an undertaking will be rewarded by a mutually exciting sharing of ideas. The ideas can be collectively juxtaposed and recombined in new patterns and fragments without self-conscious deeding of ownership. It is at this stage that truly radical thinking occurs and when effective consideration can be given to genuinely new solutions to complex problems. Yet, it is an inherently unstable state because, like our young college student analogy, these recombined ideas and ideals are not initially subjected to the "practical" test of conventional thinking. The understandable requirements of each of the collaborators to be validated in their home disciplines starts to quietly reassert itself. If not acknowledged and dealt with, the hidden hand of individual ownership with individual jealousies starts to reassert its presence. Therefore, pieces of the collective enterprise start to be taken off and jealously guarded until they can be "properly developed" with attached ownership. The chilling effect of even one such occurrence on the free flow of ideas can cast a pall over everyone in the group. Suddenly, an idealistic collection of excited thinkers starts to drift back into everyday concerns about grants, tenure, and concern about what the neighbours (in one's own discipline) might think.

While this may be the usual pattern, it is not at all clear that it is the inevitable one. Many individuals effect a translation from high school to robust adulthood while maintaining idealism and a commitment to the greater good of humanity. If our analogy holds true, there is no reason to believe that, in principle, interdisciplinary research groups must slide into a state approaching the senescence of practicality.

One of the primary charms, and strengths, of close interdisciplinary collaboration rests in the opportunity for each collaborator to see his or her colleague's discipline with clarity. Clarity comes from distance and, if not ignorance, a degree of naïveté about the subtlety that often clogs a vision of one's own discipline. The rich interplay of questions and answers marking a long and respectful collaboration can lead to a synergy that lends clarity to all partners. One can at least learn the rudimentary concepts of another discipline and, when working on a specific problem, can often explore some rather refined thinking in a new field. On the other hand, the clarity one must use in sharing concepts inherent to one's field is often of a higher order than that required to work within it. A synergy develops which has proven to be quite helpful in approaching the complex and interrelated issues with which we deal in this volume.

There is, of course, the danger that compounded views of complicated issues can yield a vision whose framework borders on the delusional. This is particularly true if the group does not acknowledge that many words have discipline-specific meanings and many shared concepts go by differing names in different disciplines. There is less of a problem when the concepts or meanings are very clearly at variance. When the distinctions are subtler, but still important, significant misunderstandings and conflicts can arise. The task force was certainly not immune to this circumstance. Such problems can generally be worked through to the general advantage of all if there exists an appropriate degree of mutual respect.

However, even greater dangers to constructive collegiality lurk at a deeper level. This is the level that moves beyond words to our particular views of the way in which knowledge is constructed.

Knowledge itself can be shaped very differently for an urban planner, a social worker, an epidemiologist, and a physician. Hence the research methods, and the norms surrounding writing and communications, are very different and subject to misunderstanding. If one extends, as we did, beyond academia to the broader community of policy makers and citizens, the structure of discourse and ethics of shared work can become even more subject to mutual conflict. There are no simple answers in this grey area where researcher and subject begin to merge in ways that challenge traditional academic reserve. The range of research methods configures themselves differently across this traditional boundary. There is often an urgent need for advice and solutions on the part of those immersed in daily decision making at the bureaucratic or community level. This action carries its own imperative that can be at odds with the desire of academicians to have their data very "clean" before sharing any of it. The closest analogy might be with the doctor-and-patient partnership in the family physician's office. Here a particular problem (usually inherently complex and frequently urgent) must be jointly addressed. It is often subject to study and analysis but perforce a decision must be taken – usually in the face of worrisome lingering uncertainty. Adequate arrangements can be made for follow-up and re-evaluation, as new experience or information comes to light. This interaction and the therapeutic interventions that flow from it (e.g., medications, surgery) may sully the "purity" of the physician's study of the health or disease status of the patient. However, undue delay in addressing factors that are known (and subject to influence) may be contrary to the patient's desires or needs. Wrong decisions can be made if information or reflection is inadequate or incorrect. On the other hand, there are frequently consequences, sometimes disastrous, of not making a decision. What, then, should we do?

Medicine has tried to follow an ancient dictum – *primum non nocere,* or, "first do no harm." This means that if one cannot reasonably expect to contribute to a better outcome than nature will supply without any intervention, one should not take action beyond supporting the patient. To be effective, the physician requires a degree of self-knowledge and humility. This is similar to what is required by transdisciplinary-community-connected researchers. Each must feel confident that they are capable of recognizing that others may see the world differently and still be dedicated to seeking a better understanding of, and solution to, the problems at hand. While research methodologies have been delineated in the volume, it is important to acknowledge that in the best tradition of problem solving, the range of tools varied according to the nature of the problem and the perspective of the researchers. As Mark Twain noted: "If all you have in your tool box is a hammer, then everything looks like a nail."

The degree to which individual task force members engaged in mutually respectful collaboration with open communication varied across the group and over time. The overall result was a reasonably effective long-term collaboration on most issues of substance. When this failed, alternative approaches using different members and methods were used to address the issues basic to our understanding of how things might work. As is obvious in the chapters of this volume, the results show a richness that might otherwise have eluded us.

Some general observations and recommendations from our interdisciplinary experience follow:

- Define the problem. The better a problem is defined, the more effective the interdisciplinary focus.
- Acknowledge language, organizational, and broad disciplinary perspectives.
- Acknowledge variance among language, organizational, and broad disciplinary perspectives.
- Bring the team together around a particular problem in order to define

and sort out the working relationships and the details of the collective approach.

- Focus on a geographic area when addressing problems such as sustainability at the community level. This can be very helpful in reducing variables and bringing collective thinking to bear on complex problems in that place (Woollard et al. 1999).
- Interact with the community. This can be very powerful in research group development by forcing joint communication and a demand for relevance.
- Create an iterative process at all levels, from problem definition to final communication; this will allow the research process to bear its healthiest fruit.
- Nurture human relationships; they ultimately determine the quality of the output.
- Do not force interdisciplinarity without a focusing problem, time to develop, and an active program of communication and nurturance. It is unlikely to be effective or sustainable.
- Refine issues relevant to the research group while avoiding a tendency to shift specific issues back to the putatively "relevant" discipline. Once significant issues are devolved in this way, it is unlikely that they will ever be effectively reintegrated into the overall process.
- Keep in mind that differing perspectives will surface and that harsh words spoken in anger have a lasting and detrimental effect.

These broad observations are made here so that readers might test and verify them as they move through their careers. It should be kept in mind that the task force has sought not only to conduct interdisciplinary research but also to reflect on the conduct of interdisciplinary research. This book should be an example of what Donald Schön (1983) calls "reflection in action."

A final observation about this experience with interdisciplinarity relates to the interface between the epistemology of modern science and a practical observation of the way humans behave in groups. Insofar as the task force worked both independently and as part of a much larger multidisciplinary research group, we were able to observe a range of enquiry. The endeavours reflected the individual scholar at various stages of development, all the way through to dozens of scholars acting in a large, somewhat loosely knit collaboration. We were also able to observe a number of group initiatives and institutes that tackled interdisciplinary issues in a variety of ways. As stated earlier, it was apparent that a scholarly group of any size requires constant communication and nurturing if it is to extend beyond individual disciplinary boundaries. There may be an optimal size for such groups, but our observations did not include a sufficiently large number of groups to comment on this specific issue (see below). The very large group tended to disperse into specific identified segments, and attempts to work across the segments were frustrating organizationally and depended upon a series of individual relationships and mutual interests.

This experience and the ecology of knowledge that tends to see it fall into ever increasingly specialized branches may have a common origin. Steven Shapin, in his elegant study of Robert Boyle and the epistemology of science, made a number of observations that may be germane. He contends that despite the trappings of experimental and observational science that have evolved since the seventeenth century, the fundamental relationship between the scientist and those who are convinced by his or her published observations is one of trust. In seventeenth-century Europe, this trust derived from the nature of truth-telling that was associated with the particular class of the gentleman scholar. Such scholars tended to carry out their experiments either where they were domiciled or very close to it, whether in the university or in the manor house. Shapin posits that with the evolution of all manner of work away from the domicile and into separate, specialized areas, the elements of trust based on the individual practitioner became attenuated. Within the twentieth century, trust has been transferred from the individual to the process and the institution. By the latter half of the twentieth century, "what underpins scientific truthfulness is said to be an elaborate system of institutional norms, whose internalization guarantees the transgressions will generate psychic pain and whose implementation by the community guarantees the transgressors will be found out and punished" (Shapin 1994, 413).

One can here make the observation that since the detailed epistemology of each of the disciplines varies to some extent, so the norms used to judge the veracity of a particular point of view will vary. The greatest comfort will be found in those disciplines whose particular epistemology best fits with the individual – hence, most likely people within one's own discipline.

Shapin goes on to observe that "the group of people mutually judged capable of participating in each of these specialized practices – what has been called the core set – may be very small. There is hardly any systematically collected information on the subject but I would not be surprised if, across the range of practices, core sets were as small as 10 or 20 individuals – about the size of an army platoon or mess group" (ibid., 414-5).

One can observe such groups developing their inclusion and exclusion criteria based on increasingly arcane language, publications, and jargon. With modern communications, such clustering of scholars may exist around the globe but still function with a comfort and trust based on familiarity. As Shapin points out, "they probably 'look each other in the eyes' with about the same frequency that members of the seventeenth century English gentry did, with the international scientific conference taking the place of the court or of the London 'season.' They function within broadly comparable systems of recognition and 'know each other's people' in ways comparable to the culture manipulated by traditional gentlemen, whose pattern of institutional training and theoretical or practical affiliation do the work done for gentlemen by family and kin" (ibid., 415).

If Shapin's observations are an accurate description of disciplinary or subdisciplinary relationships within the scientific culture, there are significant implications for interdisciplinarity. It would go a long way to explaining the time, communication, and active nurturing that must take place if a clustering of scholars from varying disciplines is to transform itself into an effective interdisciplinary team. It would also provide some evidence that there may indeed be an optimal size for such interdisciplinary teams and this size may be dictated by the opportunities members have to develop this fundamental position of trust. This may be more fundamental than the particular trappings of science attending a specific branch of knowledge and a discipline involved in its explorations.

We will close this section with the observation that such trust is hard won given the traditional reward structures of universities in which most of the scholars are embedded. For this reason, the task force has been involved in the nurturing and development of new academics, who may be more capable of incorporating the trust of other disciplines than are their older colleagues.

Beyond Hope to Action

> If you plan for a year, plant rice. If you plan for 10 years, plant trees. If you plan for 100 years, educate your children.
> – Chinese proverb

Readers who have persisted this far will have traversed a sweeping terrain of despair and hope, broad prospect and narrow detail, paths well travelled and some barely prospected. It is our intent that readers' reward be a stimulus for thought and action. As is clear from our model of nested hierarchy (Figure 7.5; see p. 209), such thought and action must take place at several levels.

If the individual reader conceives of himself or herself as being a member of a community that, taken together with other communities, is part of the ecosystem on which we all depend, this realization alone will have merit. At the very least, it will open up the possibility that thought will be given to the ecological consequences of his or her actions. The mere raising of this possibility enhances the likelihood that individual actions will not go unexamined and that avenues will be sought wherein people will behave in a manner that honours this relationship. Given the myriad choices that most of us make each day, whether in terms of food, transportation, consumption, or simply being present to those whom we meet, the cumulative impact of two million humans living in the Lower Fraser Valley is a powerful and pervasive influence on the ecosystem that sustains us.

In spite of this fact, there is a perception (and a reality) that many of the choices we would like to make are either made impossible by circumstances or made irrelevant by the thoughtless action of others. We must widen the scope for individual action into a more profound understanding of the community's role as a mediator of collective action and its impact on the broader ecosystem. The constraints on individual action come from the economy, the built form of our cities, and our political and social systems. They are not, however, immutable and inevitable. We did not slide unwillingly and inevitably into our current pattern of gross overconsumption. There are trends in the economy, and in our political and social relationships, that have served to simultaneously reinforce our consumption and insulate us from the realization of the ecological consequences of that consumption. These forces are subject to change.

Lest we fall prey to the seductive belief that we need not change because major change is impossible, let us consider one simple example. The monarchical and feudal societies that characterized Europe into the eighteenth century appeared to be implacably permanent. Talk of parliamentary democracy was seen as the prating of hopeless romantics and optimists. It was not even clear that it would be desirable to change from a system that appeared to be working well for a fair spectrum of aristocratic and bourgeois society. Nonetheless, within a matter of decades, the nostalgic apologists for a passing social order were seen as the romantic minority (de Tocqueville 1853). Even within the last decade we have seen unimagined changes in the political and social structure of former Warsaw-block countries. Therefore, let us not talk as if change cannot come; let us turn our attention to how the future should be shaped by our individual and collective actions today.

The interface between the individual and the community provides fertile grounds for promoting and shaping change. Earlier chapters in this volume have outlined ideas and methods for promoting and focusing organized action toward making our communities healthier. Others have provided descriptions of how unorganized and poorly adapted communities have seen the health of their citizenry dissipated by external forces of technological innovation without concomitant sensitivity to its social consequence. The chapter on the adverse health effects of sawmill mechanization outlines what happens when communities act as individual atoms in a system perturbed by outside forces, instead of as complex adaptive systems.

The precise nature of the organizational effort must, by definition, be specific to the problem at hand. Therefore, there is no general prescription for the political form that must be taken in order for a community to move in the direction of sustainability. However, this volume does contain tools that will be useful in deciphering whether any particular action or direction moves the community toward or away from sustainability. Like all tools, they do not replace a requirement for commitment and energy; they simply focus and make that energy's use more efficient.

Clearly the society in the Lower Fraser Basin suffers the dual hazards of overconsumption and inadequate social connection. Earlier chapters have demonstrated to readers that the development of robust social connections at the community and intercommunity level offers the greater likelihood that the Lower Fraser Basin can behave as an effective complex adaptive system. There is a great deal of hope that the development of such robust interconnections may actually reduce the demands the community places on its sustaining ecosystem. If this is the case, and the evidence in this volume would indicate that it probably is, then what appear now as twin hazards could be turned into a synergistic downward spiral of consumption and upward spiral of social caring.

If we move beyond the community to its interface with the ecosystem, we see further opportunities for mitigating the effect of our collective consumption on the ecosystems, both within the valley and globally. Earlier chapters and other books (Pierce and Dale 1999; Woollard and Rees 1999) have demonstrated that the Lower Fraser Valley's political structures are inadequate to deal with this bioregion whose lungs, kidneys, and alimentary systems do not respect political boundaries. We have outlined some of the shortcomings of current political arrangements and suggested alternative ways of distributing power and control so that communities can respond more effectively to ecological challenges. In the same way that senseless individualism can prevent the development of the community for the benefit of the individual, inappropriate individualism of communities within the Lower Fraser Valley will merely perpetuate our current unsustainable growth pattern. It is evident that many of the lessons from the actions of the City of Richmond are worthy of the reflection by other municipal governments in the Valley.

The theory of complex adaptive systems and the reality of history indicate that sustainability will occur when the individual units of a system begin to act coherently as if they were a higher order unit. This can best be achieved by simultaneous "bottom up" and "top down" approaches. Thus, individuals must have within their hands the capability to make choices toward decreased consumption and to understand the consequences of the choices they make. At the same time, leadership from the community as a whole must create, nurture, and maintain a framework sensitive to biophysical realities. We can no longer afford to have leadership committing what Eric Hobsbawm calls "economic perjury" in the mistaken belief that the citizenry cannot bear too much reality. If we have learned nothing else in the last four years, the task force has come to appreciate how much all of us need each other if we are to cure our fatal consumption. This realization may be coming belatedly to the current political and academic class. The task force sees hope for the future in the young academics and in a growing number of young people who appear to be realizing that too much is just that: too much.

References

de Tocqueville, A. 1853. "The Old Regime and the Revolution." In F. Furet and F. Melonio, eds., 1999, *The Old Regime and the Revolution,* vol. 1 (original French). Trans. A.S. Kahan. Chicago: University of Chicago Press.

Fernandez-Armesto, P. 1995. *Millennium,* 196-205. Toronto: Doubleday Canada.

Gell-Mann, M. 1994. *The Quark and the Jaguar: Ventures in the Simple and the Complex.* New York: W.H. Freeman and Co.

Heaney, S. 1995. *The Redress of Poetry: Oxford Lectures.* London: Faber and Faber.

Hobsbawm, E. 1994. *Age of Extremes: The Short Twentieth Century 1914-1991.* Toronto: Michael Joseph.

Kauffman, S. 1995. *At Home in the Universe.* New York: Oxford University Press.

Pierce, J.T., and A. Dale, eds. 1999. *Communities, Development, and Sustainability across Canada.* Vancouver: UBC Press.

Schama, S. 1995. *Landscape and Memory.* Toronto: Random House of Canada.

Schön, D. 1983. *The Reflective Practitioner: How Professionals Think in Action.* New York: Basic Books.

Shapin, S. 1994. *A Social History of Truth - Servility in Science in 17th-Century England.* Chicago: University of Chicago Press.

von Bertalanffy, L. 1968. *General Systems Theory: Foundation Development, Applications.* Rev. ed. New York: George Brazziler.

Waldrop, M.M. 1992. *Complexity: The Emerging Science at the Age of Order and Chaos.* Toronto: Simon and Schuster.

Woollard, R., and W.E. Rees. 1999. "Social Evolution and Urban Systems: Directions for Sustainability." In J.T. Pierce and A. Dale, eds., *Communities, Development, and Sustainability across Canada.* Vancouver: UBC Press.

Woollard, R., M. Wackernagel, W.E. Rees, A. Ostry, J. McIntosh, S. Manson-Singer, J. Lynam, C. Hertzman, L. Green, M. Carr, and P. Boothroyd. 1999. "The Community as Crucible: Blending Health and Sustainability." In M. Healey, ed., *Seeking Sustainability in the Lower Fraser Basin: Issues and Choices.* Vancouver: Institute for Resources and the Environment / Westwater Research.

Contributors

The designations of the authors are for identification purposes only and the views expressed in this book are those of the authors and do not necessarily represent the views of the designated organizations to which they belong.

Peter Boothroyd is a Professor in the Department of Community and Regional Planning, University of British Columbia. He is an active advocate for participatory and sustainability-oriented transportation planning in the Vancouver region.

Michael Carr recently completed his PhD dissertation, "Diversity Against the Monoculture: Bioregional Vision and Praxis and Civil Society Theory," at the School of Community and Regional Planning, University of British Columbia. Currently, Dr. Carr is an instructor of Environmental Ethics at Capilano College in North Vancouver. In addition to his academic interests, Dr. Carr has been involved in environmental and social advocacy on behalf of civil society for more than two decades.

Lawrence W. Green, formerly director of the University of British Columbia Institute of Health Promotion Research, recently joined the US Centers for Disease Control and Prevention, where he is Distinguished Fellow/Visiting Scientist in the Office on Smoking and Health, National Center for Chronic Disease Prevention and Health Promotion. While at UBC, Green received the Killam Faculty Research Prize, the Alumnus of the Year Award from the University of California School of Public Health, and the Award of Excellence, one of the two highest distinctions of the American Public Health Association. He previously served on the public health faculties of the University of California at Berkeley, Johns Hopkins, Harvard, and the University of Texas.

Clyde Hertzman completed training in medicine, community medicine, and epidemiology at McMaster University in Hamilton, Ontario, between 1976 and 1985, and has been on faculty in the Department of Health Care and Epidemiology at the University of British Columbia since 1985. He is a Full Professor in the Department and Associate Director of the Centre for Health Services and Policy Research. Nationally, he is a Fellow of both the Program in

Population Health and in Human Development of the Canadian Institute for Advanced Research. He is also Director of the Program in Population Health.

Shona Kelly is a Research Scientist in the Department of Health Care and Epidemiology and a PhD candidate in the Individual Interdisciplinary Studies Graduate Program at the University of British Columbia. Her research interests include real and perceived effects of pesticide exposure, perception of risk, biological measures of stress, and gender differences in the determinants of health.

Janette McIntosh, MHSc, was formerly the Research Coordinator with the Task Force on Healthy and Sustainable Communities. She is now a mother of two children and a researcher/consultant involved and active in the areas of health promotion and sustainability research and community projects.

Jennie L. Moore is an Air Quality Planner at the Greater Vancouver Regional District, where she works on climate change issues with a focus on building local capacity to implement actions that reduce greenhouse-gas emissions and foster sustainable communities.

Aleck S. Ostry is a Research Associate in the Department of Health Care and Epidemiology in the Faculty of Medicine at the University of British Columbia. He has a PhD in epidemiology, an MA in history (with an emphasis on the history of public health), and an MSc in health services planning. Dr. Ostry's research interests include environmental health, occupational health, and the history of public health.

William E. Rees received his PhD in zoology (ecology) at the University of Toronto and has taught at the University of British Columbia's School of Community and Regional Planning since 1969. Professor Rees' teaching and research focus on the public policy and planning implications of global environmental trends and the necessary ecological conditions for sustainable socioeconomic development. Much of his work, including his ecological footprint concept, is in the domain of ecological economics and human ecology. Professor Rees recently received a UBC Killam Senior Research Prize for his research contributions.

Jean A. Shoveller, PhD, is an Assistant Professor in the University of British Columbia's Department of Health Care and Epidemiology and the Centre for Community Child Health Research. She also is a BC Health Research Foundation Scholar. Dr. Shoveller's research interests include health behaviour with a particular emphasis on environmental health promotion among children and youth.

Robert F. Woollard, MD, CCFP, FCFP, Royal Canadian Legion Professor and Head, Department of Family Practice, Faculty of Medicine, University of British Columbia, is Cochair of the UBC Task Force on Healthy and Sustainable Communities. He has worked at national and international levels in medical education, environmental health, and international development. Dr. Woollard continues in the clinical practice of medicine.

Index